13⁹⁵

The
Western Way

John Matthews has made a special study of the Arthurian legends and has completed two books on the subject: *The Grail: Quest for the Eternal* (Thames & Hudson, 1981) and *At the Table of the Grail* (Routledge & Kegan Paul, 1984), as well as a collection of poems, *Merlin in Calydon* (Hunting Raven Press, 1981). He was co-founder in 1979 of the arts magazine *Labrys*. He has contributed widely to literary journals such as *Temenos*, *Literary Review*, *New Celtic Review* and *From Avalon to Camelot*.

Caitlín Matthews attended the Webber-Douglas Academy of Dramatic Art between 1969 and 1971. Her first collection of poetry, *The Search for Rhiannon*, was published in 1980. She is a trained singer and often accompanies her readings and lectures with songs and music on the Celtic harp. She has contributed essays to *At the Table of the Grail* (details above) and to *The Underworld Initiation* by Bob Stewart (Aquarian Press, 1985), and has written for *Temenos*, *Poetry London*, *Resergence* and *Labrys*.

Frontispiece: The Emblem of the Great Work – the Philosopher's Stone: 'visit the interior of the earth — seek and rectify the hidden stone'.

The Western Way

A Practical Guide to the Western Mystery Tradition

VOLUME II
THE HERMETIC TRADITION

Caitlín and John Matthews

London, Boston and Henley

First published in 1986 by ARKANA
ARKANA PAPERBACKS is an imprint of
Routledge & Kegan Paul plc

14 Leicester Square, London WC2H 7PH, England

9 Park Street, Boston, Mass. 02108, USA and

Broadway House, Newtown Road,
Henley on Thames, Oxon RG9 1EN, England

Set in 10 on 11 pt Sabon
by Inforum Ltd, Portsmouth
and printed in Great Britain
by The Guernsey Press Co. Ltd,
Guernsey, Channel Islands

Library of Congress Cataloging in Publication Data

Matthews, Caitlin, 1952–

The Western way.
Includes bibliographies and indexes.
Contents: v. 1. The native tradition — v. 2. The
hermetic tradition.
1. Mysteries, Religious. 2. Occult sciences.
I. Matthews, John, 1948– II. Title.
BL610.M38 1985   291'.09182'1   84–18325
British Library CIP data also available

ISBN 1–85063–017–8

To
Gareth Knight

And all who seek to rectify the Hidden Stone

'You are all one, under the stars'
Merlin in John Boorman's *Excalibur*

Contents

Illustrations

Acknowledgments

Thanks for advice, support and cups of tea go to: Dolores and Michael Ashcroft-Nowicki, all the Caldecott clan, Joscelyn Godwin, Marian Green, Deirdre Green, Helene Hess, Adam McLean, Kathleen Raine, Anthony Rooley, Wolf and Johann van Brussel, Roma Wilby, The St Mary Cray Green Circle and, again, to the Company of Hawkwood. The illustration on p. 69 is reproduced with the kind permission of T. & T. Clark Ltd, Edinburgh.

INTRODUCTION
The Outward Spiral

Hear with the understanding of the heart.

Thomas Vaughan: *Anima Magica Absondita*

The soul of each single one of us is sent, that the universe may be complete.

Plotinus: *Enneads, IV, 8,1*

The Roman cult of Mithras has associated with it the figure of Aion: a lion-headed god swathed by a serpent. He represented boundless time, which held sway over the ages and the cyclic divisions of the year. In his hands he carried the keys of the solstices: a silver one which opened the Gate of Cancer, the Way of the Ancestors, and a golden one which opened the Gate of Capricorn, the Way of the Gods, which lead beyond the processes of birth and dying and through which the gods could descend to earth. (104) (fig 1.)

These two ways represent eternal laws, as unchanging as the universe itself, and they can also be seen as akin to the two traditions which are the subject of the present work. On the one hand the Native Tradition, which looks to the Ancestors, now elevated to the status of gods, for guidance. On the other the Hermetic Tradition, which looks outwards to the stars, and to the angelic presences which inhabit them, as mediators between mankind and God.

These are different but complementary approaches to the same end: a fuller understanding of our place in the scheme of things. Both have helped to preserve an ancient wisdom which would otherwise have been lost to the world. In Herman Hesse's novel, *The Glass Bead Game*, a group of esoteric philosophers known as The League of Journeyers to the East were said to have 'contributed new insights into the nature of our culture and the possibility of its continuance, not so much by analytical and scholarly work, as by their capacity, based on ancient spiritual exercises, for mystical identification with remote ages and cultural conditions' (142). The same can be said of the explorers of the Western Esoteric Tradition whom we call Hermeticists, who have helped almost single-handedly to preserve

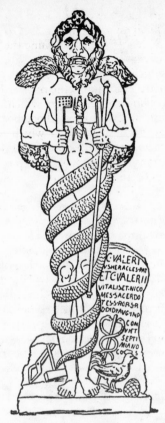

Figure 1:   The Aion

and transmit the ancient mysteries into our own times. It is the Hermeticist who continues to work of the Native shaman, and who expands our knowledge of the universe through his use of just such 'ancient spiritual exercises' as the philosophers of Hesse's novel.

The path of the esoteric tradition has veered sharply through many centuries in order to preserve its teachings: sometimes it has been paved, at others it has appeared as no more than a dirt track, kept open by the tread of a few solitary walkers. It has at no time been a common highway; yet it has rerouted itself time and again in order to accommodate travellers of many kinds. It has explored new and different traditions so that 'however its continuity may be broken by opposing systems, it will make its appearance at different periods of time, as long as the sun itself shall illumine the world.' (325)

We have spoken of the path of the Native Tradition as the inward spiral of a maze which leads into the heart of ancestral earth-wisdom. The Hermetic Tradition is the outward spiral of the same maze: a path of evolving consciousness which is informed by the inner resources of our ancestral roots. Together the two traditions form a glyph of the Western Way, in which neither tradition is 'better' than the other, but where each can inform and teach the other (figure 2). They are complementary opposites between which the esoteric experience of the individual can be measured and balanced. As the Native Tradition saw a move from primitive, tribal or collective consciousness towards an appreciation of individual, self-aware consciousness, so the Hermetic Tradition takes individual consciousness on the journey towards cosmic consciousness, where-in that first, collective awareness is augmented in a macrocosmic way. Such an evolution is the work of many millennia and can only be judged from our present standpoint. The movement has not always been a progressive one, by any means. Both traditions have a tendency to pull out of true: the Native Tradition, as we noted in volume one, has a tendency to atavistic reversion; the Hermetic Tradition tends to pull in the direction of speculative projection and mystifying obscurantism.

The unit of the Native Tradition was the tribe – forged from people, ruler and shaman – and it was held together by genetic blood

The inner spiral   The outer spiral

Figure 2:   The Spiral Maze

linkage in which shared ideas and concepts took the place of religion. But 'when blood became mixed by exogamy (marriage out of the tribal unit), . . . close connections with his ancestors was [sic] severed and man began to live his own personal life.' (321) This severing of the direct link with the ancestral realms and the introduction of new blood, enabled the transmission of new messages into our consciousness, allowing it to develop away from the purely tribal heritage. The collective consciousness of the tribe was open to new influences. In place of a succession of shamans and shamankas, a 'philosophic clan . . . moved across the face of Europe under such names as "the Illuminati." '(23) Instead of a blood descent, a new relationship was established, not with the ancestors, but with teachers upon Inner Planes. The kinship began to be one of brother and sister initiates – a subtle lifting of the tribal relationship.

This concept is thought by some to have a sinister implication, although this is due to its political application. Bands of hooded Hermeticists are *not* out to rule the world. The truth is much simpler. The fellowship of esotericists is a mystical, not a blood relationship. (Although, at a deep level, this latter understanding is also true.) We must rather, for clarification, look to the Jewish concept of the Just Ones who sustain the world by their hidden lives, or to the company of Grail-hermits who, throughout the Grail-quest, advise the questing knights and live obscurely in the woods and deserts. Such is the role of the esotericist in this age (cf. chapters 1 and 3).

The fear and distrust of the shaman and magician throughout the ages has not been ameliorated by the almost aggressive secrecy with which the Western Way has been surrounded. Periods of persecution have, perforce, been responsible for this reserve, but we have also become estranged from esoteric understandings: 'what is natural in psyche has in our culture become unique, occult, and mysterious.' (273) There is also the fear that the esotericist is dealing with forbidden things, terrible powers which could prove destructive.

The Fall of Atlantis is to the esotericist what the Fall from Eden represents to the Jew or Christian – a precocious striving for knowledge which oversets the natural order. According to tradition, Atlantis fell due to an abuse of priestly power which so disturbed the delicate balance of the environment that the continent was submerged in a mighty cataclysm. In Eden, the Fall was brought about by disobedience to God's commandment not to eat of the Tree of the Knowledge of Good and Evil. It does not matter whether we see Atlantis or Eden as geographically locatable in time and space, or as mythic paradigms of lost knowledge; they remain states which have been withdrawn from us – golden ages which cannot return. We stand now on the higher arc of the Atlantis/Eden experiment, at the mercy of our technology, the knowledge of whose uses can heal or hurt depending on how it is harnessed. The danger of pride – spiritual or otherwise – is before us once again.

Yet while these paradigms are known chiefly because of their sudden destruction, Eden and Atlantis remain hauntingly in the consciousness as states of primal perfection. The inner Atlantis reminds us of potentialities which are lost or lie dormant in us. Before the taking of the apple from the tree in the garden, Eden was a place of joy and innocence.

> If Atlantis had never existed, the student of tradition would have found it necessary to invent such a region, as in none of the lands of Western Europe do we find a nucleus from which the adjacent countries received their earliest ideas of religion, myth and magic. (316)

The Mystery Schools from the time of Plato onwards, have ever looked towards Atlantis as the source of their knowledge. The scattered seeds of Atlantis seem to have been blown by the winds and carried by the tides throughout the world. Rationalists have sought to find the Lost Continent itself, and researchers of more or less scholarly repute have tried to assemble the fragments of languages, pot-shards and ethnographical types to account for the great subsidence. While such treasure-hunting is no doubt engaging, it has little bearing on our story. We deal in metaphysical currency here (cf. fig. 3).

Hope keeps us ever watchful for a new Golden Age – indeed, the New Age movement already shows a bright tomorrow blended of such hopes. On the side of despair are the millennial pessimists who foresee the destruction of the world and everything in it. Neither pattern of behaviour is very balanced. As we have stressed throughout this study, we must be wary of seeking to inhabit a new Golden Age: those who try to set up communities of perfection know this to their cost. Yet neither do we wish to live under the futility of ultimate despair. We are neither saviours of the world nor victims of the gods, but intermediaries who can synthesize and mediate the wisdom of the earth and of the stars. This ability is figured again in the image of the Aion, who holds the keys to enable us to correct the over-emphasis implicit in millennial despair and Golden Age hope.

We may perhaps grasp this concept more easily if we realize the interpenetration of microcosm with macrocosm. The interrelation of these two mighty realities is the key to the Hermetic Tradition. The macrocosm represents the eternal reality of Light, the realm of God: the microcosm is its reflection, a fragmentation of the Light, the realm of humanity in creation. This theme has been at the core of mystery teachings of all traditions, represented as a Body of Light which is scattered throughout the universe. Each created thing bears a spark of the divine light. Some forget their original condition, while others remember and become walkers-between-the-worlds, and make the reassembling of the Body of Light their overriding aim. These latter live by a story – the rending of a god, the apportioning of a goddess – whose sacrifice brings creation into being and whose redemptive virtue, resident within the individual spark of divine light, will bring creation back into the Body of Light once again. Yet the Body of Light, like that of Humpty Dumpty, is so fragmented that it seems impossible to reassemble the pieces. Between inertia and the multiplicity of ways determined to achieve this end, the task looks impossible. For some, the realization that their individual divine spark is trapped in flesh brings about a denial of the body itself.

Yet there remain those who seek to reassemble the Body of Light by religious or esoteric means. In whatever generation there are a number of dedicated people who form a quorum sufficient to form a launch-pad for such an enterprise. These Just Ones, as we have already said, are not necessarily in touch with one another, but their work has a cumulative effect. The task of the Hermetic Tradition reflects this aim: to rectify and unite the microcosmic light with the macrocosmic light, to discover the Hidden Stone, the Holy Grail, to forge the seeds of light into a cube of true gold. This is the Great Work and is the end of esoteric philosophy.

The foregoing may confirm some readers in their opinion that esotericism is an escape from the world – an accusation that is likewise levelled at those who enter contemplative religious orders. As the philosopher Frithjof Schuon, has observed:

All esotericism appears to be tinged with heresy from the point of view of the corresponding exotericism, but this obviously does not disqualify it if it is intrinsically orthodox, and thus in conformity with truth as such and with the traditional symbolism to which it pertains; it is true that the most authentic esotericism can incidentally depart from this framework and refer to foreign symbolisms, but it cannot be syncretistic in its very substance. (294)

Hermetic esotericism is concerned with just such traditional symbologies and the truth of their wisdom. Hermeticism is in the peculiar case of guarding the mystical traditions of those religions and systems which have become mere exoteric carapaces or which have fallen out of history as living systems themselves. Exotericism and esotericism need each other. Without its mystical tradition, an exoteric system is like a rose without its perfume. Without the structures of exotericism, esotericism is an image without a temple. High, mystical knowing must percolate through to everyday life or forever be separate from it – a temptation to spiritual pride and elitism.

The problem which confronts any newcomer to the esoteric is that of motivation. Few people are raised in an environment which is informed by a mystical tradition, fewer have any experience of a living spiritual tradition at all: their ethical values and attitudes are shaped by social modification and the underlying ethical conventions of their individual culture. The exoteric world views the esoteric as evil, pertaining to the devil, morally corrupted and sexually depraved. It is all very well for the experienced esotericist to deny these projections – which is what they are – but for those venturing along this path for the first time there is the underlying suspicion that they are involved in something which might be 'not quite right'. The esoteric hinterland has been firmly closed for so long, except to bold explorers, that any expedition thither is held to be foolhardy. Certainly, without the experienced guide at one's side, this is true. The means towards finding a teacher or inner guide are discussed in chapters 3 and 4 of this volume. What was once familiar territory is now virtually uncharted; attitudes and certainties once widely held are now unknown to the modern explorer who shies at every rock and stranger on the way.

How then is the beginner on the Hermetic path of the Western Way to steer a course? By common sense and sensitive intuition, in the first instance, and by resonating with the wisdom of the tradition, in the second. Those who seek to walk the path alone, without the guidance of their tradition, without the sustenance of spiritual bread, are more likely to stray from their way, never to arrive at their destination.

We are all marvellous microcosms wherein matter and spirit are mixed to form totally individual expressions of humanity. During incarnation we will each meet certain very necessary initiations of a mundane kind: we struggle from stage to stage of our lives, learning the lessons of childhood, adolescence and adulthood. Depending upon our experience within each of these initiations, we will formulate a personal philosophy by which we seek to live. We arrive at an optimum point of experience and maturity at which we may decide to try the esoteric way. How do we know that this is 'white' and not 'black' magic? Will we truly be treading the right or left-hand path, as it often called?

'The left-hand path . . . is the path of progress for substance or matter,' reads Alice Bailey's *Treatise on White Magic*. (21) If our path does not lead us to an evolution of consciousness, to a kindling of spirit within matter, then we are indeed walking the left-hand path which diverges from the Western Way in its intent.

As a rule, the Hermeticist does not talk about 'good' and 'evil' because these terms are qualitative and misleading. What is 'good' to one is another's 'evil.' We must see things in terms of balanced polarities. We are not saying that there is *no* expression of good and evil in life – we know very well that there is – but we must not think of these in terms of absolute realities. We shall be seeing how the ancients polarized two eternally opposed causes of good and evil – a dualism which is still hard to escape from in common speech. God and Devil, angel and demon are still polarized sets of images in our consciousness; we are all aware of how destructive this application of image can be in the ascription of feminine images to matter and masculine ones to spiritual states. Such ready definitions of good and evil should be resisted.

This is not to ignore the very real horror of evil as we all experience it: evil remains a name for something unbalanced; whose origins are obscure, like those of the divine spark within us. In our souls we can perceive the evil or unbalanced forces about us, like a bad smell. The appearances of evil are deceptively smooth and charming: they appear in the forms of what we most wish for, but they are paid for in the currency of our own integrity. They lead us from the work of meshing the microcosmic and macrocosmic worlds, into the 'deepening of the plane' (107) – selling our pearl of great price for ready cash.

Those wishing to read more of these matters – and they are not easy to speak about or understand – would do well to read *The*

Cosmic Doctrine by Dion Fortune (90), which has this to say: 'evil is simply that which is moving in the opposite direction to evolution. (It) is that which . . . tends to revert to the Unmanifest. Evil can be viewed, if this is helpful, as the principle of inertia which binds "the good". Good can be seen as the principle of creative movement,' which resists inertia. We arrive at the expressions 'Negative and Positive' which will perhaps enable us to grasp these principles in a more helpful and less relative way. The way of Chaos, as an expression of the Negative pole, can be cleansing and effective, just as the way of creativity as an expression of the Positive pole can represent an imbalanced fertility. Which of these can be said to be good or evil?

So what does the Hermetic way offer as its contribution to the balanced way of evolution? We all have to face situations and decide whether to grasp the nettle or to flee, like the Fool of the Tarot, or the young man in the gospel who left his garment behind him – leaving everything, if necessary, in order to live and fight another day. All disciplines have their martyrs and their survivors. Those who follow the Western Way are not the elect, they do not offer a dogmatic package to salvation: they are co-workers, mediators between micro- and macrocosm who believe in their tradition as a means of spiritual progression. This essential work is not the sole province of esotericists, but of all religious traditions, crafts and skills. The mystic, poet, artist and every member of that Secret Commonwealth we spoke about in volume I – indeed, anyone who has an impinging of Inner realms upon the Outer world – contributes to this work.

The safest means of travelling the Hermetic Path is by means of a spiritual tradition – whether it be one of the orthodox religions or not.

For it is the height of evil not to know God: but to be capable of knowing God, and to wish and hope to know him, is the road which leads straight to the Good; and it is an easy road to travel. Everywhere God will come to meet you, everywhere he will appear to you, at places and times at which you look not for it, in your waking hours and in your sleep, when you are journeying by water and by land, in the night-time and in the day-time, when you are speaking and when you are silent: for there is nothing which is not God. And do you say 'God is invisible'? Speak not so. Who is more manifest than God? (302)

This comes, not from a Christian, but from a Hermetic text: its truth is universally applicable for the pathwalker.

In volume one we spoke of three different levels of reality known to the Native Tradition: the Otherworld, Middle Earth and the Spiritual Realm. These terms are inappropriate to describe the levels operative within the Hermetic Tradition, so we have used the words *Inner* and *Outer*, to signify the Inner Plane and the Outer or mundane realm of common existence. Depending on which system one is used to working, the Inner Plane can be divided and subdivided into more and more complex parts: we have chosen to use one word only to define 'inner' things. The Spiritual Realms of the Native Tradition can be glossed, hermetically, as the macrocosmic level. However, there is an increasing trend which perceives Inner influences as having a psychological source in the unconscious. This is misleading in esoteric terms: make your own metaphors for these realms, by all means, but do not mistake their origins or confuse them with the workings of your own psyche.

Where the word 'God' appears in the text, this is to signify the ultimate source of reality, which is neither male nor female but pure spirit — unless otherwise stated. We have used the terms *the God* and *the Goddess*, to signify the divine masculine and feminine principles operational within mythological or other systems. Within the Hermetic Tradition, the Emerald Tablet of Hermes Trismegistos is the Rosetta Stone which interprets many mysteries: as a symbol it is balanced by the Rose of Aphrodite, signifying the esoteric wisdom of the divine feminine — a badge which identifies the fellow pathwalker.

We begin our journey in the temenos of the Mystery Schools, where we see how Native Tradition flows into Hermetic Tradition, and how these traditions have been preserved and fostered from ancient times up to our own day. We consider the spiritual traditions and their seeming divergence from the Mystery Schools, in chapter 2, while in chapter 3 we see how the role of the magician is a continuation of both shaman and mystery-priest. In chapter 4 we consider the cosmologies and symbol systems which have informed the divergent Hermetic traditions, and give a list of Inner guardians or contacts with whom the reader can work in a practical way. Chapter 5 sees the goal of the Great Work through the eyes of the alchemist, while in the afterword, *Tomorrow's Tradition*, we attempt to take the next step upon the Western Way.

As in volume one, the chapters have practical exercises and meditations appended so that the reader who is not an initiate of this tradition can experience for him or herself the realities presented here in a first-hand way. These exercises are based upon Hermetic sources, though they are original to this book. If many New Age movements and techniques have been omitted, this is only because we do not yet stand at a point where they can be seen in perspective. Certainly the Western Way will continue by means of many such channels, but we cannot forecast which will have greatest power to effect change and yet still be continuators of tradition.

We have attempted to view the Western Way in the context of tradition but, in a book of this size, much has been omitted in the interests of cohesion. There many facets which we have not dealt with and which the reader can investigate further, given the loose framework which we have provided.

New readers are directed to start with volume one of *The Western Way* before reading about the Hermetic Tradition in order that they may fully grasp the two halves of its totality. The Western Esoteric Tradition is known chiefly through the Hermetic path which has preserved many facets of the Native path. Yet the Native Tradition should not be ignored or neglected for this reason.

To those who have read the first volume and feel that the Native Tradition is indeed their way, we would say this: there are many treasures within the Hermetic way which you would do well to seek. Neither way is an end in itself. We do not leave anything behind by progressing on the evolutionary way to cosmic consciousness: the loved, familiar landscapes of home, the earthy wisdom of the ancestors accompany us still. Dion Fortune, that forthright walker-between-the-worlds had it right when she wrote:

> Do not let us forget that there is our own native esotericism hidden in the superconscious mind of the race, and that we have our own holy places at our very doors which have been used for initiations from time immemorial. Potent alike for the native contacts of the Celts, the work of the Hermeticist, and the mystical experience of the Church of the Holy Grail. (91)

NOTES ON THE EXERCISES IN THIS BOOK

Before attempting any of the exercises in this book, please read these instructions and those given in volume one of *The Western Way*.

The Hermetic Path is not an easy one to follow, although it is based in the Native Tradition and draws its primal impetus from it. Historically it has been syncretic, full of pied meanings and tangles of imagery, involving complex systems of correspondences. We hope to make some of these things a little plainer without throwing the mysteries to the four winds. There is much to be said for simplicity upon this path and for inner balance in the pathwalker who follows it. The complexities of the Hermetic path can be overwhelming for some, while others may get the impression that they are becoming ever more exalted, when in fact they are walking in circles. The cardinal danger of spiritual pride is to be avoided. It is not a bad idea to perform the Self-Clarification exercise (exercise 9, vol.I) before attempting any practical work on this path.

The material in this volume is more intellectually demanding than that found in volume one, where the Native Tradition can be felt as a gut-response or a yearning in the heart. This being so, it is particularly important that the exercises concerning the Hermetic Path are applied practically. This way has had its share of theoretical pundits and armchair esotericists, who sap the vitality of the Western Tradition and give nothing in return.

This volume differs from the first in that we refer to more than one tradition, although all those mentioned fall within the broad boundaries of the Hermetic way. If you work out a scheme of study and practice for yourself, please ensure that you do not mix traditions. Certain systems – like the qabalistic – may correlate well with others, but this practice should be used cautiously. When you have had some experience of both Native and Hermetic traditions you will be aware of the subtle interplay of resonances between them, and be able to utilize this knowledge with good effect.

All meditations should be performed seated in an upright chair unless otherwise specified. Your visualizations are not guided fantasy, as it is often called, so make an effort to be truly present within each meditation. See through your own eyes, not as though you watched yourself appearing on a screen. Lone workers who attempt meditation for the first time get nowhere because they have failed to observe the basic rules: quietness of body and mind; controlled direction of the psyche; and an active, attentive spirit. As with all things, a routine time for daily meditation helps. Set yourself a reasonable régime e.g. entering your own inner landscape and mapping it out over a period of weeks; contacting your guardian and listening to any instructions or teachings which the Inner may mediate to you; meditating around a particular mythology or symbology. A Qabalistic text gives this advice about meditation:

> Make yourself right. Meditate in a special place, where your voice cannot be heard by others. Cleanse your heart and soul of all other thoughts in the world. Imagine that at this time, your soul is separating itself from your body, and that you are leaving the physical world behind you, so that you enter the Future World, which is the source of all life distributed to the living. (168)

Meditation is not an exotic technique derived from some far-out Eastern source, but your contact with *your own inner life*.

The reader will be disappointed if he or she looks within these pages for a complete magical system. There are so many books which deal with the classical methods of ritual magic: if such methods are required then you could do worse than consult the works of Gareth Knight, William Gray, and Melita Denning and Osborne Phillips which are listed in the bibliography. The trend, as we enter the Aquarian Age, is away from rigid systems towards freer methods of working. There are as yet few systems which are suitable for the lone practitioner, although Marian Green's *Magic for the Aquarian Age* (118) offers a practical schema. We have given an initiatory exercise, *The Four-Square Citadel* (exercise 5), which gives the reader a magic circle, hermetic chamber or tower of art to work from, as well as giving a first-hand initiation into the power of the elements. Many of the exercises can be adapted, within the limits stated, to create the bases of further work. The reader is at liberty to follow his or her own path, according to individual preference and requirements. The strength of the Western Way lies in the diversity of its practice, and the unity of its aims.

The prerequisite for all meditation and inner work is intent, preparation, conscientious practice and performance, mediation and service. These practices should be self-explanatory, but mediation may need a few words of clarification. Inner work is never done solely for the benefit of the practitioner. Insights, gifts, realizations received from meditation or ritual work are to be mediated to those who need them in the Outer world. This should always typify the initiate's willingness to serve and can take many forms – a short formula or ritual gesture during which the gifts of realization are mediated with understanding and intention to the world. This formal act is the prayer of the Hermeticist. Even if you have not begun to meditate or work formally, you can share in this meditation. At midday, everyday – when the sun is at its zenith, regardless of what clocks designate as noon – people all over the world, from multitudinous traditions, elevate their thoughts to the Inner spiritual sun. They are tuning into their spiritual source and sharing a brief communion with all others who share the aim of the Great Work, the reassembly of the Body of Light, the redemption of the world – whatever their metaphor is for the Great Work. You can share this moment everyday. You need only shut your eyes and silently affirm, in your own words, your dedication to the work and your willingness to serve. Your thoughts and aspirations join those of others. If you have received an Inner gift or realization, offer this in mediation at midday, that others may share it and tune in to it. So the healing of the world may be accomplished.

This is part of a commitment which Hermeticists call 'the unreserved dedication', which is not a gory sacrifice upon an altar, but an unbloody offering of oneself and all one's resources to the service of God – however that term is understood. The unreserved dedication is not offered and indeed is not acceptable, until the initiate *has* something to offer: he or she must first serve an apprenticeship in patient learning and arduous practice. Our Inner and Outer teachers can help us accomplish much, but they can only train the willing candidate.

The work of creation is the continual mediation of life itself. Our contacts on the Inner are the servants of the mysteries, gatekeepers who allow initiates to pass through and experience Inner worlds. When those initiates are properly trained, they in turn stand at the nexus of the worlds as potential helpers and gatekeepers who teach the mediation of Inner energy to those who come after them.

Those who are drawn to the Hermetic Tradition only in order to wear gaudy robes and wield ritual implements will find that possession of these inflates only the ego and not one's prowess in ceremonial magic. Implements and robes are props which condition the practitioner: they set the mood and can represent the inner correspondence to be worked with. While they are helpful and are far more suitable than a boiler-suit or a string vest, robes are not essential. Clean garments are all that the beginner requires. Expensive swords and pungent incenses are not practical for the suburban magician now that a temple or working area is a luxury that few can afford. More often a bedroom, garden-shed, attic or hastily-converted living-room must suffice. The use of the great outdoors is something which the Hermetic Tradition could learn from its predecessors.

While Hermeticists have traditionally met indoors in secret chambers and hidden temples, a secluded outdoor working space can be quite as effective. In a crowded world, only the space inside our brain seems solely private.

With all your work, remember to keep a written record – even if your impressions seem trivial – they may be real realizations. You will find such a record very useful over the years; it will enable you to see an Inner pattern in your work. Like dreams, realization from meditation fades very speedily.

Do not endanger your health or your sanity by an excess of Inner work. If you feel that any image, system or contact is becoming obsessive to you, then do no more work with it. Our remarks about obsessive contacts made on page 102 of volume one hold good here. We have given a revitalization exercise on page 229, but this should not be a substitute for medical help or wholesome rest.

Many meditation suggestions are scattered throughout the text which the reader can work into exercises if required. A list of training centres and established mystery schools is appended at the end of the book.

CHAPTER 1
Schools of Mystery

There is every reason to believe that the so-called secret societies of the ancient world were branches of the one philosophical tree which, with its roots in heaven and its branches on the earth, is like the spirit of Man – an invisibly but ever-present cause of the objectified vehicle that gave it expression.

Manly P. Hall: *Secret Teachings of All Ages*

Happy is he who passed through the mysteries: he knows the origin and the end of life.

Pindar

FLASHES OF FIRE

The Mystery Schools, ancient and modern, are way-showers; they possess the maps and compasses with which to explore the inner realms of creation. Through them, those seeking initiation in the temples and lodges of the Western Mystery Tradition are offered training in the use and mastery of these tools: no one is cast adrift in an open boat to sail uncharted seas, or sent forth on a highway that has not already been walked by others. The mysteries *are* the inner life of the people, and to discover them is to read the story of a divine spark kept burning in the temple of the human spirit.

Once, there was no purely 'Native' or 'Hermetic' tradition; only a universal response by the Firstborn to the Earth-lore and Star-magic of their shamanic priests. Later, as the single religious impulse of the Foretime split into separate cults, these two approaches, which we may think of as chthonic (earthly) and stellar, grew further apart, until the beginnings of the Hermetic traditions were seeded in Egypt and the Hellenic world, while in Europe the Native traditions remained more or less grounded in the magic earth.

However, we have to be wary of assuming that because much of the later Hermetic philosophy originated in Greece and Egypt, these areas possessed no Native tradition of their own, or that the development of religion and magic in the Celtic West was so primitive and slow that it required cross-fertilization with other sources to pull it into more subtle realms of experience. In mankind's development, tribal consciousness and Hermetic philosophy are inextricably linked; it would be a mistake to think that one developed smoothly while the other did not.

Certainly, when Alexander of Macedon died in 323 BC, there was already a high degree of interrelation within the mysteries. Alexander's vast empire extended from the Straits of Gibraltar to the Indus Valley on the one hand, and from Germany to the Russian Steppe, the Sahara and the Indian Ocean on the other. Over this huge area, which included Persia, Egypt and Mesopotamia, the Greek cultic religions were laid down, some on already existing foundations, others springing up from a combination of several cultural sources. As F.C. Grant points out in his excellent survey of the period:

> It is important to realize that only very rarely, if ever, did an ancient cult come to an end, supplanted by the dominant cult of the conquerers. Instead the old cults lived on, some of them extremely primitive, others more advanced. (109)

Some, he adds, were changed, either for better or worse, by the effect of the philosophical bent of the Greek mind; others as a 'result of that mysterious inner source of change and development that affects all our civilizations. . . ' (ibid). Professor Grant is a historian rather than an esotericist, but he makes a point here which can be understood in relation to the inner guidance which helped formulate the mysteries. It is indeed to this mysterious inner force that we must look, rather than to any specific geographic or historic point of origin.

This does not, however, obviate belief in a kind of 'table of descent' within the mysteries. They were, as Manly Hall suggests, 'branches of one philosophical tree' (133) and as figure 3 shows, a complex web of interaction does exist, linking schools far apart in time and space. This is not to suggest that there was ever a literal, historical succession involved, but rather that all drew upon a common, inner source of teaching. Nor should we envisage any one of the schools as superior to another: there should be no hierarchies of this kind in the Western Way, whatever the claims of superiority advanced by various orders in our own time.

It has often been said that the Egyptian mysteries are the true foundation upon which the Western Hermetic systems are built. This

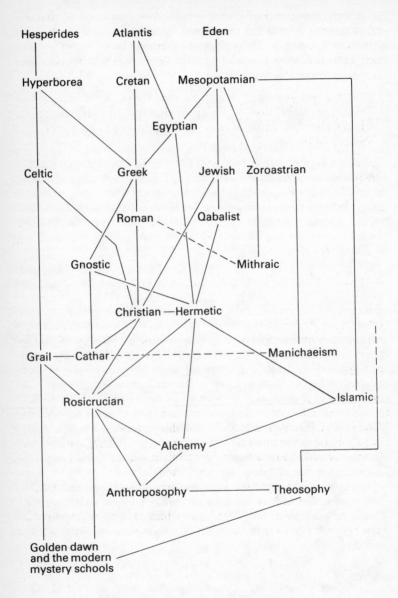

Figure 3: The Tree of the Mysteries

is due in part to an early identification of the Egyptian god Thoth, the scribe and guardian of the mysteries, with Hermes Trismegistos, the supposed founder of Western occult practice. Thus in the Hermetic text known as *Kore Kosmu*, we find Hermes addressing his 'son' Asclepios in the following words:

> Art thou not aware, O Asclepios, that Egypt is the image of heaven, or rather, that it is the projection below of the order of things above? If the truth must be told, this land is indeed the temple of the world. (186)

The truth is less grandiloquent, and by no means easy to reach, so great is the intermingling of sources in the Western tradition. There is certainly evidence of the extreme antiquity of the Egyptian mysteries: persistent traditions relating the Sphinx to a period long before the foundation of religion in Egypt, and the appearance of the four beasts aspected in the Sphinx within later esoteric practice, are an indication of this. (147)

Other traces of Egyptian mystery teaching are to be found in the Western Tradition, however, including the red and white pillars before the temple of Osiris at Memphis, which echo the black and white pillars of justice and mercy in qabalistic teaching; and the symbolic regalia of the God-King Pharaohs – sceptre and ark, sword and mace – which recall both Grail traditions (cf. chapter 5) and the four suits of the Tarot. (Other aspects of Tarot symbolism have been attributed to Egyptian influence or origin, but there is little hard evidence for this (cf. chapter 4). It is also possible to see, in the conical head-dress so often portrayed as worn by Hermes Trismegistos, a recollection of the double crown of Upper and Lower Egypt. None of this, however, adds up to anything more than a systematic borrowing from Egyptian beliefs and practices which has somehow become crystallized into a semi-mythical image of Egypt as originator of the greatest Western mystery teachings.

Egypt indeed had many mysteries, none more important than those of Isis. Her name is said to mean 'throne', 'wisdom' or 'saviour', though she possessed many other titles which testify to the universality of her cult. Above the entrance to her temple at Sais appeared the words:

> I, Isis, am all that has been, that is or shall be: no mortal man has ever seen me unveiled.

The Roman author Apuleius, in a famous passage from his novel *The*

Golden Ass (11), describes her as crowned with the moon and clad in a robe of stars. (cf. Fig 11) In Hermetic lore she became identified as the daughter of Hermes, standing for the innermost secret of the mysteries. Many have sought to obtain a glimpse through her veil, but only she may choose to show herself: like the mysteries, she hides from all but the most steadfast seeker.

The deeper mysteries of Isis, and of her consort Osiris, the god of the sun, revolve around his death at the hands of his brother Set, who cuts Osiris' body into fourteen parts and scatters them through the world. Isis undertakes a terrible journey, suffering great hardship, to seek out the broken body of her lord and to reassemble them. She does so, save for one part, the phallus, which was thrown into the Nile and consumed by a fish. Despite this, such was the creative power of Isis that she was able to conceive by means of an artificial phallus, and bore the child Horus who avenges his father by killing Set.

This is an archetypal mystery-telling, introducing themes found later in the teachings of the Hellenic schools and in the work of modern esoteric orders. It prefigures the death and rising of many gods and shows forth the power of the creative principle. It also establishes Isis as Queen of Heaven, more powerful in the eyes of many of her followers than the great god Ra himself, whose representative-upon-Earth was the Pharoah.

According to one theory the period over which the Egyptian pantheon ruled corresponds to the entire history of the world, so that the Sorrows of Isis, in which she mourns the death of Osiris rather in the manner of Mary mourning the death of Christ, relate to the agonies of our own time. The dawning of the Aquarian Age thus heralds the birth of Horus, who will come as a saviour and introduce a reign of peace and plenty.

The great student of Egyptian esotericism, R.A. Schwaller de Lubicz, described the *magnum opus* of the Egyptian mysteries as 'the reconciliation of Set and Horus', which since it has yet to occur in time could be said to reinforce the idea of the time span of the gods. (298) The reconciliation of opposing forces, and the emergence of a divine principle to bring about the redemption of mankind, are familiar themes which appear regularly in the great mystery cults of the West. From them comes belief in a divine spark in man, a fragment of godhead buried in each of us.

In Egypt this was personified in the person of the Pharoah, the son of the god on earth, whose task it was to perform the rites which would one day restore the world to the perfection of the First Time (*Tep zepi*), a lost Golden Age which existed 'before anger, or noise, or conflict, or disorder made their appearance.' (Eliade) There was no distinction between King and Priest, religious and secular office in Egypt. It was to the 'King in man', the spark of inner fire, that the people addressed themselves in their worship of the Pharoah. He, the King, was a manifestation of higher orders of creation – what de Lubicz calls *anthropocosmos*, cosmic man. In the complex structure of the Egyptian mysteries, every part of the temple, as well as the regalia of the God-King, pointed towards fulfilment, of reaching a god-like state through the enactment of the mysteries. Colours, statues, reliefs, obelisks, were all indicators of the stages of an ongoing process of perfection. Like the steps in the Alchemical Great Work, or the Architecture of the medieval cathedrals, or indeed the standing stones and circles discussed in volume one, these things were concrete externalizations of the highest mysteries.

In the many histories of the ancient world, only one figure is described as being of greater importance than Hermes. This is the Persian mage Zoroaster, who may actually have lived *c*. 1000 BC or even earlier, but who clearly did not predate the foundation of the Egyptian mysteries from which he drew significantly for his own system.

It is from the Persian mysteries, of which Zoroaster is the chief author, that we derive the dualistic spectre which has haunted esoteric philosophy and teaching ever since. In the Zoroastrian pantheon these opposing forces are Ormuzd and Ahriman, who derive ultimately from Ahura Mazda, the divine principle. Known as the Holy Immortals or Amesha Spentas (*spenta* = bounteous, the effulgence of God's goodness) they correspond to the levels of creation, clearly foreshadowing the teaching of later mystery schools such as those of Orpheus and Mithras.

Against the Spentas are arrayed the Devas, the companions of the Evil One, who are seen as ruling over the earth. They are comparable to the Qabalistic qliphoth.

The position of Persian dualism is confused by a Zoroastrian heresy called Zurvanism, which is often mistaken for mainstream Zoroastrianism. In Zoroastrianism proper, Ahura Mazda is supremely god: his Spentas are not on the same footing; Zurvanism, however, made Ahuramazda into a lesser creator or demiurge, hence the cosmic struggle of good against evil which takes place in the world of matter. In Zoroastrian teaching a saviour or *saoshyant* was to be born who would combat evil and bring the struggle to an end once and for all, betokening the *Frasokereti*, the making perfect at the end of time (cf. chapters 2 and 4).

In this we already see both an echo of the Egyptian mysteries, and a prefiguring of the later gnostic position, as well as much that has dogged the feet of recent esoteric practice where the latter has fallen into dualistic thinking. Occasionally, however, there have been moments in which the seemingly endless struggle is balanced by the appearance of a third figure – the Messiah, which as one commentator has already said, becomes a requirement of all dualistic thinking sooner or later. (109)

In Mithraism, which descended from the Persian Mysteries, Mithras stands as a mediator between light and dark, a position adopted by his followers – as, generally, by both the modern magician (see chapter 3) and the follower of Christ (see chapter 2). In humanity, the battle for the soul is fought out in the territory of the flesh. Mithras, entering there, keeps all in balance.

In this he indeed prefigures Christ, with whom he shares a number of other similarities – at times to a startling degree. Mithras is born in a cave on 25 December, watched over by shepherds, and at the end of his earthly life held a last supper with his elect followers before departing mysteriously for heaven. According to some sources he is supposed to have suffered crucifixion and to have risen again three days later: he will come again as a judge at the end of time and lead his followers to heaven. (340)

Joscelyn Godwin, in his authoritative work on the mystery religions, suggests that Mithraism is a clairvoyant prefiguring of Christianity, an idea which sits well with the inner connectedness of the mysteries. Certainly, when one reads the following extract, from a Persian Mithraic text, one is given pause to wonder. Mithras states: 'he who will not eat of my body and drink of my blood, so that he will be made one with me and I with him, the same shall not know salvation.' (104) Beyond this, the similarities are only superficial. Christianity has certainly never been as tolerant of other beliefs as Mithraism, nor has it guarded its secret half so well. On the other hand, it has survived while Mithraism has not, and to this day little is known of the Mithraic mysteries.

Still, the theme is there: the interpenetration of the physical world by the divine: macrocosm entering microcosm, God sending forth an emissary into the world. Certainly Mithraism, which was taken up by the armies of Rome and through them spread to most parts of the world, left its mark on the Native Traditions wherever it went.

While the Mithraic mysteries succeeded those of Zoroaster they followed those of Dionysius, through which the core of Hellenic mystery teaching found its way into the Western Mystery Tradition. Indeed, two streams of consciousness are discernible within the Classical mysteries which we might call, respectively, Dionysian and Apollonian. The mysteries of Dionysius were those of the sacrificed king: they pertained to the underworld side of things, the chthonic and ecstatic cult of maenads and bacchantes. The Apollonian mysteries on the other hand, related to reason, to the heavens and to order; in contradistinction to the chaotic mysteries of Dionysius. Orpheus, whose mysteries grew out of the preceding cults, combines both facets within one. He has the lyre and the gift of music from Apollo, yet ends like Dionysius, torn apart by Thracian bacchantes: the shamanic practices of the Native Tradition overlapping the priestly function of the mystery school.

In the mysteries of Dionysius we again meet the theme of the divine spark trapped in matter. In this case the divinity is literally torn apart by the Titans and eaten by them after being cooked. Zeus, the Demiurge, seeing this destroys the Titans, and from their fragmented substance creates mankind. Thus elements of both Titanic and Dionysiac force are present within man; the Titanic element holds sway, creating the warring nature of mankind. Only when total harmony and balance exist is Dionysius reborn and the perfection of all things brought about. In cosmological terms the Titans are represented by the twelve signs of the Zodiac which rule over our lives: Dionysius is the sun which warms us and causes the fruition of matter.

Dionysius belongs with those gods who descend into the underworld, either in search of enlightenment or of some lost aspect of themselves. Psyche's quest for Cupid, that of Ishtar for Tammuz, of Isis for the scattered members of Osiris or of Orpheus for Euridice, are all synonymous with the search for the absolute by the initiate. In the mysteries this is interpreted as the fragment of divinity within the seeker – through ritual he or she follows the god or goddess on their journey, returning either successful or not, according to their individual merits.

At Eleusis, where the mysteries of Demeter were celebrated every five years, the candidate of the lesser mysteries underwent a symbolic journey in which the quest of Demeter for her lost child Persephone in Hades was re-enacted with the would-be initiate in the role of

Demeter. The journey within was that of the darkened soul: the candidate passed through a door into total darkness: if he survived the experiences met within he passed through a second door into brilliant light – symbolizing rebirth into the heavenly sphere. Here he actually met the gods, experiencing Demeter's journey as his own recovery of lost enlightenment.

In the inner truth of the Elensinian mysteries the birth of the soul into matter is seen as death; only through participation in the mysteries can the initiate rise to a timeless reality where he is utterly free and alive. The soul sleeps in the body for most of the time, awakening only when it has been transformed by ritual and the use of an initiatory drink. To die without this experience is to sleep forever or to wander houseless in the caverns of Hades.

In the broadest sense all such quests and descents represent the theme of the spirit trapped in matter: the lower Ishtar, or Demeter, descend in their search, the greater their suffering; the lower man descends into matter the more he suffers his exile from the blessed realms. The fact that Psyche, Ishtar, Persephone, and Orpheus are able to return from the underworld is a symbol of hope, implying that mankind too will one day escape the prison of the flesh and be assumed again into the glory of the empyrean.

Above all it is in the Orphic mysteries that we first come to terms with this perilous descent into darkness and re-emergence again into primal light. The suffering of Orpheus, who loses Euridice (through fear, first pitfall of all mystery knowledge) and is then dismembered by the Maenads, is a paradigm of the suffering and rebirth of the sleeping soul. As a descendent of Dionysius, Orpheus is the intellectual image of a demi-god raised to deity by his sufferings in the underworld: a perfect symbol for all who follow the path of the mysteries.

The movement from the cult of Dionysius to Orphism, marks a change from a more primitive response towards an ethically-based philosophy and mysticism which included belief in the transmigration of souls, reincarnation and final assumption into godhead. In the Orphic mysteries the first real moment of stillness comes into being: the Dionysian frenzy is stilled; peace reigns. Through the strains of Orpheus' lyre is tamed more than the beasts: the beast in man, the Titanic element, is also at rest for a time.

In some senses the Orphites were 'the first real Christians' (104) – in some senses more Christian than Jesus' own followers. For this reason, perhaps, Christianity borrowed much from Orphism through the agency of the neo-Pythagorean schools of the first century – among whose initiates were Plutarch and Paul of Tarsus: there is considerable borrowing of Orphic matter in the Pauline Epistles.

The Orphic mysteries (or rather the theology built upon them) are complex in the extreme. Those desiring a full account are recommended to consult G.R.S. Mead's *Orpheus*. (226) Here, it must suffice to say that each of the energies ruling creation, the movement and delineation of the cosmos, are tabulated in series of 'Triads', 'Dodecans' and 'Monads'. Descending from the ineffable One, the Godhead, are a number of lesser powers, demigods and deities, who are each related to one another both within their separate triads and cross-related outside these triplicities. The overall rate of movement, of communication, within these correspondences, is so swift and so total as to defeat the grasp of the intellect. Only through the attainment of a super-sensible state of awareness – through initiation – can a proper understanding be arrived at.

Orphic cosmology also suggested that each star or planetary sphere contained aspects of *all* the deities. Thus there were, for example, a lunar Ceres, a saturnine Apollo, a mercurial Hera and so on. And of course there were planetary aspects present within each of the deities, so that an aspect of Dionysius also contained lunar, solar, saturnine declensions within him. The gods themselves thus formed a constantly shifting matrix of planetary influence, which meant that an initiate who invoked a lunar deity was at one and the same time in touch with all the gods and thus all the planetary influences of the heavens.

This complex organization kept the cosmos turning and insured that, however intricate Orphic theology and cosmology became, the most important aspect could be grasped through direct experience. This was that mankind and the gods are related; at a most subtle and sensitive level a blurring of edges occurs, an overlapping of human consciousness and divine awareness. 'Everything that lives is holy' becomes a reality in the interaction of the divine and the mundane. The hierarchy of spiritual creation is supremely complex, but the gods are like a ladder, a system of related possibilities, the potentiality of which is seeded within the whole of creation. We are all, indeed, related – not only in a familial scene (cf. volume one) but also to everything: earth and water, sky and stone; not only because all of creation is made up of different combinations of molecules, but because we are all a part of the divine hierarchy.

This is the true meaning of the mystery teaching concerning the divine spark; the god-like potential of humanity is far better expressed by this means than by any discussion of man as Superman. The divine fragment is that part of us which is always seeking reunion, a reassembly of separated parts into the whole from which they were created; a return to the paradisial state before the Fall. The torn body of the God, scattered through creation, must be restored.

> Man then is of twofold nature, the Titanic and the Dionysiac, the earthly and the divine. The aim of the Orphic life is by purification, asceticism and ritual to purge away the Titanic part of us and prepare ourselves to become fully divine. The body . . . is a tomb from which the soul of the Orphic initiate will finally be released to find the true life. (353)

It sometimes taking as many as a thousand year cycles before the Orphite at last flees the weary wheel of incarnation.

The Orphic school was, above all, syncretic. Orpheus is credited with the dissemination of the mysteries, with passing on rather than inventing, much that became the basis of subsequent Greco-Roman theosophy. Pythagoras followed many of the Orphic teachings and made Orpheus the central deity of his own esoteric system, establishing a canon of Orphic Hymns which were to influence esotericists as far apart in time and persuasion as Pico della Mirandola (351), Athanasius Kircher (102) and Thomas Taylor the Platonist (325).

This is not surprising when one considers that 'the Orphic method aimed at revealing divine things by means of symbols . . . a method common to all writers of divine lore' (270). In later times Orpheus was widely recognized: particularly for the symbolism of the seven stringed lyre and the perfect harmonies he was believed to have produced from it. Combined with Pythagorean knowledge, the Orphic mysteries became central to the Renaissance arts of music and masque, and to the doctrine of the Harmonies and Signatures set forth by writers such as Jacob Boehme (1575–1624) and Marcilio Ficino (1453–99). Orpheus was recognized as a son of Apollo and Calliope, the Muse of harmony and rhythm; Euridice becomes humanity slain by the serpent of knowledge (perhaps an instance of later borrowing from Christian sources) imprisoned in the underworld of ignorance from which only Orpheus could free her. The rending of Orpheus becomes an image of the warring factions of knowledge, nominally pacified by his music. The seven strings of his lyre are the seven keys of the spectrum, or of universal knowledge. (116)

Figure 4: Hermes Trismegistos

We can see how this wealth of symbolism must have delighted the minds of the Renaissance philosopher-magicians, who sought to reintroduce the mysteries into the world and like Orpheus harmonize them into a single system. That they failed to do so was not for want of effort, as we shall see in chapter 3. They came as near as anyone could to achieving a synthesis of mystery school teaching, magic and philosophy – a goal still sought by many today, though with a good deal less understanding of the common points of balance between one discipline and another.

Between the Orphic mysteries and their partial revival in the Renaissance there is a long gap, not only in time but in understanding. In part this was bridged by the figure of the magician, whose role will be discussed more fully in chapter 3; and the Alchemist, whose work we shall investigate in chapter 5. The magician, in particular, is related to the earlier mystery schools, while the Alchemist draws upon a far wider range of sources, including Arabic metaphysics and Christian mysticism. The single force which unites all these elements is the body of teaching attributed to Hermes Trismegistos, 'Thrice Greatest' Hermes, whose doctrines stand at the very heart of the Western Way.

THE HERMETIC REALITY

Hermes saw the totality of things. Having seen, he understood, he had the power to reveal and show. And indeed what he knew, he wrote down. What he wrote, he mostly hid away, keeping silence rather than speaking out, so that every generation on coming into the world had to seek out these things. (302)

This strikes the keynote of Hermeticism: the coming of the human soul into matter without knowledge, and the search for the hidden mysterious truths seeded throughout the world, through which freedom might be gained. In particular we note that 'every generation' has to 'seek out these things'. The mysteries are not calcified, not frozen in time; they change and grow with the changes that occur in mankind. It is another side to the idea that humanity contains a spark of the divine, seeking always to return to its point of origin. Though the quest here is more one of abstract knowledge, behind it we may detect a deeper goal: 'A desire for the truth, especially about the gods is in reality a yearning for the Deity. For the study and search (for these things) in a reception, as it were, of things sacred. . . ' (270) This is the Hermetic quest: it is reiterated throughout the whole vast spectrum of wisdom, mystery text and inner-directed learning which is the true *Corpus Hermeticum*, the reality behind the texts which have come down to us. These are really only a gathering of fragments, attributed to Thoth Tahuti (later called Hermes) but few of genuine Egyptian origin. They have been copied, recopied, edited, altered and in part destroyed by a succession of Hermetic 'scholars' and exegetes down the ages. As Iamblichus noted, the earliest philosophers and mystics used to ascribe their own writings to Hermes, as god of wisdom and learning, in such a way that one would suppose that he had written them personally! (152) This has given rise to much confusion over the origins of the *Corpus* – added to which Hermes often appears as a character in the texts, making it even harder to discover actual sources for the material. Hermes, we remember, hid much that he had written: enough still remains to be uncovered to make it difficult to write with authority about the existing *Corpus*.

It is, however, safe to say that it was in the melting-pot of Alexandrian mysticism and philosophy during the first three centuries after Christ that the original Egyptian Hermetic writings became cross-fertilized with Judaic and Greek teachings of the Gnostics. The influence of the *Corpus* on Gnosticism was considerable, and it is probably this more than anything which helped preserve the Hermetic tradition, though it cast it permanently into a pseudo-Christian mode (So much so that in the sixteenth century the Humanist philosopher Francesco Patrizi petitioned Pope Gregory XIV to allow Hermes to supplant Aristotle as the arbiter of learning in the universities as he would resonate more harmoniously with Christian doctrine. (107).

In Gnostic literature Thoth became Hermes Trismegistos and Maat his wife was identified with the figure of Sophia or Divine Wisdom. The three grades of initiation recognized by the early Hermeticists – Mortals (probationers), Intelligences (vision seekers), and Sons of Light (perfected ones) – were renamed Hyle, Psyche, and Pneuma (cf. Chapter 2). Hermes became tutor to Isis and Osiris, and was known as one of the sacred ogdoad of the Gnostic cosmology; four pairs of male and female syzygies whose task it was to maintain balance in the cosmos. According to Mead this is the oldest form of the Gnostic structure of deity, and within it Hermes has the supreme task of keeping order amongst the rest.

The title Trismegistos or Thrice Greatest has had several different meanings attributed to it. One of the most interesting is found in the writings of the monk Syncellus, who claimed to be quoting from the writings of Menetho, whose works, though lost, were probably the earliest gathering of Hermetic lore. (147) He, according to Syncellus, refers to certain monuments of the *Seriadic* country, which contained the original teachings of the *first* Hermes. These were later translated and set down in writing by the *second* Hermes ('sometime after the Flood'). From this it is possible to posit the existence of a *third* figure, also called by the name of Hermes, who again worked on the texts, perhaps rendering them into a form of system. All of which indicates three stages of transmission. Hence 'thrice greatest' refers to a *third* avatar bearing the title of the God, to whom came to be attributed the whole lore and writings of the original Hermeticists.

Of what, then, does the *Corpus Hermeticum* consist? Basically it is a series of exchanges, purporting to be between pupil and master, or between Hermes Trismegistos and his 'sons' (i.e. disciples) of various names. They are often repetitive and cover much of the same ground in varying degrees of complexity. The first, and perhaps the best known, is the *Poimandres*, a description of the creation cast in the form of a dream. The (here unnamed) adept falls asleep and is visited by Poimandres (Mind of the Sovereignty) who explains to him all that he has wished to know concerning 'the things that are, (how to) understand their nature, and get knowledge of God' (302):

> When he had thus spoken, forthwith all things changed in aspect before me, and were opened out in a moment. And I beheld a boundless view: all was changed into light, a mild and joyous light; and I marvelled when I saw it. . .

There follows a description of the creation, a mingling of light and dark from which comes forth 'a holy Word . . . and methought this Word was the voice of the Light.' When the seeker desires to understand what he has seen, Poimandres tells him: 'That light . . . is I, even Mind, the first God . . . and the Word which came forth from the Light is the son of God.'
When the dreamer asks how this may be, he is told:

> Learn my meaning . . . by looking at what you yourself have in you; for in you too, the word is son, and the mind is father of the word. They are not separate one from the other; for life is the union of word and mind. (ibid)

Again and again this message is affirmed: there is a god within which gives life to the body and inspiration of all that we do: events in the sphere of incarnation reflect those in the heavenly sphere. It is this emphasis on unity rather than disharmony which marks out the Hermetic mysteries: unity of all things, of God with man, of higher with lower, of divine with mundane. It finds its clearest expression in the *Emerald Tablet of Hermes* with its famous injunction 'as above, so below', so often quoted and so little understood by occultists throughout the ages.

Various legends exist concerning the origin of the Emerald or 'Smagdarine' tablet. According to one source it was found by Apollonius of Tyana (cf. Chapter 3) who entered a hidden cave and took the tablet from between the clasped hands of the corpse of Hermes himself. Another version recounts how it was Alexander the

Great who found the tomb and carried off the tablet to Alexandria – an interesting memory of the transmission of the Hermetic mysteries from its possible place of origin to the city where its truths became disseminated widely. (197)

In reality, the text of the *Emerald Tablet* was for a long time known only in Latin versions dating from the time of the philosopher Albertus Magnus (1193–1280) who was believed to have written the material himself. Subsequently Arabic texts were discovered which dated the *Tablet* to the time of the Alchemist Gebir (722–815) or even earlier, so that the traditional ascription of its composition to Apollonius may in fact be closer to the truth than any of these theories.

Whatever one chooses to believe there is no getting away from the fact that the *Emerald Tablet* is one of the most profound and important documents to have come down to us. It has been said more than once that it contains the sum of all knowledge – for those able to understand it.

The *Tablet* outlines a doctrine of signatures and correspondences which reflect the mind of the Creator. The Greek word from which we derive cosmos means 'order', and we live in an ordered creation through which we are able to move at will yet always find a point of recognition. This is because the cosmos is the product of a single act of generation which has set a signature upon everything. In the finite world in which we attempt to bind ourselves this is scarcely recognized by anyone; yet the youngest mystery school initiate would have known it once, no matter how many different gods he worshipped.

The Smagdarine Tablet describes just such an ordered cosmos: it tells the story of creation, its history and its goal in terms of such blinding simplicity that, in common with other, equally simple statements ('love thy neighbour as thyself', for example) it has been subject to frequent misinterpretation. Our own suggestions as to its meaning will be found in chapter 5, while the text itself has been placed at the end of the chapter, where it forms an exercise in controlled meditation and may be studied free of any commentary.

Initiation, it is said, is always a one-to-one experience: the seeker stands alone (however supported by his or her brethren) before whatever principle he seeks to know. In the Western Way, as we have tried to show, all knowledge and experience thus gained is part of a single initiation we must all undergo. It was for this reason that the Temple of Thoth was called the House of the Net, meaning the enclosing snare of matter. To escape this the captive (the initiate) must learn the parts of the net – its poles, ropes, weights and so forth – in order to turn it to his own use, as a means of catching the food of the spirit. An ancient prayer reads: 'Hail, ye net-inverters, fishers and catchers of the spirit which alone nourishes! By refining your higher selves, ye have produced that which produced you.' (227) Again the familiar theme: discover yourselves and you discover God. It is not strange that the imagery here echoes that of Christ's 'I will make you fishers of men' (Mark, Chap.I,17) which can be read as meaning that those who follow the way will find themselves, and in themselves find God.

This is why Hermetic teaching places such importance on the place of man in the cosmos. He is seen as central in that he touches the boundaries of creation at every level, and because he possesses within him the encoded mysteries of matter, spirit and mind. Plato recognized this in the *Timaeus* (67) which he is believed to have derived from Egyptian sources. Here he defines the cosmos as a living creature, formed after the manner of the most perfect synthesis of creation – the human cosmic being, anthropocosmos, Adam Kadmon. According to Proclus' commentaries on the *Timaeus* (54) this is to be equated with the Orphic Man of Light, who is threefold and contains the essence of all creation. This threefold division of matter into *Phanes* (shining), *Erikepaois* (power, male), and *Metis* (wisdom, female), represents a profound understanding of the breakdown of matter into its component parts, which when reassembled make up the perfection which is the closest we can get to understanding the nature of God.

It is on this doctrine of unity that the foundation of Hermeticism rests. We have grown used to a dualistic tendency in Western philosophy since Zoroaster, but in the Orphic and Hermetic schools the emphasis was on balance, polarity, the coming together of elements into a unique whole. This is why the gnostic Hermes is represented as being the uniting principle in the system of the ogdoads. As one ancient text has it: 'One is the All . . . and if the All did not contain the All, the All would be nothing.' (22) Once again we hear the echo of the divine interaction between God (the One) and creation (Matter, the All). It is not just incidental that Hermes' symbol is a staff with twin serpents of wisdom and understanding coiled about it. As in the Qabala, where the central pillar holds those of left and right in balance, here too the principle is the same.

The mysteries were always intended to be understood in a threefold fashion: with the spirit, the mind and the senses. Such a threefold division has continued to be recognized in Western esoteric practice ever since. Sacred words, uttered in temple or lodge, echo through three worlds: the divine, the intellectual and the physical, bringing all three together in a *rapprochement* which causes them to vibrate harmoniously one with the other.

The universe (or God) is always willing to respond to an harmonious note emitted by those in tune with the infinite Word of creation. To find that note within the self has ever been the most important action of the mystery seeker. Initiation leads towards just this point; study and self-observation, discipline and obedience, self-abdication: all acts of the adept are aimed first at realizing the divine harmonic within himself and then in tuning this to include the whole of the creation in which he stands.

The elements of creation may well be divided and scattered, as the myths of the Titans and the rending of gods like Dionysius and Osiris suggest, but what has been divided can be joined again – in the story of Isis and Osiris even the absence of the phallus did not prevent the creation of the divine child, Horus, the uniting principle which ushered in a new age of peace and harmony.

In this sense the passions of Christ, Baldur, Tammuz, of all the saviour gods, can be seen as a wholly natural process in which matter seeks out its component parts and reunites to form the whole which was the original design of the cosmos. God is lonely for the children that are lost to him, the fragments of himself created so that he could know himself. We should not be surprised, therefore, to find him sending forth his beloved Son – the nearest aspect of himself – into matter to seek out those lost ones.

Christ and Hermes with all of the shepherd gods, are come to gather in their flocks. But they cannot do so unaided. We must be willing to co-operate, to harmonize with them as we do whenever we celebrate the mysteries. Thus the glorious anamnesis of the Eucharist, the love-feast of the Agathadaimon, are aimed at giving us a glimpse outside the walls of our chaotic, fractured universe at the peace and tranquillity which can be ours – if we wish it to be.

This, then, is the Hermetic reality: the maintaining of a divine unity within the mundane sphere, which in turn raises that sphere to divine heights. As above so below, always. God imprints everything at the moment of creation with a divine signature, the DNA of the cosmos, which makes every rose a rose, every man a man, every beast a beast. And this signature contains the very essence of the creator, his message to all that he has caused to have being: like to like, very like to very like, the One and the All contained in each other. As a seventeenth-century Hermeticist put it:

> The Sun and the Moon I see above me influence me neither for good nor bad, but the Sun and Moon and Planets (with) which God's providence has adorned the heaven *in me*, which also is the seat of the Almighty, these have the power to rule and reform me according to their course ordained by God. (84, our italics.)

The methods by which such a point of realization might be attained, the practice behind the theology, are what we must look at next.

THE LANGUAGE OF DESIRE

The Mystery Schools are really containers for certain concepts and images designed to assist in the building of inner worlds where the perfection of humanity and eventually of all material things can take place. A fully functioning and active Mystery School is a power house generating energies from which both the individual seeker and the great teachers of the age can draw strength and sustenance. We must be aware that:

> The highest of our initiations here below is only the dream of that true vision and initiation; and the discourses (on the mysteries) have been carefully devised to awaken the memory of the sublime things above or else are of no purpose. (228)

In other words the 'sublime things' must be reflected by those who attempt to realize them; they must be remembered by the initiate so that he or she can embody the divine truth in themselves. (96)

But entrance to the mysteries is first dependent upon a degree of maturity. In Egypt, it was said that before one can know the spiritual Isis one must first know her terrestrial aspect. This meant that a thorough grounding in knowledge of earthly and mortal existence was necessary before the inner mysteries were opened to the initiate. The same is no less true today, and nothing should be attempted by the serious student until he or she has 'put their house in order', learning to cope with the stresses and strains of the ordinary world. If you cannot survive the daily grind of living you will certainly find it hard to sustain the rigours of a magical working. If, on the other hand, you master both aspects of being, there will gradually begin to be an overlap – your normal life will become permeated with magical understanding, and your magical life with the fruits of human wisdom. In the end, both will be transformed.

> The beginning of wisdom is the most sincere desire for instruction, and concern for instruction is love of wisdom. . . . For she is a reflection of eternal light, a spotless mirror of the working of God, and an image of his goodness.(Wisdom of Solomon 6,17)

Desire is a beginning, but once contact with the invisible hierarchy is made, it is for the initiate alone to keep the flame of his or her intention alive and to learn to be a reflection of 'the working of God, and an image of his goodness. . . '

Without that initial spark of desire, there can be no progress; and even then the journey will seldom be easy or swift. Years of study, discipline and concentration lie before the would-be seeker. He must come to terms with his innermost longings, fears and hopes before he can even begin to reach that state of consciousness where he may expect to walk with gods and converse with angels.

An initiation, by its very nature, is a form of inner pressure designed to 'shock' the initiate into a sense of his or her inner capability. In almost every instance we find that the mysteries contain the dramatic reconstruction of a primary myth, in which the would-be initiate takes his or her part, playing either the central role or the part of an onlooker, but always involved directly or otherwise in the events. At Eleusis human procreation and birth were shown to be the first steps on an initiatory journey: a preparation for the soul's passage through life and the voyage into the Underworld. The little death of initiation prepared the way for the greater life and the greater death. Persephone returns from Hades, but is subject to Pluto thereafter; the initiate survives his ordeals but will never be the same again. Finally, the soul is freed to return to its origin. This world is but a reflection of the Elysian fields, as Plato saw. In its mirror, we see ourselves – but transformed.

Nevertheless, initiation is not a ceremony or set of rituals which automatically ensures enlightenment. It merely marks the ingoing of the candidate; a transition period. The knowledge gained thereafter is of an interior and instinctive kind, purely personal in the way and shape it manifests itself. Though the path is by no means an easy one, certain common practices are as much a part of contemporary training as they were in the great Classical schools.

Apart from preliminary suitability, good health, a sense of integrity, dedication and so forth, the candidate will have to resign him or herself to patient effort during the seemingly tedious period of technical training. Whatever is required by the teacher must be met, in equal measure, by the student. What is important is not the success, but the honest effort at attainment. What took one student six months may take another two or three years, depending upon ability and circumstance. Speed is not important: seemingly brilliant students often spurt ahead in the early stages and then lose interest because they are insufficiently mature to plod through the donkey-work, whereas a seemingly dull and conscientious pupil might take longer to assimilate training but achieve a higher standard of under-standing.

Basic to early training is a thorough acquaintance and mastery of the elemental qualities within the student. Fire, Water, Earth and Air is the four-square basis of magical competence, and without a complete understanding of the elements within the self, the student will be as the Sorcerer's Apprentice (who incidentally could not control the element of water in either an Inner or Outer capacity). W.G.Gray gives many excellent exercises in his *Magical Ritual Methods* (115) for familiarizing oneself with one's elemental strengths and shortcomings. Work with the Elemental kings and kingdoms is often scorned and neglected as too basic for the Herme-tic student; but like breathing and relaxation it is an essential quality for the esotericist (cf. Exercise 5).

One of the first requirements of a magical school once the initial training is over, is to set the candidate to making a set of ritual implements. These are the mainstay of the occultist – the extension of his personality and the elemental symbols of his or her craft. The Wand, Sword, Chalice and Pentacle or Patten signify the elements of Air, Fire, Water and Earth respectively. The initiate is expected, if not to work the metals himself, at least to work upon the naked blade until it resembles the sword of his will. Likewise, he or she will cut the wood and fashion the wand, engrave or cut the pentacle, paint or scribe the sigils on the cup or chalice. A practical mastery of the elements is basic at this point.

As we shall see, the Gnostics and Mandeans left instructions for their initiates as to how they should leave the earthly sphere and progress through the spheres or levels of the Archons – the rulers of the planets. In the mysteries also, the next step is often a familiarity with planetary powers and influences. The initiate may acquire this by many means, becoming, as we have seen, familiar with the correspondences devised in the Orphic schools. But the method most likely to be used in our own time is the investigation of the planetary attributions on the qabalistic Tree of Life. Each sphere or sephira on the Tree has its ruling planet, its vice and virtue, whereby this power can be usefully or destructively applied. The charity of Tiphareth can easily fall over into selfishness, the dynamic strength of Geburah into destructive violence. The candidate for higher initiations will be expected to progress through these sephiroth one by one as stages along the way, and to equilibriate the positive and negative qualities within him or her self. (See fig. 117)

Gradually the initiate is refining many levels of the self, attuning them to the Inner. This task is never really complete in the lifetime of the initiate, any more than any human being should expect perfection. It is ongoing and repetitious. The basal urgings of our lower nature are never completely rooted out, though they can be kept under control and even used positively as a thrust-block to our attainments. Periods of trial come even to the adept, who is by no means exempt from the trivial or earth-shattering problems of human life. From those who receive, more is required, goes the occult adage. The failings of the humble go unnoticed; those of the famous or infamous are the subject of newspaper headlines.

The responsibility of the adept, the true walker-between-the-worlds, is not just to those students and co-workers on the Outer, but to the forces of the Inner who rely upon their mastery of the Outer, as well as their aptitude in mediating the work of the Inner thence forward. We shall discuss this important aspect of training more fully in the chapter dealing with the Magician and his work.

The Mystery Schools demand firstly 'know thyself'. The Lesser Mysteries are spent in clearing the ground ready for the dawning of this event. The Greater Mysteries come only when this basis is established, when the initiate can stand alone, in command of his inner fortress; when the threshold is swept and made ready for the descent of the Holy Guardian Angel or the Inner Master. The preparation complete, the levels of the self clearly perceived, the initiate is then ready for the identification with the god-forms or archetypes of his or her school.

Identification with an archetype demands a great deal of objectivity and cannot be attempted in early stages of training. Like a dancer or actor who has spent years perfecting the body, the voice, the numerous forms of their art, and who steps upon the stage at last before a live audience, so it is with the initiate. There can be no confusion between theory and practice, no running to the wings to consult a book or a teacher on a point of technique or a personal problem. The initiate is alone with the archetype and the identification one with the other must be a total communication so that the energies of the archetype can be mediated successfully. It is easy to spot an actor who is not really acting: his eyes lack conviction, like a person telling a lie, his movements are not carried through, his voice veers away from the sense of the script, he does not truly interact with the other actors on stage and often hinders their performance. He does not convince the audience either, who sit and shuffle. An initiate's mediation can suffer in just such a way, but he does not just fail his fellow ritualists. The audience, in this instance, is the Outer – for whose benefit a ritual is performed. The producers are the Inner, who are quite justified in taking their work elsewhere and seeking a new cast.

The first kind of identification required of an initiate comes in an acceptably easy way – he or she is asked to officiate as the officer of a quarter, mediating a particular quality to the lodge or circle. We say easy, but it is often hard work: the qualities of the elemental kings must be present and operative within the quarter-officer. One becomes a doorway or channel through which the quarter-guardians (who may be either god-forms or angels) can come. This requires concentration and alertness, not a passive overpowering by the Inner contact. It is work of a privileged kind, and reveals to the initiate the priestly qualities inherent in his craft. The circle or working area is a division of matter into elements, and those most at home in one quarter with one element will feel drawn there. Nevertheless, an ability to work from *any* quarter is important and should be cultivated; it will anyway follow naturally if the inner elements have been properly balanced. A very good breakdown of this kind of work will be found in Gareth Knight's *The Rose Cross and the Goddess*. (184) and in W.B. Gray's *Inner Traditions of Magic* (114)

Later, the initiate may be asked to participate in ritual dramas which enact the stories of the gods employed by his or her school. Here, just as in the ancient schools, the initiate will represent the Mighty Ones themselves. This is an awesome function which is not assigned to the unready; dangers of over-identification or ego-centric appropriation are present, but may be avoided by a simple procedure prior to the rite in question.

This can be done in two ways. First, the archetype to be assumed is visualized as a mask which the initiate will put on. Just as in the

Greek mystery dramas, the initiate will go apart silently before the ritual and contemplate the mask, possibly holding a dialogue with it in imagination, establishing it as a separate entity from him or herself. The symbolism surrounding the archetype can be rehearsed objectively, the stories and correspondences of this figure compared with those of other pantheons and traditions. Then the mask is assumed, in the wings, as it were, of the working place. The second method takes this a stage further: it may not be suitable in all cases nor be appropriate to certain kinds of individuals. The mask is visualized before one and enshrined: flowers and incense are placed before it, prayers said, invoking the qualities required in the rite – the archetype in question becoming, for a time, one of the 'masks of God'. The assumption of the mask is correspondingly a more awesome thing for the initiate, but there is no danger of over-identification.

Relinquishing the mask at the end of the ritual, the initiate performs the same procedure, only in reverse, returning the mask to the shrine, or visualizing it, face away from him, returning to the Inner. Such an identification is never done for the gratification of the individual – a fact which few appreciate who have not stood in the circle dropping from exhaustion and Inner pressure resultant from the technique. Dion Fortune spoke wisely when she recommended the work of a blacksmith as lighter than that of the ritualist. The pressures and strains are many, not only on the physique but upon the astral and etheric bodies. Depletion of energy is usual at the conclusion of a ritual: energy is built up and mediated properly, not left to slew around in a vacuum. There is nothing abnormal or sinister in this: particularly important pieces of work require more energy than others, and the re-energization of the individual will take correspondingly longer. This will be less so when working with a larger group, where the energies will be shared out and the demands are less great on the individual. In cases where extreme exhaustion is suffered, a good night's sleep and an intake of nourishment will normally suffice to replenish the spent ritualist, otherwise the use of exercise 9 is recommended.

Little enough emphasis is given by modern mystery schools to the training of the body as well as the psyche. A good ritualist should be deft in hand-gestures, have a supple torso, good posture and carriage and be able to operate without falling over his or her feet. Physical clumsiness is often the result of mental unpreparedness or lack of concentration. The demands upon the body are immense and if insufficient training is given to keep the physical instrument in good working condition, then the magical work will suffer also. Sport and dance are obviously helpful here, but they cannot cater for the peculiar requirements of the esotericist, who has to consider *all* his or her bodies! Schools would do well to consider introducing classes of ritual movement and ask their experienced members to speak more openly about the physical side-effects of ritual work. The mature body is, strange to relate, better equipped for the strains of ritual than the young. The ageing body depletes quicker than both but often has greater staying-power. (263)

On the other hand, rewards can be great – provided you do not expect them to be material. Aspirations are high indeed – but then the watchword of most contemporary mystery schools is 'responsibility' – care, that is, for the self and for the divinity within – not in a selfish way but in an effort to bring humankind into line with its infinite potential. It is this end to which the trials, tests, rituals and initiations must lead.

Within each individual is the possibility of becoming, microcosmically, Adam Kadmon. The final outcome of this will be the uniting of all humanity in one being – the Body of Light which Poimandres speaks of as the source of the Word. For this reason many modern schools describe themselves, variously, as 'servants' or 'societies' of light – and the theme has become prominent within New Age movements of recent times. To be a servant of the light is to be, as the initiates of the original schools were, dedicated to the freeing of the divine spark.

This has sometimes led to an ecstatic response, and the ultimate experience of the divine has been sought through both asceticism and an ecstatic sexuality. But if, as the Dionysian mysteries suggest, we are made up in part of the stuff of the Titans, it is little wonder if our response to the infinite arises as much from a sexual as a religious basis.

So often the archetypal presences invoked within the mysteries translate into the basic elements of life itself – sperm and ovum – and we see a sexual polarity problem of the kind we spoke of in volume one (cf. chapter 5 of this volume). Sexuality could be used as an ecstatic method in which union with another human being becomes an expression of the divine union of the Saviour-god with his or her beloved. This was often utilized ritually when a priest or priestess represented the deity in themselves. The abuses of temple prostitution were remarked upon with distaste by several Classical authors who travelled in the Middle East and saw their own mysteries in later ascetic forms which were devoid of the earlier and earthier celebrations which were a part of the Native traditions.

In earlier times, the identification of the priest or priestess with the deity enabled the people or their ruler to have congress with the divine guardian of the tribe. The Classical mysteries still bore this understanding subtextually within their celebrations, yet within the mysteries of Eleusis, for example, the hierophant drank a draught which specifically inhibited his sexual function. He was always chosen from an Eleusinian family and was himself married in the normal way: not, as with many of the Eastern cults, castrated in the service of the Goddess. (356, 339)

Sexuality within ritual is thus a constant reminder of earlier resonances: it should never intervene in the flow of energies in any operation whereby the work becomes earth-bound. The esoteric Judaic and Qabalistic practice of union with one's wife in order to mirror the union of God with the Shekhina, comes nearer to an understanding of how sexuality can be made to express the deepest religious impulse upon earth. The abuse of this in magic occurs when the levels are confused. On the ecstatic or tribal level of consciousness, sexuality is an honest expression of religious fervour translated into human terms.

All of this may well lead one to ask: what does this exalted work have to do with me – surely it is for the highest adepts, dedicated to a greater service than is possible for the ordinary follower of the Western Way. Not so: we are all, if we so desire it, servants of light, and dedication is possible to all – to a greater or lesser degree according to our personal capacity.

All mystery schools and orders, of whatever kind, exist to train the mind and the heart, the intellect and the soul, until they are working together at the highest level of perfection. Such things may take more than one incarnation, depending upon the stage of development already reached by the student. When all have been trained and have fully realized themselves then the work of the Schools, Fraternities and orders will be completed– there will no longer be any need for them since humanity will have reached the point of development intended for it, to aid which those we call Masters have been sent. (91)

The Western Way is one means to that end, one among many, but it is a means only and not an end in itself. Those who think of it in this light will travel no further than the first few steps – they will find themselves traversing the same section of the road again and again, endlessly travelling but never arriving.

Although the emphasis in this book is on the practical, it should not be considered in any way a substitute for proper training or belonging to an order or lodge. There is an increasing tendency towards solitary working, and this is well supported by the habits of the Renaissance, where more often than not a group of people *could not* meet to celebrate the mysteries. So, if you are a lone worker either from choice or circumstance, this book is aimed at giving you a grasp of the essential requirements of the would-be initiate. However, if the opportunity to work with a group comes your way, do not pass it up – providing of course that it appears to be properly organized and governed.

The choice of a school can be fraught with difficulties: there are so many and their approaches are often bewilderingly different. Instinct and inner awareness alone can tell you when you have found one that feels right – though it does not follow that you will feel right to them. If all goes well, however, and you are accepted as a candidate, this should be the beginning of a satisfying and rewarding association, You should have gained at least some idea of what to expect from the foregoing pages; however, we have yet to bring the picture up-to-date, to follow the thread of the mysteries foward in time to the present.

GUARDIANS OF TRADITION

Just as the Medieval and Renaissance mysteries can be traced to a Hermetic impulse, so the schools and fraternities of our own time owe their origin primarily to what may be termed the Rosicrucian impulse. Yet, by one of those paradoxes which seem to govern the transmission of the Western Way, there is no evidence that either the Rosicrucian Brotherhood or its founder Christian Rosenkreutz had any physical existence at all.

The first that anyone in the outside world knew of the Rosicrucians was in 1614, when a curious document entitled *Fama Fraternitatis of the Meritorious Order of the Rose Cross* (6) appeared in Germany and was widely circulated. It purported to be a description of the life of one Christian Rosenkreutz, philosopher, mystic and magician, who had lived to the age of 106 and whose body was then concealed in a secret tomb which was not discovered for another 120 years.

This places the life-time of Rosenkreutz at the end of the four-teenth or the beginning of the fifteenth century, though there are no records from that – or indeed any – time which relate to his actual existence. The description of the finding of the vault containing his uncorrupted remains is written in highly symbolic language which reads like an initiatory text. (Certainly, to follow the steps leading to the discovery of the body, followed by the description of the vault itself, and to mediate upon them, can be a richly rewarding experi-ence.)

The opening of the vault is, in the *Fama*, likened to an event of far-reaching effect: 'for like as our door was after so many years wonderfully discovered, also there shall be opened a door to Europe . . . which already doth begin to appear, and with great desire is expected of many.' (6) Judging by the reaction across Europe to the *Fama* and the manifestos which followed it, the desire and expecta-tion must have been considerable. A new hope was seeded thereby which had nothing to do with the effects of the Renaissance – medieval attitudes were still abroad and enlightenment battled uneasily with a mysticism which retained the blinkers of dogma and superstition.

The authorship of the first Rosicrucian manifesto has been traced speculatively to the University of Tubingen and more precisely to one Johann Valentin von Andrae, yet behind the human authors we can detect the beginning of a powerful new stream of inner teaching which found an outlet in this manner. (195) No one knew the whereabouts of the Rosicrucian brotherhood but this did not stop many who read and understood the true value of the manifestos from trying to make physical contact. The fact that there were writings which spoke of a brotherhood of adepts who could be contacted 'through proper channels' was enough to prompt many to advertise in newsheets for more information. Even the philosopher René Descartes went to Germany to seek out the brotherhood and, not surprisingly perhaps, found nothing. Yet on his return to Paris in 1623 he was forced to show himself publicly in order to prove that he had not become invisible– i.e. that he was not a Rosicrucian – for so had the rumours circulated. (365)

When no reply was forthcoming to the various inquiries sent to non-existent addresses or people, enthusiasts were driven to publish their own books and pamphlets to see whether their ideas resonated harmonically with other would-be Rosicrucians similarly situated. Thus the original manifestos spawned a succession of imitators and commentaries, constellating their writers into the formation of a mystery school whose doctrines were set out for all to read who could understand them – an odd reversal of the classical schools who hid their teachings from all but their initiates.

This is surely a prime example of the way a mystery school receives its formatory impulse: it has certainly been a much repeated method since the age of the Rosicrucians. Not that their own writings can be in any way described as clear statements of intent or belief. The language employed is allusive and full of symbolism which must have prevented all but those in the know from understanding what was being said. Ever thus do the mysteries guard themselves from idle curiosity.

Initially we may see von Andrae and his fellow philosophers at Tubingen reacting against the climate of the times, so that when the writer of the *Fama*, who had long since admitted its composition, while denying its importance as a document, included in his will the words: 'Though I now leave the Fraternity itself, I shall never leave the true Christian Fraternity, which, beneath the Cross, smells of the Rose, and is quite apart from the filth of this century.' (207)

At its heart the Rosicrucian impulse was a combination of esoteric Christianity with straight mystery-school teaching as it had been kept alive in the work of the magician and the alchemist. That it transcended both points of origin is an indication of the power of the inner impulse which brought it into being: the symbols of the Rose and the Cross combined to make the first real synthesis of magical and mystical teaching since the original Hermetic impulse.

The idea of an invisible college of adepts is, as we shall see in chapter 4, not so rare as we may think. Rosicrucianism survived because it had no visible foundation, no headquarters, no officers, no dogmas and no rules of membership.

The effect of this on the European world of the seventeenth century was deep and lasting. It paved the way for the French esoteric revival of the next century, which was thus able to draw upon both Native and Hermetic Traditions at a deep level. This was aided in part by the operations of another body of initiates – the Freemasons; for though a conjunction of Rosicrucianism and Freemasonry cannot be ascertained with any surety, Freemasonry became an important vessel of Rosicrucian survival.

Freemasonry itself grew out of the crafts-guilds and friendly burial societies of the pre-Reformation. The Master of his 'mystery' or craft-profession was a powerful man, and together the crafts-guilds exerted a considerable pressure on society. This is still observable today where an ostensibly esoteric movement exerts a high degree of political influence. Masonry's origins, like those of Rosicrucianism, are retrospective in their construction. The supposed 'life' of Christian Rosenkreutz, like the building of Jerusalem's temple and the Murder of Hiram, are all thematically important – yet to claim these resonances as historically traceable is to confuse Inner with Outer realities.

If Rosicrucianism is the Germanic Protestant impulse, as many have seen it to be, then Freemasonry is a British esoteric one: their fusion was not entirely curious. The Protestant ethic had left sad lacunae in the life of medieval confraternities whose esoteric pursuits had probably been no more than an occasional mass celebrated by the guild's priest, or the usual kind of initiatory high-jinks practised upon freshmen at university or apprentices in crafts today. The guilds remained, but their ritual life was severely curtailed. Masonry may well have been formed upon the principles of the crafts-guilds, as an 'inner circle' by masters of their crafts and thence permeated through to learned gentlemen of leisure whose antiquarian and classical background would give them ample scope for the creation of rationalizing legends to accompany these new 'mystery schools'. God was the architect of the macrocosm and Christ, his apprentice, was a carpenter in that microcosm we inhabit. The idea of co-inherence was thus carried forward into a new era of esoteric belief.

There is something fundamentally Protestant in the conception of the Divine Architect which is akin to the more puritan lines of certain Judaic traditions, as well as those of Mithraism, of which Masonry had many echoes. As Mithraism rose through a tangle of syncretic cults to become a unifying principle within the Roman Empire, so Freemasonry today has tended to follow a similar course. Military and Chivalric orders certainly found continuance within Masonry, as did the idea of monarchic restoration and ritual chivalry; and the unfolding translation of Qabalistic texts enabled much Judaic esotericism to be assimilated herein. The theologian and apologist Philo of Alexandria once asked, of the pagan mystery schools:

> Why, O initiates, if these things are good and profitable, do you shut yourselves up in deepest darkness and render service to three or four individuals alone, when you can render it to all by presenting these advantages in the public market? (261)

In our own time, perhaps, this question is being answered. Reliance on authority or tradition is a Piscean trait. The gradual dismantling of the awesome temple scaffolding, the secrecy devolving upon initiates in times of ignorance and persecution, the solitude of the seeker are largely behind us now. Instead of temples, the concert or lecture hall, the spontaneous gathering of seekers; instead of robed occultists, the free dissemination of hidden wisdom, which nonetheless remains intact; instead of isolation, the growing network of those sensitive to cosmic purpose.

There have always been guardians of the mystery traditions, however elusive they may have seemed; teachers have always been on hand to impart the eternal truths. With the gradual relaxing of the inner laws governing the open dissemination of esoteric beliefs in the last two centuries, many schools have come forward, each one claiming the right to train and initiate its followers into the divine mysteries of creation. Some have proved false, having nothing of value to teach; others have grown, flourished, and then faded with the passing of their founders. Still others have passed on their knowledge to those who came after.

When, in the late nineteenth century certain members of the Theosophical Society – then the most prestigious occult organization of the time – began to tire of the emphasis given to Eastern mysteries, they looked elsewhere, finding within the newly translated Egyptian papyri and the wealth of Classical MSS, a fund of Western wisdom to be explored in a practical way. Enthusiastic explorers rather than scholars, they delved deeply into the neglected heritage of the past, and came up with a whole system of magical and theurgic mysteries.

Thus the 'Hermetic Order of the Golden Dawn' was born, admitting Freemasons, poets, clergymen and thinkers to its ranks. It was to outlast many of its own offspring, and became, in the next few generations, the most prestigious organization of its kind since the Renaissance. Most modern esoteric schools trace their descent from the Golden Dawn, and through it, knowingly or not, make contact with both the Rosicrucian impulse and the great Classical and pre-classical foundations.

Behind the often over-elaborate nature of the Golden Dawn rituals lie a multitude of sense-experiences unattainable to those who follow meaning rather than understanding. The incantatory power of these rituals goes far beyond the sum of their elements. It matters not that we can distinguish Chaldean, Egyptian, Geraeco-Roman and Gnostic elements within them; one has only to glance at the 'knowledge-papers' of the Order, edited in a single compendious volume by Israel

Regardie (283, 285) to understand that here is a valid system of working esoterically which has not been exceeded by any other modern-day school.

Theosophy, which indirectly gave birth to the Golden Dawn, had, in the early nineteenth century, already begun to awaken aspects of Western esotericism which had long lain dormant. Its contact with the East brought in a language and conceptualization which helped define areas which had remained indistinct since the Renaissance or had been relegated to the crypt of Christian mysticism. Its leader, Madame Blavatsky, achieved the reputation of a typical shaman with her travels to the East and meetings with Hidden Masters. She bluffed her way through areas of ignorance and contacted the light of the perennial wisdom in ways which now seem haphazard. She believed beyond all else that whatever was true must come from outside her own consciousness. This lead her to fabricate much that was untrue about her sources for *The Secret Doctrine* and *The Veil of Isis*, her two monumental studies of esoteric tradition. (29) Her sources were and still are often traceable, but her studious refusal to admit that they came from elsewhere and were written down but not actually composed by her, led many to doubt her in the end. Sadly, perhaps, because she has much to say that is worth listening to, and had she only admitted her own part in the composition of her writings she would probably have reached a wider audience who would have taken her pioneering more seriously. As it is, and despite the sometimes farcical organization and petty bickering within Theosophy, Blavatsky appeared at the right time to bring a revitalizing influence to bear on the Western Way.

The schools which post-date Theosophy and whose founders were trained therein, are continuators of the work begun by Blavatsky. Anthroposophy, which is still a thriving movement, resulted from Rudolph Steiner's break with Theosophy, which he found too overtly Eastern for his taste. A recent commentator calls Anthroposophy a 'demythologised Theosophy' (75) because it rejects the magical in favour of education and the arts, as well as holistic living.

Steiner emphasized Western elements however, and in his autobiography describes anthroposophy as 'a path of knowledge, leading from the spiritual in man to the spiritual in the universe'. (318) He sees the universe as living and hierarchical, and is thus very much in line with the teachings of the Classical schools. He was also convinced that the ancient mystery knowledge was communicated in picture-dreams, 'pictures which revealed the spirit-world' (ibid). He saw imagination as a door of communication between the worlds, and consciously encouraged the entrance to the ancient mysteries through allowing the subject to experience its spiritual contact directly by means of the senses stimulated by art. His concept of 'Erkraftung des Denkens', or putting force and life into thinkers, through thinking within thinking, and other exercises designed to liberate thought from the bodily instrument, also recalled traditional techniques – although the original mystery teaching was to stimulate the subtle body centres from below upwards, while the Steiner method, in common with other newer schools, is to liberate them from above.

Steiner also, interestingly, developed three forms of higher knowledge: *Imagination* – a higher seeing of the spiritual world in revealing images; *Inspiration* – a higher hearing of the spiritual world, through which it reveals its creative forces and its creative order: and *Intuition* – the stage at which an intuitive penetration into the sphere of Spiritual beings becomes possible.

This kind of structure, which recalls the grading practised by some Golden Dawn offshoots, is perfectly workable by any group sufficiently experienced in working with the mysteries. At the same time it is rather artificial in its formation of levels, which do not always mesh with the intentions of inner impulses behind any contacted school. It is easy to be discouraged when faced with a plethora of complicated hierarchies within any school – though there are obviously instances where such structures are valid. (91)

The Golden Dawn worked a system of grades based on the Qabalistic Tree of Life, starting with Zelator (Malkruth) and rising to Ipsissimus (Kether). (183) This is still used by many magical schools today and there are certain initiatory ceremonies connected with each grade. Many are disappointed to find that their teacher is not an Ipsissimus – such a claim should be cautiously questioned in any case. But the grades are symbolic of the initiate's efforts to attain proficiency, just as Bachelor, Master and Doctor are conferred on individuals in the academic world. But just as Doctors of Philosophy do not know everything, neither do those who have had high grades conferred upon them by their schools. There is no end to knowledge, nor to the number of initiations we all take on the Inner.

The division of the mysteries into 'Greater' and 'Lesser' is another form of structuring practised by contemporary Mystery Schools. In any such there is a period of probation followed by the lesser and greater mysteries. These can be seen as three basic levels of work, although about the latter it is difficult to generalize. The lesser mysteries are usually the initial 'outer court' work of the group wherein the images and symbols are embodied in a mythical framework. In the greater mysteries, this earlier work is subsumed in the personality of the initiate – it becomes a living reality about which there can be no question. The initiate enters the 'inner court' of the Temple and finds him or herself in an empty room. Here no deity is enshrined, no great teaching written; here is no symbol to distract or enter the consciousness – only the emptiness of the cosmos: which is, of course, far from empty. Initiation into the Greater Mysteries is indeed a confrontation with the self and with the summation of the divine presence within everything. (cf. afterword) There, macrocosm and microcosm conjoin and are reflected. Even so, there can be no sublime merging with the divine principle yet: the initiate must return to the outer world again, continuing to act as a mirror of the macrocosm.

Many such *psychotechnologies*, to borrow a term from Marilyn Ferguson, (82) are practised today by the hundreds of modern mystery schools extant in the Western world. All attempt to mediate the inner mysteries of life in some way. We have lost much in the way of methodologies, but tentative New Age experiments are reviving them, in part analeptically, to a standard of efficiency. It is obviously not possible to discuss even a tenth part of the schools offering training today, and even if it were we should feel restrained to do so only of those we had personally experienced. There is no hard and fast rule about joining such a group. Common sense and clear sight will guide you in your first steps and after that the inner guides should be in a position to take over. The Rudolf Steiner School combines elements of Christian esotericism with Rosicrucian, Hermetic and Native mysteries. If you prefer to seek a Qabalistic training, the Servants of the Light organization offers a thorough and effective way into the mysteries of the Tree of Life and the symbolism of the Grail. (12) The Alice Bailey School is strongly Theosophical in origin, subscribing to belief in masters and hierarchical cosmology. It propounds an evolutionary development through mundane as well as esoteric means. The vast underpinning literature, dictated by Master D.K. to Alice Bailey, is read by many outside the school, where it has contributed widely to the spread of Aquarian consciousness and cosmic consciousness. The Rosicrucian Fellowship and AMORC are rival schools following the teachings of Christian Rosenkreutz. The former was founded by Max Heindal in 1906. Active in Theosophy, he was contacted by a Rosicrucian Master and took instruction. The school teaches world evolution, reincarnation, inner helpers and masters. AMORC was founded in 1915 by H. Spencer-Lewis and is based on Freemasonic lines with a developed philosophy and practice: it declines the titles of religion or cult. Its glossy literature and vastly public headquarters in San Jose, California, do not lead one to suppose that a mystery school is in operation here. The Builders of the Adytum, founded by Paul Foster Case after he was expelled from the Golden Dawn for publishing their secrets in his Tarot publications, is probably the most Hermetic of those mentioned above. BOTA was founded on Inner contact in 1920 and still uses Tarot and Qabala as its main implements.

Another interesting school which has released its teaching papers is the Aurum Solis or Order of the Sacred Word. Since its reconstitution in 1971 it operates as a private magical group and not a school. It was founded in 1897 by Charles Kingold and George Stanton, two occultists who were in touch with Qabala, as well as Greek and early magical systems. *The Magical Philosophy* (68) which comprises these teachings is, like the Golden Dawn collection, a complete magical system which can be studied and worked by the esotericist who does not belong to any group.

Schools and magical groups are still organized. This normally comes about when one adept is contacted by the Inner and gets his or her 'go ahead' to organize a preliminary meeting with those close to him. A scheme of operation is noted down and the signs and sigils of the company meditated upon. In its early stages the whole project may abort for various reasons: the adept or his company may prove unstable. But if the group fulfils the required dedication the impetus to get organized can be tremendous, sweeping aside daily events or problems as insignificant distractions. Then, having fulfilled its function – which may only be a short-term project – the whole apparatus is disbanded. Thus groups and schools will last only as long as the Inner intends they should, after which the dismantling process begins, often showing itself in the form of personality clashes, changed circumstances, death of leading members and the scattering of those who may be led to found their own organizations and teach others.

The non-initiate may be baffled by such procedures, seeing only half of the picture, and may vow to have nothing to do with such activities. The above statements refer more to magical groups than to training schools which are used by the Inner as a foundation of more important work, and which will not be abandoned in the cursory fashion of the nonce group. The work of Gareth Knight and William G. Gray is of a parallel kind, yet each have different approaches to magic training. Here the beginner can enter in the knowledge that he or she is in the hands of trained and knowledgeable adepts who are able practically to convey much that a training school should impart.

Without a teacher or training school behind one, the work is uphill and cannot be correlated with the student's development. Clearly, medieval magical systems which go in for long and barbarous means and incomprehensible conjurations are not practical. Intent, clear and easy steps which follow logically from each other, careful preparation and self-discipline go a long way. The groundwork of self-training is not book-learned, although it may often be inspired thereby to begin with.

The vexed questions of an Inner teacher will be dealt with in chapter 4. But is an Outer magical teacher necessary? Nothing can replace the guidance of an experienced fellow-worker, but finding one willing to take on students is another matter. Most people proceed without one in the earliest stages of training, keeping their eyes open, reading, studying and correlating their life's experiences with the strong Inner impulse which leads them deeper into the mysteries. Some students join groups unadvisedly and regret it, leaving with their illusions shattered. Others work alone for what seems a lifetime and then suddenly find doors opening for them. There is no rule or set timing for finding a teacher but, once you find one do not expect it to be easier from then on. A teacher will demand regular work and certain results: if you, the student, do not measure up to your teacher's expectations, you will be considered a time-waster, someone who is unworthy to transmit the traditions which are being inculcated within you.

There is certainly no shortage of schools, some better than others, some worse. But as the theologian Don Cupitt expressed it in a recent TV series: 'the truth now is no longer in fixed positions – it is in the quest.' The modern quest for knowledge, whether within the mystery schools or elsewhere, takes many forms. For many the mysteries are now best taught in open court, in small groups or seminars where the mysteries are discussed and practically engaged upon by gatherings of interested people. Both the authors can testify to the remarkably powerful and effective nature of this kind of work, where seemingly random combinations of people are brought together by the Inner to do some specific piece of work and then separate again, sometimes not to meet for long periods.

This way of working is growing in popularity, and many more opportunities exist which combine lectures with practical applications of magic techniques. It has been said that the time of the Mystery Schools is over, and while this may not necessarily be true, the old closed orders of adepts are growing fewer in number. However, as we have tried to show throughout these books, the solitary worker or the small dedicated band of workers can be just as effective as a fully fledged school – especially once Inner contact is established. There is a great need for those willing to put up with occasional discomforts in return for the satisfaction of the work.

All myth, legend and poetry derives from the Mysteries in some sense: they are the potential sparks to ignite a sense of the wonders of creation and the purpose of life. Almost any of the countless themes, characters, fragments of tales – whether from ancient Greek, Egyptian or Welsh Triads (cf. Vol I) can be quarried and utilized for exploration individually or with a group. Once you begin to work with the matter of the mysteries you will find it like controlling a team of eager, high-stepping horses. Feel the reins in your hands and the pull of their heads at the bit. Your chariot will carry you far, across land and sea, both in Inner and Outer realms. The mysteries are not something locked away in dusty tomes on a libraryshelf – they are here and now, living lines of contact with which to enter a wholly different dimension.

> The object of the Hermetic search is that life which is capable of being transmitted to a specific being in order to lead that being *to its own perfection*. . . this available 'life-essence' is called the King, cosmic man; but it must be recognized that attaining the aim of the Hermetic opus is not an end; it is the beginning of the light that illuminates reality . . . the true King, is the living being who has reached the stage of immortal and conscious return to the source of the Soul that animates him. . . (298)

This return to the source is the objective that animates all magical work, fuelling Orphite and Hermeticist, Gnostic and Cathar alike. As we shall see in the next chapter, it is present in esoteric Christianity as well as the Hermetic schools. Divine knowing is all important if we are to find our way further than the first few steps on the road we have elected to travel.

EXERCISES

EXERCISE 1   THE MAZE OF THE GODS

The Roman historian Ammianus Marcellinus gives an interesting account, in his discussion of the mysteries, of 'certain underground galleries and passages full of windings which, it is said, the adepts in the ancient rites (knowing that the Flood was coming, and fearing that the memory of the sacred ceremonies would be obliterated) constructed. . . . These, he says, contained buildings 'which were mined out with great labour. And levelling the walls, they engraved on them numerous kinds of birds and animals . . . which they called hieroglyphic characters.' (147)

This may well be a distant memory of a visit to one of the great pyramids of Egypt, on whose walls were cartouches relating the history of its one-time occupant – or it may again be a fleeting reference to the great labyrinth at Mareotis, mentioned by Herodotus and other ancient historians. Whatever the truth, it conjures up a fascinating image of a vast and secret maze, containing on its walls the knowledge and history of the Egyptian mysteries – perhaps even of an earlier Atlantean mystery centre. The purpose of the exercise which follows is to enter such a place and there to encounter the living forms of the gods who will be our guides and instructors in this particular area of the Western mysteries. As we saw in volume I, the gods are many things: they await the moment when we are sufficiently in tune with ourselves to recognize that we are living vessels of the ancient wisdom – to be filled with as much as lies within our capacity to hold. In this exercise we will make our first contact with some of the powers with which we shall find ourselves working in times to come. In this instance we shall come under the guidance of Hermes, who will conduct us on the first steps of the Hermetic way.

Much of the imagery here comes from Egyptian sources, but this should not be seen as the only way into the Hermetic tradition – there are many other doorways just as valid through which we may gain admittance. As with other exercises in this and in the previous volume, no attempt should be made to embark on an inner journey until you feel sure the time is right. Once you feel ready you should begin by making yourself relaxed, breathing to a regular rhythm, comfortably seated in an upright chair. This done, you are ready to proceed.

Fig 5: An ankh

You are standing at night on softly yielding ground. At first it is quite dark, but as you grow accustomed to the place, the moon comes out from behind a cloud and by its radiance you perceive that you are standing on fine white desert sand, which stretches away on all sides to the horizon in softly sculptured waves. Ahead you see several vast shapes, rooted in the desert and rising towards a sky filled with stars. . . They are strangely familiar, and as your eyes grow accustomed to the subtle light you recognize their shape. You are in Egypt and before you lie the Pyramids of Ghiza. . .

Filled with awe you walk towards these vast and towering monuments, which gleam softly silver in the light of the moon. As you draw near you see that they are not quite as you may have seen them pictured, crumbling and aged by time and weather, but smooth and sharp-edged and faced with white marble upon which you dimly discern hieroglyphs in seemingly endless rows. The whole pyramid before which you stand is covered with writing, but though you may long to pause and examine what is written there, you are drawn onward towards a dark entrance which opens before you. At first you hesitate, for the way ahead is very black and there is no light to show what lies within. Ancient fears of the dark and of becoming lost beneath the great weight of stone stir within you and you feel reluctant to proceed further. Then as you stand uncertainly before the dark entrance, a figure detaches itself from the shadows and comes towards you. You recognize him from his shaven head and white kilt as an Egyptian priest. He holds out his left hand, in which he carries the symbol of his office, an ankh, the ancient Egyptian symbol of life. You see that he is smiling in welcome, and you reach out and take the proffered sign in your own hand. It feels warm and smooth to the touch, and as soon as you have hold of it, begins to glow brightly.

The priest now stands aside and indicates that you should proceed within. You find that your earlier fears have left you with the touch of the ankh and that you are eager to discover what lies within. You enter through a narrow stone door, and as you pass further into the heart of the pyramid the ankh glows brighter, illuminating your path.

With the symbol of life in your hand you go forward unafraid. The passage-way is narrow and twists often to right or left, doubling back upon itself more than once until you have lost all sense of direction. Time, also, seems without meaning here. Is it only a few moments since you entered, or have hours passed? You walk on, holding your glowing ankh before you, until at last you feel a draught of cool air on your face and emerge into a larger, open space.

You are now standing in a long, narrow hall, its roof upheld by an avenue of pillars, those upon the right painted red and those upon the left, black. As you walk forward between them you see that the walls of the hall are painted with brightly coloured figures. Some are in Egyptian dress, but others seem clad in costumes of other lands and times. Though they are only painted scenes they almost seem to move with a life of their own. You do not feel moved to stop and look at them in detail, but much that you glimpse there may return to you later, either in sleep or meditation.

Your feet are drawn onward toward the end of the hall, where you see a door, flanked by two great red and black pillars carved with symbols and hieroglyphs. As you approach, the door opens and a figure comes forth and stands waiting for you, arms folded on his breast. He is manlike, tall and powerful, but from his shoulders rises the head of a jackal, its ear pricked and its eyes gleaming in the light.

You recognize the figure of Anubis, guardian of the mysteries of Egypt and keeper of the threshold of the gods. You stand before him, waiting to hear what he will say. He may ask you your name, or he may wish to know your reason for coming to this place. Think carefully and take time before you answer. You may not lie or speak falsely before Anubis, for he can read the heart as you might read a book. (Pause)

When he is satisfied, Anubis stands aside, welcoming you to the place of the Mysteries, then he steps aside and bids you enter by way of the door through which he came.

Before you do so, Anubis softly speaks the sacred password which will admit you to what lies beyond. Thus prepared, but still not without some trepidation, for it is a great step you now take, pass forward, and find yourself walking down a short corridor connecting the door through which you came with another some little way ahead. Here you pause for a moment to collect your thoughts and to weigh your intention, for behind this door lies the chamber of the Inner Mysteries and you must be certain of your reason for coming before you enter in. You may take your time over this and if you do not feel ready as yet, may turn back at this point and retrace your steps without fear or shame. Many have reached this point before you, and have turned away. If you decide to do so, you may return at another time. (Pause)

Assuming that you decide to go on . . . you step forward and open the door before you. Stepping through, you find yourself in a small, many-sided room. As you hold up the ankh before you, you see by its light that the walls are faced with mirrors of bronze which, as you advance slowly towards the centre, give back a thousand images of yourself. But not all the images are the same. As your vision grows accustomed to the strangeness of the place, you see that there are many different aspects of yourself reflected back from the walls. You may see yourself at different stages in your life to this moment (but never beyond: the future is not for you to read) and perhaps also of other lives. But you must be careful of how you interpret the images you see, for it is easy to become dazzled or glamourized by a particular form or image. If you feel drawn towards one or another you may look closer, but always hold the ankh symbol before you as your sign of life and intention.

Look now towards the centre of the room. There you will see a circular platform with steps leading up to it. Upon it stands a mighty figure holding a book and writing implements. You recognize Thoth, the scribe of the Gods, keeper of the sacred mysteries, teacher of wisdom, known by some as Hermes Trismegistos, founder of the Hermetic mysteries.

As you approach he demands by what right you come there and you respond with the word or phrase given you by Anubis. Thoth then asks your intentions in seeking the mysteries and whether you are drawn to any one aspect. You should answer this as truthfully as possible, but do not be afraid to say that you do not know. Thoth records your name and response in his great book and bids you step up to the platform at his side.

As you do so the walls of the chamber begin to turn slowly, gradually speeding up until they are a blur. Only the platform and the wise head of Thoth, shaped like the sacred Ibis, remain unchanging. As you stand at his side you realize that this is a centre from which all the Mystery teachings are spun forth. All are contained in the great book which lies beneath the hand of Thoth.

Now in the blur of the passing walls, images form, flickering there for a moment and then disappearing again. You see the faces of those with whom you have worked before on the inner planes, and others who are strangers to you. You should try to notice and to remember as much as you can, since these things and people may well become important to you later on. (Pause)

At last the spinning slows and stops. You see yourself again in the mirrors and realize that you are alone. There may be subtle changes now in the way that you behold them, for Thoth has entered your name in the Book of the Mysteries and you are a part of them from now onward.

Slowly you descend from the platform and depart from the chamber by the way you came. In the outer chamber Anubis awaits you, and as you pass before him he places upon your brows a plain circlet of silver or gold. You understand that this is a token of the Mysteries upon which you have now entered. It is plain as yet because your journey has only just begun, but in time it may bear symbols or letters acquired by you on your way.

Taking leave of the jackel-headed god you return to the open air, finding no difficulty in retracing your path through the maze. At the entrance, return the symbol of the ankh to the priestly guardian and go by the way you came, slowly allowing the scene to fade from your consciousness to be replaced by the surroundings in which you began your journey. Wherever you go forth upon an inner journey, or take place in some magical activity, you should imagine the circlet given to you by Anubis, and this will be your sign to others that you have passed through the maze of the gods and returned.

EXERCISE 2   BUILDING THE BODY OF LIGHT

This is a ritual of great potential power, designed to awaken a sense of the cosmic dimension of the Hermetic path. We make no bones about including what is in effect an advanced technique of working. Those who are ready to undertake work at this level will find themselves drawn to approach it; those who are not should still be able to perform the working and obtain from it a sense of well-being and inner fulfilment. It should, however, not be performed more than once when it has proved effective, and it is advisable to eat and rest afterwards.

Begin quietly, seated or standing, in a place prepared. Build the circle of force about you and hallow it with the light of love. Centre yourself and then begin to stretch upward from your psychic centres – further and further until your physical body is far below and a new self, hazy and without substance as yet, stands with head and shoulders in the heavens. Slowly stretch forth with your senses feeling them newly cleansed like windows that have had the grime of centuries wiped from them. Look about you and be aware of the vastness of the heavens, of the mighty beings who guard the cosmos, of those who have responsibility for our own solar system, for each planet that whirls about the star which is our own sun. Take time to hold this new reality and fear nothing. You are, as is each one of us, an immortal soul whose right it is to travel the uttermost reaches of the universe under the protection of the Holy Ones who helped in its formation. Listen and you may hear their voices raised in the music of the spheres.

Now stretch forth your hands and find before you in the uttermost blackness and singing darkness of space a shape which your senses tell you is a vast bowl or Krater. You cannot perceive this with your sight, only feel its outlines beneath your hands. Its surface seems wonderfully worked and you wonder for a moment what scenes are depicted upon it. But it is not yet for you to see such things, and there is another purpose for you now.

Look now into the depths of the bowl, which is perfect blackness and impenetrable dark. Far below, as though you were looking into the uttermost depths of the cosmos, a tiny gleed of light begins to form, impossibly far away and bright. Like a jewel it shines there and as you look it begins to grow gradually larger. Stretch your hand down into the bowl and take forth the glowing thing which is there. It may look like a living flame (which cannot burn you) or like a jewel of surpassing brightness. As you hold it in your hand its light begins to spread through your insubstantial form, filling you with a sense of peace and joyousness.

Look about you now and see that on all sides in the vastness of space are other figures, invisible to you before, but now revealed in a glory of light. They greet you in many different tongues which you have no difficulty in understanding, and you understand that you are now like them, that you share in a common radiance which is both within you and fills the corners of the universe.

Gradually begin to draw in upon yourself and to shrink down towards your body far below. Keep the light within you, for it is a spark of that divine fire from which the cosmos was formed and which has always been a part of you. You are now part of the Body of Light which surrounds and dwells within all of creation. Wherever you go you will take it with you, and you will always be able to recognize it within others. So, too, will you be able to hold converse with the myriad souls who inhabit the vastness of space, and who have welcomed you among them as brother or sister.

Become aware of your surroundings once more, feel the ground beneath your feet and the chair upon which you are seated. Close the circle of power and perform a suitable closing ritual which you have devised. Reaffirm the Light within you by performing a brief ritual of attunement at least once daily.

CHAPTER 2
The Divine Knowing

In their religion they are so unev'n,
That each man goes his own by-way to Heav'n.
Tenacious of mistakes to that degree,
That ev'ry man pursues it sep'rately,
And fancies none can find the way but he,
So shy of one another they are grown
As if they strove to get to Heav'n alone.

> Daniel Defoe: *The True-Born Englishman*

Wisdom reaches mightily from one end of the earth to the other,
and she orders all things well. . .
For she is an initiate in the knowledge of God,
and an associate in his works.

> *Wisdom* VIII, 1 and 4

THE GIFTS OF WISDOM

Gnostic, illuminatus, hermeticist, magus, mystic – what a glorious muddle the Western Way must appear to the outsider! The multifarious nature of the Western Tradition has caused many problems of acceptance among those who prefer their concepts in tidy packages. Yet Dr Dee's medium, Edward Kelly, reminds us that what we see as a fragmented and often back-biting set of disciplines is indeed derivative of those great mystery schools we have been considering:

> This Art found its way into Persia, Egypt and Chaldea. The Hebrews called it the Cabbala, the Persians Magia, and the Egyptians Sophia and it was taught in the schools together with Theology: it was known to Moses, Solomon, and the Magi who came to Christ from the East. (121)

He is appealing to a common tradition across a breadth of disciplines, specifically relating his argument to alchemy and to the completion of the Great Work.

But the Great Work can be achieved through many disciplines; through the science of alchemy, through the art of magic or through the philosophy of the mystic. There has been much dispute as to which is the correct means by which to proceed because the disciplines of the Western Way have been fragmented and split off from each other. Science, magic and religion seem to be eternally estranged, yet each of these disciplines corresponds to a cosmic law which everyone must obey: science observes the law of Nature; magic, the law of correspondences; and religion, the law of God. None of these laws is irreconcilable. Science and religion seem to have passed beyond the time where they each held as complementary to the other, while the esotericist is now regarded as a godless creature by one and as a crank by the other.

In order that we may appreciate all sides of this problem we shall be examining the science of alchemy and the art of magic in their proper place, while here we wish to scrutinize the philosophy of religion, the spiritual science. But before we do so, let us first examine the Western Way from the standpoint of the Perennial Wisdom.

The term *Sophia Perennis* or Perennial Wisdom was first coined by the German philosopher, Gottfried Leibnitz (1646–1716) who understood that different religious traditions were not only valid in themselves but that they could inform each other. The syncretism of the Classical mystery schools comprehended something of this understanding, as does the modern Ecumenical movement today, but the Western Way is left out of the reckoning because few class it as a valid tradition at all.

The problem confronting us today is that most religious traditions have become empty structures: exoteric walls and empty esoteric space within them. Yet the Western Way suffers conversely: it is made up of a rich store of esoteric wisdom which has been discarded by religious traditions, yet it has no structure in which to house this treasure. While this is to some extent a generalization, and the state of neither religion nor the Western Way is as parlous as that, we must consider the means by which the ancient wisdom is being preserved and transmitted.

A tradition begins to die when it becomes theoretical: that is the danger not just within the Western Way but in religious traditions the world over. Once they begin to be studied for their own sake rather than being applied directly to everyday life, they lose their impetus to transmit wisdom. More than ever we need skilful mediators who know how to blend traditional wisdom for our own time. The professional defenders of tradition – once the poet and shaman, now the academic and priest – often fail to preserve the essential quality of tradition; they have lost their ability to communicate the wonder and wisdom. Where then are the visionaries of note who can show us the divine truths? We seem to have reached a plateau period when the old metaphors have been overhauled and found wanting, yet new metaphors are harder to find. All things change and evolve, and it is good that they should do so, but when a tradition is confined within narrow, rigid forms, it cannot easily reach those for whom it is intended. As religion takes a nose-dive into the fundamental and popularist, many self-made cults come into being at the request of those who want to see their own visions and dream their own dreams.

It may be asked whether we are not promoting some kind of new religion in these pages. We do not propose anything of the kind: the Western Way includes the whole spectrum of paths from the overtly esoteric to the inherently mystical. We encourage you to find a tradition and inhabit it. (40) Only tradition has the ability to preserve mystical and symbolic teaching in a safe manner, giving transformative realization of the Inner Kingdom. Those who are outside traditional systems are vulnerable in that they seek the Inner Kingdom by means of their own maps and from the the basis of their own efforts: they try to go it alone. Yet the need to explore inner worlds does not decrease with succeeding generations: rather it is on the increase as traditional systems sell themselves short and offer quick and unsatisfying answers to those who come hungry with questions.

The impulse of the Hermetic path of the Western Way derives from this predicament: the need to evolve and the need to preserve. It has produced the natural philosopher, the amateur theologian and the ritualist to counterbalance the stasis of many religious traditions. It has encouraged the skilful adapter, the cunning preserver and the quiet reconciler. Few of these men and women have left the tradition into which they were born; indeed the most successful among them made their way within it and even despite it. Mystics and saints such as Clement of Alexandria, Vladimir Soloviev, Nahman of Bratislav, St Hildegard of Bingen, Blessed John Ruysbrock were not renegades determined to show up their traditions, but explorers and revealers of the way for others. They were not afraid to retain the esoteric riches of their tradition often in the face of exoteric disapproval. Yet it is also true to say that very few have the ability to respond to the esoteric depths of religion while recognizing the necessity for an exoteric structure.

This splitting off of mystical and mundane, esoteric and exoteric has become pronounced in our own day. Many followers of the Western Way would put the blame squarely upon the advent and promulgation of Christianity in the West, which is seen by them as the disturber and destroyer of Native Tradition. This view has blinded many to a true appreciation of the treasures of Western wisdom which took seed within Christianity and grew to maturity there. These lie in profusion about our feet and we cannot see them. We must consider that Hermeticism grew up within the Christian era and that most of its proponents were not Christian due to fear of persecution, but because that was their means of religious expression. We shall be considering more closely the reasons by which the Church became suspicious of its own mystical tradition in the next section. Basically, however, this was due to a division between the ways of faith and knowledge or *gnosis*.

Neither faith nor knowledge can gain us entry into the Inner Kingdom on their own: we need, primarily, the gift of wisdom to guide us, and to bind faith and knowledge together as harmonious travelling companions.

> The Lord himself created wisdom:
> he saw her and apportioned her,
> he poured her out upon all his works.
> She dwells with all flesh according to his gift,
> and he supplied her to those who love him. (*Sirach I, 9–10*)

Those who yearn after eternal things and wish to know the Inner Kingdom for themselves, speak the language of wisdom which transcends the limitations of human speech. It is the common tongue of mystics and esotericists everywhere, spoken above the snowline where the many-sided mountain of Deity is revealed at the peak. Followers of the Western Way, whether of Native or Hermetic Traditions, know themselves to be of this number and so are the company of *Sophia Perennis*. Included also are followers of the Eastern Way, as a close study of mystical texts both Eastern and Western will confirm.

Some readers will be concerned that the esoteric side of tradition seems exclusive and cliquey. The truth is much simpler. Any *practising* member of a religious discipline is free to enter deeper into the mysteries of his or her tradition at any time. It is a matter of involvement, of identification with and dedication to its inner wisdom. It is often a matter of finding the right key. Frequently one meets sincere religious people who go through the motions prescribed by convention, yet who never touch the inmost heart: they travel by faith alone, in blind hope. Yet if they ever contact this inner heart by means of prayer or meditative awareness, they become knowers as well as believers. They do not migrate from their adherence but are confirmed within it.

On the other hand it is also possible to meet those who steer solely by the means of knowedge, who spurn the way of faith. Some esotericists see themselves as the Children of Light, the race of the new Aeon: such are not the inheritors of the Inner Kingdom. These have succumbed to the sin of spiritual pride which marks them off from the common run of humanity and places them in the same category as those fundamentalists who see themselves as the Chosen Ones, the Elect of God. The true initiates of gnosis are those who have learned by the preliminaries of faith, who have become teachers and nourishers of wisdom wherever it struggles to be made manifest: those who encourage the growth of inner potential in others, not those who boast of their own spiritual achievements.

The companion on the way to the Inner Kingdom is Wisdom, who is the law of knowledge and the mother of faith. She keeps the former within safe boundaries and distributes it to all gnostics; she guides the latter, encouraging it to grasp and realize the true nature of eternal things. A firm Wisdom-contact is essential in esoteric work, especially for those outside a living tradition. To this end we have given exercise 3 which may help the reader focus upon his or her traditional affiliations.

Childhood faith is now threatened, traditional working metaphors are jettisoned, power is syphoned from spiritual to political ends with many fundamentalist cults, and the deep magic of the Inner Story is despoiled. There arises, in response to this fragmentation, a kind of vocational consciousness from among the peoples of the world. The Secret Commonwealth (cf. vol. I) arises again, no longer in a nationalist but in a global response. Whatever aptitudes are available, whatever their traditional or non-traditional provenance, many ordinary people perceive the danger our world is in. Often their response is humanist or ecological, rather than spiritual, yet it is motivated by the earthy ancestral wisdom which is the birthright and gift of every human being who loves the creation.

Together with them, the mystics and esotericists strive to mediate the healing of the Inner world to our world. Awareness of the danger and responsibility for finding a way out of danger, brings humility enough to the children of Wisdom, whether they steer by means of faith or knowledge.

The *Sophia Perennis* is not a religion nor an end in itself, but a bond between riven traditions. It can easily sink to an intellectual appreciation of comparative religion or a collection of woolly New Age aphorisms where one tradition can easily be substituted for another. Each tradition has its essential character: the Western Way is made up of many such. Wisdom is eternally true, however traditions change: if we love the truth, she will ever accompany us, her philo-sophias, (literally 'lovers of wisdom'). Those who have never considered the Western Mystery Tradition in the light of religion, may find it helpful to see it as an esoteric philosophy, along these lines.

Perhaps we may start by admitting that we are wounded: 'The metaphysician (is a) wounded man. A wounded man is not an agnostic – he just has different questions arising out of his wound.' (232) Like the shaman, the wounded healer is one who knows that the true cause of pain is loss of Inner reality – the Inner Kingdom. This realization fired the Gnostics to go upon their own voyage of discovery, just as it later inspired those who went on quest for the Grail and the healing of the Waste Land. Truly, there are many ways of achieving the Great Work.

THE FRUITS OF GNOSIS

'The life of the Gnostics is, in my view, no other than works and words which correspond to the tradition of the Lord,' wrote Clement of Alexandria. (291) This early Christian theologian was a lone voice rising from a sea of discontent and disapproval at the Gnostic experiment. Since Gnosticism, the Western World has never been the same. Its suppression left the Christian tradition poorer, although fragments of its teachings are still to be found in the Hermetic Tradition. Gnosticism still rises periodically to haunt orthodox religion, but its coloured tatters stir painful memories and provoke bigoted reactions. What was Gnosticism that it still has power to awaken the hopes and fears of later generations? The fruits of the Gnostic experiment are often bitter to taste: some have never ripened, others are over-ripe, so it is necessary to be discriminating.

First of all, let us not confuse gnosis (which just means knowledge) with Gnosticism. It is possible to say of St Teresa of Avila that she was gnostic, but not that she was a Gnostic, for instance. Gnosis as divine knowing is the birthright of all spiritual traditions and does not imply their connection in any way with historical Gnosticism.

Gnosticism can be seen as a synthesis of the mystery schools which preceded it. It is 'perhaps the first religion, at least in the West, which is wholly non-tribal and centred upon the discovery of infinity within the (individual) psyche,' (75) and that makes it a vitally important link in the development of the Western Way. It is not without reason that the Gnostics have been claimed as spiritual predecessors by many revival mystery schools in the modern age, rather as the classical mystery schools looked back to Atlantis for their inspiration. Perhaps because Gnosticism did not attempt to explain 'the sacramental rituals ... as mere magic performed in memory of (historical) events, but as the externalisation of internal psychic alchemy,' and because it regarded the 'Bible not as history but as mythology of the most sublime and valuable kind' (ibid.) that modern Mystery schools have warmed to its teachings. The Gnostic thread runs exotically through the whole Hermetic tradition, as we shall discover.

What we know of Gnosticism today emerges from an incredibly complex welter of traditions: in the melting pot of Gnosis it is possible to find Persian, Egyptian, Hellenic, Platonic, Christian and Jewish elements. These fuse together at the nexus of the Mediterranean culture, at Alexandria in whose environs were to be found the great proliferation of traditions and teachings. Although the great Alexandrian Library was fired in AD 391 and its remaining wisdom subsequently destroyed forever in the early seventh century under Moslem occupation, the accumulated teachings within its rolls had already made good their escape into the living traditions which had made their home in Egypt.

The chief features of Gnosticism were inherited from Zoroastrian sources as well as from the many baptising sects such as those of the Essenes, both of which were functioning before the onset of Christianity. The seeds of Gnosticism took root in the garden of Christianity, where its plants flourished in a riot of colour and spectacular abandon in contrast to the more sober seedlings being trained up. Gnosticism already had the conceptual apparatus of the Mysteries behind it, while Christianity was still finding its feet. Christian

Gnosticism expanded from the middle of the first century AD and had its demise during the sixth century, although its influence post-dated this period. The only true lineal descendant of Classical Gnosticism operative today is the Mandean sect of Iraq which preserves the ritual purity of the early baptising sects: however, it is non-Christian, nearer in type to the Zoroastrian than to the neo-Judaic kind. It is doubtful whether its primitive traditions will outlast this century. (291)

As Gnosticism developed it rejected the Jewish basis of Christianity while yet retaining figures from Jewish scripture – Seth, Melchizedek, Adam and Eve – as forerunners of its traditions. The rewriting of received texts is not of course merely a Gnostic phenomenon; it occurs today in many New Age groups and Christian-based cults which strive to purge mainstream Christianity while retaining some elements from it, especially the figure of Christ himself, about whom new tales are spun, from whom come new sayings and commandments which, in reality, often emanate from that cult's leader rather than from divine sources. It is natural that all religions should seek to promote their antique antecedents, and Gnosticism was no exception.

If Gnosticism has had a bad press, this is because it has been known mainly through its detractors. Such texts as survived were so fragmentary that a full picture of Gnostic belief was impossible. However, the discovery of the *Nag Hammadi* in 1945 and the Qumran texts in 1947 have enabled scholars to begin piecing together the fragments into an astonishing cohesion. The Gnostic codices, like the contents of a time-machine, have survived miraculously to land in our own century. The extraordinary story of their discovery may be read in John Dart's *The Laughing Saviour* (62). Prior to their availability the meagre evidences of Gnosticism could be gleaned mainly from invectives penned by church fathers. Needless to say, such evidence was not from the horse's mouth. Their almost universal detestation by the orthodox wing of the Church ensured the infamy of the Gnostics for all time. Their championship by Clement of Alexandria brought him little reward: this attractively balanced theologian who foresightedly saw the truth within other traditions, especially within Platonism, was demoted from sainthood by Pope Clement VIII in the sixteenth century, because of his doubtful orthodoxy.

The Egyptian alchemist, Zosimus, wrote about a race of wisdom-lovers who live forever at the Inner Door (227). This image applied

neatly to the Gnostics whose existence was regulated by communica-
tions which came from behind the Inner Door. The Gnostics were
Knowers – possessors of an inner wisdom, guardians of a tradition,
inheritors of the mystery schools. They envisaged humanity as a set
of divine sparks entrapped in matter. The true God was unknown
and hidden – he alone was the origin of the light. Creation was the
work of a false god, the Demiurge. Every Gnostic lived in the hope of
rejoining the true God in the fullness of the Pleroma (heaven). They
believed that such a journey was possible, but that the way of return
was fraught with difficulty because the divine spark within each
individual lived in the forgetfulness of the flesh. It was necessary to
combat the King of the World (the Demiurge) by whatever means
were possible. He could be denied by means of asceticism, which
denies the currency of creation, or by licentiousness which scorns the
created order. Some Gnostic sects were so extreme in their practices
that they doubtless earned the censure heaped upon them. However,
not all sects used either of these means. Similar accusations have been
levelled against modern practitioners of the Western Way, but there
has been little evidence to support these claims: then, as now,
unscrupulous individuals use the cover of esoteric ritual to front their
sexual practices, none of which has any bearing on the practice of
dedicated initiates.

It is important to bear in mind that though there are common
elements within the Gnostic sects, the variations are so numerous
that we cannot generalize. Here there is only space to present the
barest outline of Gnostic belief and practice, in so far as an understanding of Gnosticism can highlight elements within the Western
Way.

The complex apparatus of Gnostic practice was designed to
stimulate the divine spark within, to prepare it for the release from
flesh and for the hazardous journey of the soul through the kingdoms
of the archons, the servants of the Demiurge, who ruled every sphere
between earth and that of the Pleroma itself. This journey through
the spheres is dealt with in more detail in chapter 4, where we will
also unfold something of Gnostic cosmology. (see fig.6)

The descent of the soul into flesh and its eventual return is
epitomized in the *Song of the Pearl*, from the apocryphal *Acts of
Thomas* (10) in which a prince (the messiah) journeys from his home
in the East (the Pleroma) into Egypt (the earth) in order to 'bring
back thence the one pearl which is there . . . girt about by the
devouring serpent.' In order to achieve this, the prince puts on the

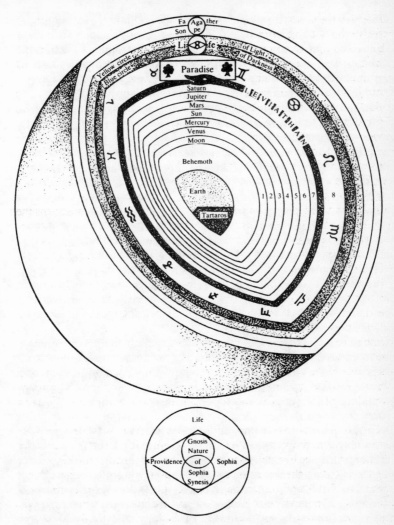

Fig 6: The Gnostic Cosmology

garments of Egypt (the flesh) in exchange for his own glorious robe (the divine nature). He forgets who he is, whence he came, or the purpose of his quest. A secret scroll is sent to him by means of an eagle, bidding him awake and remember that he is the son of kings.

He wins the pearl (the divine spark), strips off his filthy garments and takes the way of return, guided by the secret scroll (the hidden gnosis). As he returns, the jewels and robes which he put off at the various stages of his journey thither, are restored to him. (Just as Ishtar had to put off her garments at each of the gates of hell.) 'But suddenly, I saw the garment made like unto me as it had been in a mirror ... and I knew and saw myself through it.' He remembers totally and is brought before 'the brightness of the Father' fully equipped as a royal prince.

The parallels between this and the parable of the Prodigal Son (St Luke 15, 11–32) are not accidental. Present too are the resonances with the captivity of Joseph in Egypt whose imprisonment and subsequent change in fortunes are all undergone on behalf of his brothers who have forgotten their divine spark. (Genesis 37–45) Christ himself is figured in this Gnostic parable, in his own flight into Egypt, obscure childhood and subsequent return to his Father bringing with him the Pearl of Great Price, the fruits of Redemption. Robert Southwell, the sixteenth-century Jesuit poet, recalls this theme in his poem on *The Nativity of Christ*:

> Despise him not for lying there:
> First what he is enquire.
> An orient pearl is often found
> In depth of dirty mire. (315)

This is a theme to which we will be returning when we examine the inner resonances relating to alchemy and the quest for the Grail (chapter 5). We have presented this mystery story in some detail in order to give a flavour not only of the Gnostic mind, but also of the timeless nature of this theme down the centuries.

The Gnostic was obsessed with the need to know 'Why am I born? What is my purpose? How does evil originate?' These philosophical questions are the forerunners of the kind of scientific enquiry which dictated the shape of the Renaissance and which brought about yet another clash between believers and would-be-gnostics. The Gnostic prefigures the alchemist in his ability to believe in the possibility of transformation, and to use the images and archetypes close at hand to attain this state. The imaginative resources of the Gnostic creation dramas are staggering in their conceptual scope.

Central to the return of the divine spark of the soul were the dual themes of Anthropos and Sophia, both of whom represented that continual obsession of the Western Way – the interpenetration of the microcosm by the macrocosm. The Anthropos is the Adam of Light, otherwise known as Adam Kadmon, within Qabala. He is the first man, the mirror of the macrocosm, but he is deceived by the Demiurge and his archons into forgetting his heritage. Together with the spirit of Sophia (Wisdom), whose daughter he partners – the Eve of Paradise – he is lost in matter. Adam's body is the body of the world: his soul the totality of souls. Likewise the sufferings of Sophia, the exiled wisdom of the true God, were analogous to the sufferings of the created world. Her ultimate union with Christ – her Saviour and that of the world – was the expected portion of Valentinian Gnostics who conceived of their union as the signal for the *apocatastasis*, or the restoration of all things. Adam and Eve, and Christ and Sophia, were seen as types of *syzygy* (partners or consorts) whose reconciliation was important for the balancing of creation. This theme is also of critical importance within the Western Way: we discuss it further in chapters 4 and 5.

It is evident that Gnosticism fostered many levels of dualism which, at the one end, merely reflected the contemporary concern with the fallen nature of humanity, and at the other end polarized an eternally warring good and evil. These were not only the concerns of early Christianity, but are to be understood as deeply ingrained in the Classical world. Saviours, redeemers and messiahs of both sexes were to be found in almost every mystery school and religion at this time: these kept some degree of order in the precipitating superstitions then current. They were the symbols of hope and release from the vagaries of inexorable Fate – the obsession and scourge of the Classical world. The fusion of elements as disparate as Platonic, Orphic, Zoroastrian and Christian models made Gnostic dualism particularly confusing, especially from our modern standpoint which is comparatively naive in its conceptualization of good and evil. The stoic purity of Orphism, the endless battles of Zurvanist gods and demons, the semitic dualities of male and female, all appear in Gnosticism in different forms. The Gnostics may not have had all the pieces of the cosmic jigsaw, but they certainly enjoyed trying to make those pieces fit.

Having established their own idiosyncratic gospels and rich cosmology, they were free to relate to it. They considered themselves to be 'the kingless race' or, conversely, 'the king's children,' the offspring of the true hidden God – a relationship to be prized over that of the evil Demiurge and creator. The neo-Platonist, Plotinus (3rd century AD) was shocked that they should class themselves

with the divine: 'brothers and sisters of those above!' (268) The
Gnostics had the assurance from the mouth of Christ, no less, who,
in conversation with the apostle Andrew, states:

> Know ye not . . . that ye and all angels and all archangels and
> the gods . . . are out of one and the same paste and the same
> matter and the same substance, and that ye all are out of the
> same mixture. (264)

This spiritual elitism rose from the way in which Gnosticism divided
humanity. There was the *hylic* or fleshly man, the *psychic* or
partially-enlightened man (usually understood as one who was
nominally Christian), and the *pneumatic* or spiritual man, who was
fully gnostic (one who had heard the secret revelations of Christ and
his disciples). This concept is described in *The Origin of the World*
(239) as the three Adams. The enlightenment of the Gnostics was of a
predestined order – an element which was to appear in the form of
Calvinism in later centuries. The pneumatics were variously called
'the elect' or 'the perfected'. As representatives of the then new aeon,
the Gnostics strove to utilize the tools provided by Christianity, to
work with a system whose catholicity and impact was immense. But,
the promotion of knowledge over faith was too unbalanced. Having
envisaged a fallen Sophia (wisdom) their gnosis was correspondingly
less applicable to daily life. 'The beginning of Perfection is the
Gnosis of Man, but the Gnosis of God is perfected Perfection' (227)
might stand for the ideal which the Gnostics strove to follow.

Apart from Marcion and possibly Valentinus, there was no
attempt to codify the complexities and varieties of expression within
Gnosticism itself. Marcion (?–AD 160) was the only one who tried to
institute a church after the Christian model, rather than the rather
loosely-based cults into which Gnosticism was organized. Gnosticism appealed to the intellectual and cultured section of society – the
same section which had been the mainstay of the mystery schools.
Christianity appealed to a universal need and even accepted slaves,
which had been rare within the mysteries. The Gnostic priesthood
was both male and female, after the ancient manner, whereas
Christianity maintained a male priesthood. Gnosticism was suppres-
sed for a variety of reasons: its lack of well-distributed literature, its
elitism, its reluctance to proselytize and its uncodified nature, are a
few contributory factors. Crucially, it did not offer the kind of
Imperial cohesion which orthodox Christianity was to give to the
empires of Rome and Byzantium. Its suppression was swiftly effected

though not finally effective: Gnostic traces, like the tares in the parable, could not be separated from the wheat of orthodox Christianity.

Many of St Paul's letters to the churches in Asia Minor and Greece reflect a manful struggle with the unruly effects of Gnosticism among his proselytes: 'Avoid the godless chatter and contradictions of what is falsely called knowledge, for by professing it some have missed the mark as regards the faith.' (I Tim. 6, 20) Here is the heart of the dichotomy between Gnosis and Christianity.

Christianity has ever afterwards had a love-hate relationship with its own esoteric tradition, as we shall go on to discuss. The effect of the Gnostic experiment was to widen the gap between knowledge and faith to the extent that St Ignatius of Antioch could write:

It is better if a man knows nothing and does not perceive a single cause of things created but abides in faith in God and in love, rather than that, puffed up by such knowledge, he falls away from the love that makes man alive . . . and rather than that he falls into godlessness through the subtleties of his questioning and hair-splitting. (291)

The way of gnosis is indeed fraught with such dangers, but its dismissal was a prelude to the church's continual distrust of its own saints and mystics. The Gnostic experiment may have been unbalanced, but then so was the reaction against it.

Christ's words: 'Let your light so shine before men, that they may see your good works' and 'I come not to abolish (the law and the prophets) but to fulfill them' (St Matthew 5, 16–17) was to become the lost Christian legacy. The challenge of Gnosticism reappeared to haunt orthodoxy again and again, in the form of many heresies and the words of the Gnostic Christ still echoed up and down the circles of the archons: 'I am the actual call which causes a call to resound in each one, and thus they recognize (me) through (knowledge), since a seed (of light) is in (them)' (291: lacunae in text.)

What is heresy? It derives from a Greek word meaning 'choice.' We should carefully distinguish esotericism from heresy in our understanding of the Western Way, because they are not synonymous. Tradition is never a matter of choice. The esotericist is one who explores the levels of a tradition, taking ever deeper soundings and re-emerging enriched. The heretic does not stay long enough to explore, but leaves demanding his entrance money back. Dualism can be pernicious to esoteric tradition, setting up false dichotomies, estranging the seeker from a holistic perspective. The fruits of Gnosis, like that paradisial fruit, bring knowledge of good and evil. The re-membering of the Body of Light, the reassembly of the divine spark, are paradisial longings for a unity which cannot be realized while we are incarnate. We have truly 'eaten of the fruit' of our experience – this is not original sin, but an opening of the inner eyes. God and evil, light and dark, man and woman, matter and spirit – these are the *dualities* which the guardians of tradition everywhere attempt to balance, attempting to resist *dualism* into which these concepts can fall. Rejection of one in favour of the other leads to imbalance and to heresy.

Gnosticism was merely one contender for the orthodox title of Christianity during the early days of the Church when doctrinal matters were still being codified. It failed at about the same time as the barbarian hordes swept across Europe, eclipsing the rich Classical heritage. The Byzantine Empire maintained certain ancient traditions, church and State coalesced to strengthen each other against the onslaughts of armed insurrection and spiritual darkness. It was no time for personal revelation. While Christianity struggled to make its impact upon Europe, using the vehicle of Native traditional practices and customs as a teaching aid, the Gnostic vision was borne eastwards and westwards by Manichaeism and Catharism, respectively.

Manichaeism is not a direct derivative from Gnosticism so much as a parallel development. Its founder, Mani (AD 216–76), was born in Seleucia of mixed Persian and Gnostic-Baptist background. At the age of twelve he had a vision in which his heavenly companion assured help and protection. Further revelations led him to regard himself as 'the Paraclete of the Christians, as the Messianic son of Zarathustra, and as the Maitreya Budda.' (291) – no small claim! He shared the Gnostic belief in the imprisoned particles of light which must be released by spiritual means. Man was a light-bearer, one who must be active in the combat with darkness – a Mithraic concept, as well as a Christian one. All apostles of Light it was believed, saw their culmination in Mani – Noah, Seth, Enoch, Buddha, Zoroaster and Christ. Extreme asceticism marked his followers: vegetarianism, abstinence from wine and sexual intercourse, a general avoidance of harm to all potential vessels of light whether they be human, animal or plant, typified their practices.

The success of Manichaeism was due to Mani's determination that his teachings should be written down and widely circulated. His church spread rapidly, despite persecution, especially in the East. Mani was martyred by being flayed alive and his disciples were banished from Persia. While a few came West, Manichaeism developed mainly in the East where it held its own against the Nestorian church and with Buddhism. It became particularly strong in Central Asia at Turfan, in Chinese Turkestan, where it proselytized and enjoyed a tolerant hearing until its suppression in the wake of the Mongolian invasion. Manichaen scriptures, found in Turfan early this century, are still being investigated. (291)

The legacy of Manichaeism in the West seems small, probably due to the intervention of Islam which drove a wedge between West and East very effectively. Yet Mani's prophecy, 'my hope will go into the West and will also go into the East,' was a true one. Elements of Manichaen dualism can still be discerned within Christianity due to the theology of St Augustine, who, despite his refutation of his early adherence to Manichaeism, nevertheless introduced a flavour of dualism into his writings.

While Manichaeism trecked eastwards, that other remnant of Gnosticism went westwards through Bulgaria and Italy into France and Spain, where it became known as Catharism. (188) It is perhaps significant that their joint journeys came to an abrupt and bloody end during the thirteeth century, almost as though that influence had run its course for that era. But where Manichaeism developed and flourished away from other Christian rivals, Catharism was as much a product of Christian reactionism as a continuation of Gnostic principles.

The roots of dualism are very deep and difficult to eradicate: there remains an unhealthy surplus of its seasoning within the Western Way.

> Dualism carried with it . . . the need for revelation, and the need for redemption. If man cannot while living in the body, truly find god, the God must make himself known. And if the life of the body drags down the aspiring soul to its level and weakened its powers of flight, then the body and its activities can never achieve their destined end without some infusion of divine power from outside, from above. (109)

Within historical perspectives of the Western Mystery Tradition, the Cathars are often promoted as martyrs to a shared esoteric principle. But though their destruction and persecution at the hands of the Inquisition has aroused much sympathy, the full rigour of the

Cathar way of life and their spiritual stance would find little favour almost anywhere today. The way of the Cathar is not the way of the Hermeticist, though its appeal is doubtless not far removed from the kind of 'Aquarian consciousness' prevalent among those who look for the millenium to be accomplished in nuclear holocaust: a truly ultimate dualism of hopelessness wherein matter is utterly dissolved. We shall return to this point in the final chapter.

For both Manichaens and Cathars, the flesh and matter generally were creations of the evil Demiurge. Here an ultimate dualism was postulated wherein evil and good were eternally polarized. The agents of the Light had somehow been imprisoned and uniformed in the colours of Darkness. It is perhaps difficult for us to appreciate this doctrine, living as we do at the latter-end of the twentieth century, mostly ignorant of the spiritual perspectives which underlie our culture, but it is essential to avoid the pitfalls of dualism now as then.

Dualism was a recurrent problem within Christianity. The Incarnation and the Redemption were concepts which were often misunderstood and without the balance of which the extremes of heresy always flourished. The earth and its creations were not cause for joy to a peasant ploughing his feudal lord's fields, nor to his wife burdened with 'boon-work' and many children: for such as these, respite came only on feast-days and at death. The Cathars found creation as a cause of sorrow, since matter was ensnared within the flesh, seen as the prison of the divine spark. Food, sexuality and enjoyment of the world's goods were either rejected as worthless trash, or else subjected to a deep antimonianism which put the body and spirit in two different compartments, having no interaction. Elements of this attitude are still prevalent among those who have a deep distaste for the actions and function of the body: it is rooted in a fear of our humanity. Cathars wanted release from this condition: they yearned for a spiritual condition with all the zeal of the Orphite. Spiritual purity could have no truck with the body and for this reason, the Cathars said that Christ only 'seemed' to be born of a woman, and 'seemed' to die on the cross. Likewise the sacraments, which exalt matter as the gateway of spiritual grace, were rejected totally.

The Church, because it traded in the coin of matter, was seen as the agent of the Demiurge. It is interesting to speculate just what caused the development of Catharism within Provence where the Courts of Love flourished, where troubadours sang ballads of forthright love and where the cultural climate was of the bountiful South. Perhaps, 'the Cathar notion of body-soul division and the need to ascend through a cycle of purification to a dimension of non-material light had some affinities with the more idealist side of courtly love.' (198)

Like the Gnostics and Manichaens, the Cathars had three ranks of adherents: hearers, believers and the perfect. 'There was thus in effect the same division as among the Catholics between the Religious or Monks and other Believers.' (ibid) The perfect ones reached their exalted position by renouncing evil, living continently, in abstinence from flesh-meats and the fruits of sexuality. They alone could reconcile sinners by means of a ritual called the *consolamentum* – a sacramental-like means of purification. Its effect was considered final and was possibly not repeatable: if a perfected one fell into sin after having received the *consolamentum* – whether by eating meat or committing murder (both equally reprehensible acts) – all those who had received purification at his hands were rendered likewise sinful: a chain of evil had been released. Vigilance and a high degree of integrity were key features of Catharism then. Often the *consolamentum* was not received until death, when all sin was remitted. Women were admissible to ranks of the perfect ones; widows kept Cathar communities, educating children and practising the Cathar way of life. It was a form of ideal Christianity, but dualist to the heart.

Their plain life, simple food, laying on of hands, their celibacy and their adherence to the Gospel of St John, make them seem models of the faith: these very points alerted the Church to the dangers of heresy – such cases had occurred across Europe before. The Albigensian Crusade (1208–18) was launched against them: its causes and success are as much dynastic and geographical as religious. (188) By 1242, Catharism had retired to the stronghold-fortress of Montségur whence its inhabitants were led, to be burned and dispossessed of their lands. By the end of the fourteenth century, Catharism was all but dead.

We have dwelt at length with dualist heresy neither to vaunt its attractive qualities, nor to praise the inhumanity of the Church. ('Kill them all – God will know his own,' cried the Abbé of Cîteaux at the siege of Béziers in 1209 when asked how the army was to distinguish heretic from Catholic.) (125). The facts, in so far as they can be established, speak for themselves. The works of the English doctor, Arthur Guirdham who has claimed Cathar incarnations, have done much to popularize the movement. There are various Gnostic churches in America, as well as a neo-Cathar movement in Holland, known as the *Lectorium Rosicrucianum*.

We have followed the threads of Gnosis into heresy, but the trail does not stop there. Gnosis – esoteric knowledge which is gently led by wisdom – reveals itself within the mystical essence of Christianity. Because the impulse of the Western Way has been classed as heretic by the exoteric Church, does not mean that it does not resonate strongly with esoteric Christianity.

ASLAN IS NOT A SAFE LION

In his *The Lion, the Witch and the Wardrobe*, C.S. Lewis presents Aslan – a Lion, King of the Beasts, and son of the Emperor over the Seas – as a type of Christ. Some of the characters in the story expect him to be a tame, domesticated lion, an anthropomorphic, story-book beast, but they are told: 'Aslan is not a safe lion.' Some expect to see Christ in the same guise – a safe, domesticated god, familiar and expected – the reality is different. Indeed, so far from the reality have we come that many adults who read this story as a child and later realize the nature of Lewis's allegory have said, 'Jesus was a bearded man in the Bible, someone I couldn't relate to – but I could have died for Aslan.'

This shows how we have lost touch with the story of Christianity. The dynamic Christ of the Resurrection, the flogger of the temple money-changers, the one who blasted the fig-tree for its barrenness, the one who will come to bring fire and the sword, is at odds with the downtrodden Man of Sorrows in the mode of Attis and Adonis, the saviour god dead in his mother's lap: the one who has latterly become Gentle Jesus, meek and mild. Christ is *not* safe. He is the Anointed One, whose tongue is a sword (Rev. 1,16): the Logos or Word of God. As a yardstick of creativity rather than as a comfortable icon, we must see him.

Commenting on the implicit dualism of Western religion, Dion Fortune says: 'the great weakness of Christianity lies in the fact that it ignores rhythm. It balances God with Devil instead of Vishnu with Shiva,' which are the preserving and destructive aspects of Brahma. More challengingly, Jim Garrison says: 'God as experienced has been shown to possess light and dark dimensions and to be as savage and terrible as God is merciful and forgiving.' (100) What are hermeticists to make of this? Especially one to whom Christianity seems to be the deadest of dead ends?

More words have been written, and more blood spilled over the founder of Christianity and his intentions, than many can bear to contemplate. Christ has become the figurehead and puppet of both saints and sinners, and the measure of his doctrines a tawdry mockery of the gospel. With this gutless and limp effigy we have little to do here. After nearly 2000 years of substitutes, it is time to look hard at the reality.

In this part of the book we shall be looking at the esoteric *not* the exoteric side of Christianity, and we must do so from the basis of tradition. We spoke in volume one of how the Native Tradition was transmitted by means of Christianity. Just as the customs of ancestral importance and national cohesion were upheld by the Church, so, too, the Hermetic Tradition was rescued from oblivion. While it

> designed to obliterate and extinguish the memory of heathen antiquity and authors ... contrariwise it was the Christian Church which ... did preserve in the sacred lap and bosom thereof the precious relics even of heathen learning which otherwise had been extinguished as if no such thing had ever been. (16)

This is not a book of Christian apologetics. We are not concerned with the historical record of the Church as a human institution, but as a preserver of tradition and as a living mystery school. We must be in the singularly unique position, in this century, that those who join a spiritual tradition today rarely bring any spiritual baggage with them unlike the

> Greeks, and Syrians and Egyptians ... (who) came to the Church loaded with packs of their own, crammed with metaphysics and mystical experience, with cosmic lore and traditions ... nor did they dream of dropping all this on the threshold of the Church and forgetting all about it. ... On the contrary they prized these things as heirlooms, as their dowry. (108)

The validation of spiritual life does not come from some projected set of dogmas, but from inner experience resonating to a tradition. In our times, outsiders now come to gaze on the exterior architecture of tradition, and few see the vision in the sanctuary.

The Church has always taught a mystery: that Christ is both fully human and fully divine. Humanly, this is usually translated into

Christ, the man *or* Christ, the god – rarely both together. But the implications of the Incarnation (the taking of flesh) and the Redemption, are of overwhelming importance to the hermeticist if he or she is engaged upon the Great Work.

Neither of these concepts appears to command universal respect even among those nominally Christian, although the Incarnation and the Redemption are the two pillars between which the world is balanced. The central point of balance is the crucifixion and the harrowing of hell – 'this central event is the meeting of many power lines: whatever their provenance before this event in time, whatever their divergence after it – all lines (of tradition) lead through the mystery of the Resurrection.' (217) The mystical content of these concepts cannot have its full effect unless the non-Christian reader is able to dispel the various ideological smokescreens which prevail in this area.

Due to a popularist Theosophical understanding, Christ is now seen as but one among many such saviours of East and West. On the other hand, he is often seen as yet another of the dying and rising vegetation gods of the mystery schools. The answer is not easy. The Hellenic notion of the Logos, together with the Jewish idea of the Messiah, as well as the mystery schools' own saviours are combined in the figure of Christ. (81) The Eastern Orthodox doctrine of *theosis* may be a key: 'God became man that man might become God,' said St Athanasius in his *De Incarnatione*. That alone, among the mysteries of Christianity is unique to its nature, although it is not one which the Church publicizes. Theosis (literally, deification) is nonetheless the key not only to Christ's actions but to Christian belief. (208) Whether one is a believer or not, something changed direction from the point of the Incarnation: not just the birth of a tradition but the opportunity for consciousness to evolve, a necessary bridge between the impacted dualisms of the Classical world and the cosmic hope of the Mysteries. Non-Christian readers are invited to proceed along the mythological consideration, if they so wish.

Saviours had come before, in many guises, but none before made the impact of Christ. 'What is this mystery that touches me? I received the divine image and did not keep it. He received my flesh to save the image and grant immortality to the flesh.' (200) This was the unique promise which has been obscured and remains to be rediscovered within Christianity which is, despite all appearances, a visibly present, though often invisibly operative mystery school. The Hermetic Tradition draws strongly upon the archetypal myths of

Fig 7.   The Resurrection – alchemical emblem of the Great Work

Classical, Christian and Native mysteries: each has become part of the other so that they can rarely be distinguished.

The occult enclosure of hermeticism has been a self-protective measure as much as a means of preserving the mysteries from the profane. The Christian mysteries, on the other hand, have become open, though inherently hidden, mysteries. Their traditional wisdom and liturgical symbolism have all but escaped through over-simplification. The *disciplina arcani*, the Christian mystery guardians, once ejected non-initiates from observing the higher mysteries of the consecration, as the medieval rood-screen kept the common faithful from becoming too familiar with the sacramental operation: now anyone can see the act of the Great Work taking place quite openly.

The Great Work is figured forth on altars daily in nearly every country of the world as the *prima materia* of the sacred elements of bread and wine are miraculously changed into the Body and Blood of Christ? How many alchemists achieve the same and show it public-ly? (cf. chapter 5) The transubstantiation of the bread and wine into

Fig 8. Lady Mary and her Son in the Ship of Faith, piloted by Wisdom

the Body and Blood of Christ is something which was not lost upon alchemists in later times who used the Eucharistic symbolism as an emblem for their own work. This central sacrament in which the Incarnation and Redemption are enacted was archetypally representative of the Great Work. Those who received the sacrament were enabled, mysteriously, to become members of the Mystical Body of Christ. (fig. 7)

The hermeticist who is aware of the indwelling divine spark and the attempt which must be made to kindle it and take the evolutionary journey into the heart of the macrocosm, has only to consider the implications of Christ's Incarnation – an involutionary journey into the heart of the microcosm in order to bring Divine Fire to the indwelling spark. The amazingly universal application of this action is not dependent upon production of a baptismal certificate, but applies to all. The story of the divine spark is our story too, as we have already seen. It is the skilful use of this story – whether one uses the Christian model or another – which brings us out of 'the vale of tears' into the Inner kingdom:

Not that one should give up, neglect or forget (one's) inner life for a moment, but (one) must learn to work in it, with it and out of it, so that the unity of (one's) soul may break out into (one's) activities and (one's) activities shall lead (one) back to that unity. (241)

The Resurrection breaks through and overturns the tides of time. As with all mysteries, the Christian one happens outside of time: all that happens *within* time is subject both to the laws of time and nature, which is why the imperfect face of the Church reveals not the tranquillity of the Inner Kingdom but the battered makeshift within the world. (189) The Redemption reconciles the two trees of Eden: the Tree of Life, and the Tree of the Knowledge of Good and Evil. The dualism of matter and spirit is reconciled into the realization that all things created have in them the potentiality of resurrection, of transubstantiation, of the completion of the Great Work itself.

Such are the possibilities of esoteric Christianity but, many will demand, where is it practised? While there have been many specifically occult Christian spin-offs from the time of the Gnostics right up until the Liberal Catholic Church with its Theosophist tenets, we will not find the mystical kernel of which we have been speaking anywhere else except within the traditional folds of the Catholic and Eastern Orthodox churches, who have hosted and preserved their spiritual traditions with rigorous care.

The mystical way of tradition has had to work hard to survive the battle which has been joined between faith and knowledge since the time of Gnosticism. We have only to look at the beginning of Christianity to see how pitiful and unnecessary this battle has been. Two sets of visitants come to the manger in Bethlehem: the shepherds and the kings. The shepherds, impelled by angelic messengers, accept the proclamation of the new-born messiah with uncritical enthusiasm – with faith. The kings, by means of their gnosis, follow a star which is the certainty of their faith until they, too, reach their destination. It is perhaps of note that the shepherds go straight to the manger, while the kings waste time calling upon Herod to suffer unwanted congratulations. (cf. chapter 3)

'The faith of uneducated men is not the less philosophically correct, nor less acceptable to God, because it does not happen to be conceived in ... precise statements..... The ears of the common people are holier than are the hearts of the priests,' wrote Cardinal Newman. (244) While faith and knowledge are not exclusive, as we have seen, the Church does not have the apparatus for coping with the mystic who has progressed beyond blind faith into certain faith, which is the gnosis of spiritual illumination.

We have seen how the Gnostic and Manichaen movements catered for the disparate needs of their followers. Modern Christianity seems saddled with a system in which only the 'minimum belief' of the faithful and the highly inflected way of the monk and nun can be accommodated. We need what Jacob Needleman calls 'intermediate Christianity.' (241) The mystical traditions are too circumscribed by experts to be richly and readily available to all; they are not widely taught as a matter of course and those who do stumble upon the esoteric side of Christianity (usually by accident) are without the guidance or assurance of experts in the field, or else are so frightened they mistake their findings for heresy.

As for those psychically gifted or esoterically involved believers – these find themselves out on a limb.

> For centuries the tradition has been to distrust the psychically sensitive people as representing the pagan religions from which the Christian faith has liberated the countries into which it has percolated. . . . But in Europe, the Church has driven the psychic into the underworld. It never disappeared; but it was always threatened, so that it allied itself with pagan rather than with Christian ideas. (259)

The infancy of the Church is over, yet it seems unwilling to push forward to new growth and adulthood; those who seek spiritual maturity find themselves held down in spiritual adolescence. It is little wonder that a mass exodus of Christians is occurring in the direction of other religions or spiritual systems which bother to teach the techniques of prayer and meditation, and which not only treasure but are willing to transmit the traditions which they have inherited to others.

This neglect of the inner life within the Church has led many to speculate as to whether a spiritual renaissance is not due. There are now many spiritual pilgrims abroad and fewer guardians of tradition. If such a renaissance is abroad then it is more likely to arise from the laity rather than the clergy who seem hell-bent on a programme of steady demythologization, liturgical impoverishment and theological inertia: the new chastity, poverty and obedience of the modern age. Few Hermeticists and non-Christians foresee any continuing hope within Christianity as a church-administered religion. The steady devaluation 'in the price of what it is to be a Christian' had so accelerated in the philosopher Kirkegaard's day that he wrote, 'at last it became such an absurdly low price that soon the opposite effect was produced, that men hardly wanted to have anything to do with Christianity.' (176) Some would see the demise of Christianity as an example of poetic justice, in the sense that it has been directly or indirectly the undertaker and executioner of many another tradition.

If the esoteric Christian mysteries are guarded anywhere it is by the unheralded mystic who lives, like a hidden hermit, within his or her tradition. We returned to our concept of 'marginal shamans' who inform the traditional values of the Secret Commonwealth. (cf. volume I) For every mystic whose realizations are written down, there are probably hundreds whose silent practice is unknown. Mysticism is still tarred with the brush of Gnostic and revelatory taint. From past records it would seem that the mystic, like the shamefully-neglected poet, is immediately lauded upon his or her death after a lifetime of being hounded from pillar to post. The incarceration of St John of the Cross and the inquisition of St Teresa of Avila are extreme instances of this practice. Stigmatics and wonder-workers, far from revelling in the reputation enjoyed by pre-Revolutionary Orthodox hermits or *startsi*, have been relegated to obscure monasteries. One feels that a real live St Francis would upset the Church as much now as once he did in thirteenth-century Umbria.

The mystical way is a trackless path on which the pilgrim seeks to encounter God face to face, believing utterly in the promise:

'I will give you the treasures of darkness and the secret places.' (Isaiah 45, 7) Finding one's own inner way is by no means dependent upon how others have travelled, but the length of the journey is considerably diminished if spent in the company of one who is also travelling. In this way, the great mystics of the church have companioned pilgrims from the medieval mystics Julian of Norwich (160), the author of the *Cloud of Unknowing* (50), Thomas à Kempis (179), and St Catherine of Siena (44), to the mystics of our own day: Thomas Merton (233), Caryll Houselander (149) and Ida Gorres. (108) The restoration and preservation of the Christian tradition has been the concern of many mystics and spiritual writers in this century. Two remarkable women, from disparate backgrounds, have contributed much to our understanding: Rosemary Haughton (136) and Lois Lang-Sims (189). Both are aware of the Christian mysteries and the 'lost' esoteric side of their faith. Their books rise solitary from a babel of theological dispute and fundamentalist cant. It is perhaps significant that they are both women within a tradition which, though it has boasted, 'there is neither Jew nor Greek, there is neither slave nor free, there is neither male nor female' (Galatians 3, 28) has held tenaciously onto the very sexual disqualifications that boast was meant to abolish.

When Teilhard de Chardin, writing in the middle of this century said, 'there is the general question of the feminine, and so far it has been left unsolved or imperfectly expressed by the Christian theory of sanctity,' (327) he was hardly underestimating his own traditions's failing in this regard. Though Christ's ministry can be understood by the feminine poles of Mary the Virgin, his mother, who accomplished his Incarnation by her willingness to serve God, and by Mary Magalene who discovered the empty sepulchre on the morning of the Resurrection, the Church has been slow to meditate on this. Much feminist theology has tried to rectify this state of affairs, but has often succeeded in setting matters on their head, substituting female for male symbology, and promoting the ordination of women over more crucial issues. These esoteric matters necessarily upset our esoteric understanding when we see a willing acceptance of a symbol for liturgical purposes: e.g. the representation of and anthems to, the Blessed Virgin, Lady Mary, and an exclusion of her daughters. Mystics have been particularly drawn to Lady Mary: 'Mary is a dimension of Jesus, a dimension which he expressed when he said, "My yoke is easy and my burden light," it is advantageous to address oneself to this dimension in order to reach totality.' (294) (fig. 8)

The Logos and his mother, as the manifest incarnations of God's love, who share in the lot of humanity, are the balances of the spiritual totality. Jung was right to acclaim the doctrine of the Assumption of the Virgin into heaven as of supreme importance for our time, for so does the dualism of male and femaleness stand some chance of being flushed out of Christianity. The spirit – symbolized frequently by Christ – is important, but so is the body – which Christ took through the help of Mary. If the body or soul of a man (i.e. Jesus) had been assumed into heaven, then it was right and fitting that the body and soul of a woman should be also so assumed, says the dogma. 'From this earth, over which we tread as pilgrims, comforted by our faith in future resurrection, we look to you. . . . O Sweet Virgin Mary.' (237) It is interesting to note that though the Protestant churches after the Reformation forsook devotion to or mention of, Lady Mary, hermeticists and alchemists never forsook her. Entrenched within the Protestant enclaves of Rosicrucianism, in the writings of Boehme, Vaughan and others, Our Lady's memory is still sweet. We shall be looking further at the Divine Feminine in chapter 5 where we shall consider the identifications of the Goddess, the World Soul and the Sophianic Lady herself, Our Lady Wisdom.

The hermeticist may often find him or herself at odds with the exoteric or dogmatic nature of the Church, but seldom with its esoteric mysteries. 'What the microcosmic heart does not tell, the macrocosmic heart – the Logos – tells us in a symbolic and partial language.' (294) Christ's parables reveal two levels of understanding – on one level a story, on another, a key to the Inner Kingdom. Jesus speaks about himself in a symbolic way, urging his hearers to squeeze the last drop of meaning out of his parables. His storytelling is aimed to provoke response from among those listeners who have the native wisdom to use the story practically. While he was an enemy of theoretical knowledge, especially when it was imposed upon people who live by simple faith (St Matthew 23), he also encouraged the faith which leads to better knowledge (St John 10). More abundant life, not less, was his saying. Whatever salvific story we live by, first we must believe in it and trust it to show us its treasures. Awareness of the macrocosm, of the Inner Kingdom lies locked within the gospels.

Mystic revelation is not a forbidden, exotic thing: it is merely the skilful understanding and use of spiritual symbolism. In volume one we spoke about the ways in which we can read the landscape, the ancestral stones of our Native Tradition; the same holds true for the Hermetic Tradition. The Gothic cathedrals were known as 'the Bible of the people,' whose architectural mysteries embodied the esoteric story of Christ. To visit one of these today is to step within a forest of stone pillars in whose nemeton are the depictions of saints, angels, and prophets, the yearly round of the seasons, the secret tokens of Christ and Lady Mary. Here, too, at Chartres, one can enter the maze which symbolically represents not only the pilgrimage to Jerusalem, but a return to the heart's home, the Inner Kingdom which is reached by means of life itself. (358, 57, 2) The maze is also our reminder of the interconnecting spirals of the Western Way which is the subject of our present pilgrimage. Within the towering pillars of this Cathedral-forest might we not glimpse the White Hart who has ever been the emblem of spiritual search, in whom the Grail-quest has its quarry? (277)

It is as though Pwyll from the Mabinogion (204) had strayed into the Middle Ages in pursuit of the Otherworldly White Hart, where Arawn's wild hunt rides in a new guise. (cf. volume 1) The quest begun under the aegis of the Native Tradition continues without break into the Hermetic Tradition. From the Gundestrup Cauldron with its depiction of Cernunnos as Guardian of the Sacrificial Hunt to St John of the Cross's 'for the wounded hart appears on the hill' (155) seems a long step, but we should not find any difficulty in reconciling these interrelated images. From within the temenos of a medieval cathedral it is easier to make this important connection. These stones were hewn and erected when spiritual chivalry was abroad – the quest which did not exclude the laity, neither lady nor knight, lord nor peasant. The virile epics of spiritual chivalry, embodied in the Grail legends, combined the Christian mythos with the vigour of native storytelling. Love, both earthly and spiritual, was present in all its complexity: from the urge to protect pilgrims by those monks on horseback, the templars, to the Otherworldly Courts of Love where Celtic paradise and medieval simplicity combined, everyone wanted to be part of the story.

St Francis of Assisi, his head stuffed with such stories, had attempted to be a chivalrous knight before he rode out in defence of Lady Poverty in nothing more than a tattered habit and a handful of ideals, yet he never lost sight of his love for spiritual chivalry and the quest. He founded two orders, one for monks and one for nuns, but, so overwhelming was this troubador of the Lord, that his storytelling set fair to empty the villages of Italy, so he founded an order for lay people, that they might not be left out of the story.

The tribal stories did not retreat, but were reworked and incorporated into that of the White Hart, Christ himself. The Classical remnant which went to found the basis of the Hermetic tradition has for its centre the story of the lost pearl and the finding of the spark of light. Both stories cross-track each other and will doubtless find their meeting in the fullness of time – unless, of course, they meet on the Inner, within the Kingdom itself, outside of time. And while both stories were to be challenged by new metaphors, they still have the power to draw in listeners.

The thirst for knowledge has been overwhelming, often engulfing what the Church saw as the more important concerns of spiritual quest. For, while the academicians and proto-scientists were not satisfied with the sum of medieval knowledge, neither were those on spiritual quest content to remain within the known limits of religion. The earlier splintering of religion from shamanism was to be unhappily mirrored once more between religion and science during the Reformation and Counter-Reformation when faith and knowledge joined battle again, with the help of new combatants – tradition against the word, laws of God and laws of nature set at odds. Too much radical experimentation in the area of physics and metaphysics resulted in an almost total schism within religion. Scientists and magicians were hard-put to reconcile their activities with their beliefs.

The importance of quest is primarily within the exploration of consciousness: however far we go in spiritual quest, we always find what we sought within ourselves. The exploration of the internal workings of man, the microcosm, was still the prime concern of the mystic, scientist and magician. And, although each sought on different levels of experience – each quest was valid. It is our

> God-given task to reconcile and harmonize the poetic and the material realms, to bring them to unity, to spiritualize the material, and to render manifest all the latent capacities of the created order. As the Jewish Hasidim expressed it, man is called 'to advance from rung to rung until, through him, everything is united.' As microcosm, then, man is the one through whom the world is summed up; as mediator, he is the one through whom the world is offered back to God. (355)

This realization is shared by Christianity and by Judaism: it has become the task of the hermeticist also by means of a wonderful ladder of light which joins the traditions of the West in a mysterious manner. We have spoken of tribe and of wandering tradition: within the Jewish spiritual tradition, the two are one.

THE SHATTERED VESSELS

> God arranged the order of creation so that all things are bound to each other. The direction of events in the lower world depends on entities above them, as our sages teach: 'There is no blade of grass in the world below that does not have an angel over it striking it and telling it to grow. (168)

So wrote the Jewish mystical leader, the Hai Gaon (939–1938). This pronouncement will be familiar to the hermeticist who will catch resonances of the Emerald Tablet. It is also a statement about the interrelatedness of the worlds which Qabalism, above all other systems, has understood and given to the world. The development of Qabala within Judaism is extraordinary because of its amazing success and acceptance not only as a mystical tradition within Judaism itself, but as an esoteric system which has been taken over by non-Jews.

Qabala is an instance of a mystical tradition arising organically from its exoteric shell, but one which remained totally integrated within it. It evolved from the oral teachings of the prophets, took on board mystical elements and techniques during the Babylonian exile and the Diaspora whence it developed in significantly localized ways. The exoteric laws of Judaism, rather than militating against its development, have welded it more strongly, keeping the esoteric secrets in the hands of adepts who were also religious leaders.

Two factors above all determine the hardiness of Judaism: tribal cohesion, as exemplified in the family unit, and the adaptability of a nomadic people – as the Jews have been forced to live until this century. The minutiae of Judaic law are often represented as a tiresome burden by non-Jews, but, for those within its folds, they are opportunities for contact with God: the touching of the sacred text of the *Shema* ('Hear O Israel', *Deut.* 6,4.) in the *mezuzah* on leaving and entering a house, the wearing of the *tallit* and *tefillin* – the prayer shawl and phylacteries – the dietary laws and seasonal celebrations, the divine rest of the Sabbath, are the interactions of the faithful people with God. (335) Judaism's mystics are not monks and nuns, but married people living in the world who understand the necessity of reconciling the lives of the body and of the spirit.

No one can date the inception of Qabala. It remained an oral teaching for centuries, the first texts appearing in early medieval Spain. The cross-fertilizations affecting the Mediterranean during the early Christian era are also apparent within the cosmological speculation and formulations of Qabala. Since worship at the Temple in Jerusalem was disrupted first of all in 586 B.C. when the Solomonic Temple was destroyed, and then in AD 70 when the rebuilt Second Temple was burned during the Roman occupation, certain religious obligations and duties could not be fulfilled. Moreover, the dwelling-place of God's Spirit, the *Ruach HaKadosh*, the Shekhina had nowhere to abide but in the souls of the faithful. This is central to an understanding of Judaism's obsession with the preservation of tradition. No matter where the chosen people lived, there also went the Shekhina to share their exile invisibly, as once the tribes had followed Moses through the desert led by a Pillar of Cloud by day and a Pillar of Fire by night – the mystical appearance of the Shekhina which dwelt between the cherubim upon the curtained Ark of the Covenant. In the new exile of the Diaspora, each member of the congregation bore the added duty of retaining a secret tabernacle for the indwelling spirit which could only be wrought by upright life and constant study of the traditions. From such intense study was born the mystical system of the Qabala.

The Qabala is a microchip in which is encoded the whole of Jewish mystical tradition. Because of its unique compression, it is a system which has been borrowed by the Hermetic tradition in order to codify its own complex symbology. But we should not forget that, first and foremost, Qabala is a Jewish spiritual expression, not a Gentile magical system. Qabala is made of many levels of mystical experience, and has had many commentators. We do not have space to list them all: the reader is referred to the bibliography where many titles are listed. (167, 168, 145, 154, 77, 127–30)

What is evident is that the techniques employed by Qabalists included prayer, fasting and the repetition of the holy names of God – the usual religious devices – alongside what we may consider to be more esoteric techniques such as meditation, rhythmic breathing, chanting, the adoption of certain postures in order to perceive the divine vision, and many means of visualization. These techniques have been carefully guarded from the uninitiated because, used without guidance, they cannot only be physically dangerous, but can mislead the practitioner into qliphotic realms – where the shells of creation are inhabited by demons.

One of the main sources of Qabala is the *Zohar* or Book of Splendour, attributed to Moses of Leon (1250–1305), but which doubtless dates before this in oral tradition. Together with the *Sepher Yetzirah* (Book of Creation) it gives us the basis for all subsequent Qabalistic study, establishing a sephirotic system upon the Tree of Life, and the means of undertaking the series of spiritual ascents known as 'merkabah' or ascents in the chariot. The sephiroth are the ten essences or 'sapphires' of God's emanations. (See fig 9) They have tended to become useful filing cabinets within Gentile Qabala, but their original meaning is of jewel-like light through which the different qualities of God's glory are manifest. The *Merkabah* or chariot, was the vehicle by which the mystic contemplated the heavenly halls of God. This form of mysticism derives from the Vision of Ezekiel whose account of the wheeled chariot and

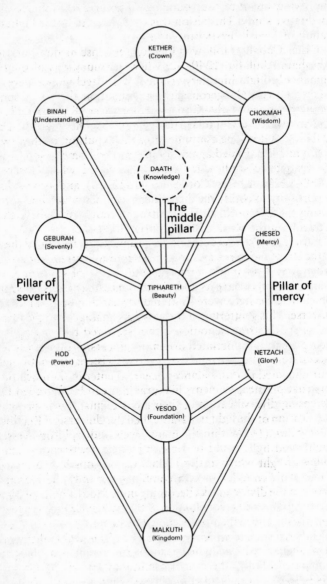

Figure 9:   The Tree of Life

the living creatures surrounding it became the object of much meditative study. This vision was considered to be the highest in the canon of Jewish mysticism. (154)

Other Qabalists followed their own intense meditations, notably Abraham Abulafia (1240–92) whose permutations of the Hebrew alphabet brought him fiery visions. (1) His techniques were considered to be very dangerous: it is possible that there was some link between him and the Christian esotericist, Ramon Lull – their systems were very similar. (cf. chapter 3) The Spanish school of Qabala did not long continue after the expulsion of the Jews from Spain in 1492. Exiled again, some returned home to found a centre for Qabalistic studies in Palestine, at Safed where Joseph Karo (1488–1575), Moses Cordevero (1522–70) and others had the opportunity to codify the disparate disciplines which had sprung up during the Diaspora. At this centre the course of Qabala changed, maturing in the work of Isaac Luria (1534–72)

Luria's system was exceedingly complex: he developed the notion of the ten sephiroth as existing within four universes concurrently. In order that God might permeate the whole of creation and that everything might have its god-like response, the vessels (or sephiroth) which held his light were shattered so that they spilled into a lower universe. This shattering of the vessels is analogous to the idea of the divine spark's fragmentation into a scattered body of light. From their primal, but unrelated origin, fragments of the vessels fell into successively lower universes, or levels of existence, until the light was so fragmented that imbalances began to enter in (in much the same way that physical elements like uranium can be degraded through increasing diversification of their constituents). Luria preached the rectification of the light of a state called the Universe of Rectification, the *Tikkun*. (16) Within the many levels and sephirotic vessels, the fragmented light could be reassembled as archetypes – miniature bodies of light which at the Tikkun would constitute an integrated whole. This complex system combines not only the Hermeticists' theory of the divine sparks becoming united into a Body of Light, but also the union and reconciliation of the syzygies,which is a feature of Gnosticism and which preoccupied alchemy.

The final state to which mystic, alchemist and Qabalist work may seem an exalted one which cannot be in any way hastened or anticipated. Truly, these are cosmic matters, yet as Chaim Vital (1543–1620), Luria's chief disciple, wrote:

In his ascent the mystic is irradiated by the light of the tree and in his descent the light finds a medium through which to flow back into the daily world. . . . In the descent a magic is worked and all the pretended way of ascent (through imaginative meditation) is rendered 'greater than reality' (121)

The meditative techniques whereby an appreciation of the Tree of Life's secrets might be understood became the means by which the Qabalist made the ascent and descent, so that the higher universes and lights of the sephiroth might be experienced with the help of the imaginative faculty. But this experience was not for individual retention, but to hasten the return of the Shekhina and her people out of exile.

Luria's teachings spread throughout the Jewish world, particularly into Russia and Eastern Europe where it influenced the Hasid movement. The Hasidim (the devout) were subject to frequent persecution but in them the living Qabala took root. They brought it firmly back from the mystical flights of medieval Spanish fantasy into the realms of everyday life. Most famous of the Hasidim was the Baal Shem Tov (1698–1760) who founded a tradition of Qabalistic wonder-working. The sufferings of the people were so great at that time, that it is no wonder that the Hasidic masters were looked upon as magicians and saviours. It is interesting to note that this same ability to work wonders was a feature of the Russian Orthodox wandering hermits, the *startsi*: their continual repetition of the Jesus Prayer, 'Lord Jesus Christ, Son of God, have mercy on me, a sinner', was in many ways similar to the recitation and permutation of the Holy Names of God performed by Qabalists. Perhaps Qabalism and remnants of northern European shamanism touched at this point? Certainly the complex systems of Qabala were brought to the people by the means of a storytelling tradition which had its roots in the Native Traditions. Rabbi Nahman of Bratislav (1772–1810) told of the Tikkun, of the creation dramas and the qualities of the sephiroth in the format of simple folk-stories. (240)

As Kaplan remarks, 'the closer one gets to the present, the less dangerous and more universal the methods of Qabalistic meditation become.' (168) The Hasid dances and sings in ecstatic oneness with God, the Lurianic Qabalist performs the mystic unifications which bring male and female aspects of God together in divine embrace, the Spanish Qabalist sits enthroned within the radiance of the Holy Names. Few aspire, in these latter days, to return to the beginnings of

Qabala, to attempt the last ascent in the Chariot of Fire to the Seventh Holy Hall where God himself sits in glory.

Jewish cabals still meet today, drawn from Orthodox or observant Jews, not Gentiles. Their work is part of the Western Way's rich heritage, presenting its face to the Inner world in order that the light of the Divine Countenance might shine more clearly upon the outer world. Their task is not unlike that of other mystics from other traditions:

> A man is born into this world with only a tiny spark of goodness in him. The spark is God, it is the soul; the rest is ugliness and evil, a shell. The spark must be guarded like a treasure, it must be nurtured, it must be fanned into flame. It must learn to seek out the other sparks, it must dominate the shell. (274)

Many Jewish Qabalists cannot comprehend Gentile or even Christian Qabalism, as it often called. (cf. chapter 3) For them, Qabala is the ultimate expression of their religion not, as for Western occultists, merely a technique. We shall be looking closer at the ways in which Qabala has passed from spiritual tradition into psycho-spiritual technique in the next chapter. Occultism has done for Qabala what psychology has done for religion. One person's mythology is another's religion, after all. Unless the reader has direct experience of a living spiritual tradition at first hand, he or she is unlikely to ever understand or even recognize the images, symbols and states which its practice entails. Those hermeticists who employ Qabalistic techniques should have more than a passing acquaintance with the tradition from which it sprang. The books of Z'ev ben Shimon Halevi (see bibliography) will give the general reader a firm background in this area, as well as providing a system of training in authentic Qabalistic method.

We wonder how often this Hebrew children's prayer has been used in other, esoteric, contexts:

> In the name of the Lord God of Israel, may Michael, the protection of God, be at my right hand; and Gabriel, the power of God, at my left; before me Uriel, the light of God; behind me Raphael, the healing of God; and above my head Shekhinat El, the presence of God. (88)

EXERCISE 3   THE TEMPLE OF INNER WISDOM

This exercise is designed to establish a temple of Inner Wisdom, a common meeting place where those of disparate traditions, or from no tradition, may meet. If 'religious loyalty is nothing else than the sincerity of our human relations with God, on the basis of the means which he puts at our disposal,' (294) then we must find and use the most skilful means. Although an accident of birth determines our cultural background, and though we may find our own tradition only after having come to maturity, there exists a companionship of the Sophia Perennis which we all partake of.

The Temple of Inner Wisdom is circular. About it are set many antechambers which give access to the central area. You will enter through one of these. The inner temple is approached through the antechamber which represents your own tradition. This will be furnished according to the appropriate symbology and correspondences of that tradition. It should be a place where you feel at home.

If you have no tradition, consider the many paths which have led you to where you stand today. These paths may not necessarily be traditions in themselves, but fragments or derivatives of one. Perhaps you have used a meditation technique which has been helpful, or read a book whose philosophy resonates with yours so that you have adopted it. You may have explored a symbol-system such as the Tarot or Tree of Life; you may have used techniques derived from Eastern religions, such as yoga or I-Ching. If you wish, you may make these the antechambers about the temple, but make sure you are at home there: do not attempt to work from a tradition which alienates you. Before entering the temple, make sure you comprehend the tradition you have chosen on more than a surface level. Each of these chambers will have a guardian who is at liberty to admit you to the temple: each is a master or mistress of that tradition, so listen to their advice.

If you are still travelling towards wisdom (and when do any of us finally possess it?) or if you are totally bewildered by the multiplicity of traditions available to you, do not hesitate to enter the antechamber of the Amethyst Sanctuary. This is a bare, holy room in which hangs an ornate silver lamp with an eternal flame burning in a glass of amethyst-colour. Anyone may enter this place. Its only furnishing is a chair where you may meditate on the Eternal Flame. If you truly wish to enter the Temple of Inner Wisdom, you must bring something of your spiritual experience with you. One will come to you from within the temenos to talk with you and instruct you. This guardian will invite you to enter the temple from the Amethyst Sanctuary when you are fully prepared, and not before.

There are as many antechambers to the temple as there are traditions in the world. To prepare to enter the Temple from your chosen room, sit in meditation and build the antechamber about you, evoking its essential qualities, using the tools of the senses. You should, in effect, be *inhabiting* your tradition before you are allowed to draw aside the curtain which separates you from the temple. The chamber's guardian – who can appear as a religious leader, prophet, mystic or established guide along that path – you will indicate if you are fully prepared.

You draw aside the curtain. The circular hall is of vast proportions. Around it, supporting a golden central dome, are seven pillars. There are no symbols of any tradition here – these all remain in the antechambers for they are the outer semblances of an inner tradition. The sanctuary of the mysteries was an empty room, representing the imageless truth of wisdom.

In the centre of the Temple is a round table on which is a dish of bread and salt, and a cup of red wine. All who enter here must partake of this meal, or they have no place here. This bread and salt of hospitality and the wine of fellowship is served by Sophia herself. She may appear as a beautiful, crowned queen of mysterious aspect, or in other guises. It is possible that the meal will be served by invisible hands, that the meditator will see no figure at all. Yet the presence of Sophia pervades this temple, making it the meeting place of all who are engaged on the search for her gifts.

You may come here to meditate and to meet with all aspects of other traditions. Because you have eaten the bread and drunk of the wine, there is concord between all who come here. You may ask questions about aspects of traditions which trouble you or which you do not understand. Because you represent your tradition in the Temple of Inner Wisdom, do not be surprised if others ask *you* questions.

This exercise may grow in importance over the years: its effect is a cumulative one. The Temple can be used as a place of tranquillity and refreshment. You may meet other pathwalkers here, as well as guardians, saints, and mystics of many traditions. You may even sit at the round table of fellowship and partake of the counsels of Sophia.

Do not despair if you are entering by way of the Amethyst Sanctuary and you cannot seem to get an invitation within. You will enter when you are ready. The Temple is by no means for those who have reached the end of their search for Wisdom. She leads us by winding roads and those who have entered by way of one tradition may find the door temporarily closed to them if the road should lead away from it. Another door will open in time, and meanwhile there is the Amethyst Sanctuary which is always open to one who thirsts and hungers after Wisdom and her gifts.

CHAPTER 3
The Magus and his Magic

Let my lamp at midnight hour
Be seen in some high lonely tower,
Where I may oft outwatch the Bear
With thrice great Hermes.

Milton: *Il Penseroso*

The magician strives to know God's mind as it is externalized in
the Cosmic patterns.

Godwin: *Mystery Religions*

THE RETURN OF THE SHAMAN

Three magicians were attendant at the nascence of Christ. As the
Gospel of Matthew tells it:

Now when Jesus was born in Bethlehem of Judea in the days of
Herod the King, behold, wise men from the East came to
Jerusalem, saying, 'Where is he who has been born King of the
Jews? For we have seen his star in the East, and have come to
worship him . . . (St Matthew II, 1–2)

The New Testament Greek calls them 'sages' but tradition has called
them Magi almost from the start. Early Christian iconography
depicts them visiting the infant Jesus in a cave, their Phrygian caps
identifying them as Persian or possibly Mithraic priests. As we saw in
chapter 6, there are at times startling similarities between the lives of
Christ and Mithras, so that it seems appropriate that the servants of
one sacrificed god should come to the nativity of another.

Who were these first visitors to the incarnate god who recognized
his kingly and divine character in a way which the Jewish people
themselves did not? We may presume little about them, save that
they came from the east, were probably Zoroastrian or Mazdian
priests, and that they followed the courses of the stars. Traditionally,

their names were Balthazar, Melchior, and Caspar: Balthazar was of the white race of Shem, and brought the gold of incarnation; Melchior, of the black race of Ham, brought the frankincense of crucifixion; Caspar, of the yellow race of Japheth, brought the myrrh of embalming and resurrection. Each stood for a race and an art; each was an aspect of ancient wisdom, coming to pay homage to its newest manifestation. They are in at the beginning of Christianity but accorded no place in its subsequent development. Yet 'they saw the child with Mary his mother', presumably in much the same way as they would have identified statues of Isis and Horus, Cybele and Attis, and other such prefiguring archetypes, and presented with the living icon of mother and child, they fell on their knees and worshipped:

> The children of the Chaldeans saw the Virgin holding in her hands Him who with His hands fashioned mankind. Though He has taken the form of a servant, yet they knew Him as their Master. In haste they knelt before Him with their gifts and cried out to the Blessed Virgin; Hail, Mother of the Star that never sets. (191)

Who then were these men, who acknowledged Christ as their master before the start of his earthly ministry? One writer describes them as men who were 'able to understand god' and who knew 'how to minister to the divinity' (270). Both of these descriptions could be applied without alteration to the role of the shaman, with which we dealt in volume one. The magi are still priests, close enough to the gods to recognize a new avatar and to wish to act as intermediaries between divinity and mankind. They are the precursors of the magician, or perhaps we should say his ancestors, and they bear within them the seeds of his craft.

Although there is a great distance in time between the shaman and the magician, there is almost no essential difference in their respective functions. Both stand as mediators of an inner impulse to the outer world: the shaman as a public figure, the centre of his tribe's relationship to the gods; the magician as a private figure, working often in obscurity, but continuing to mediate cosmic forces to his fellow men. No longer the priest of the tribe, he is constrained into a position of isolation; he lives a hidden life which touches that of the man in the street only tangentially. He is 'neither a saint, nor a saviour, nor a prophet, nor a seer. He is a shaman-in-civilization.' (75) (fig.10)

Fig. 10   The Magus

As such the magician operates in a manner wholly different from that of his precursor: where the one had a direct line to the god or gods of his tribe, the other works with different techniques, different contacts, yet is always seeking to break through into the inner realm itself, to speak directly to God, as his ancestors had once been able to do. Thus his magic is the practical extension of a philosophical/mystical underpinning, and without that foundation it would not exist. To look at the magician without taking into account his dream of unity, however partial or superficial, with deity, is to mistake his whole purpose.

We make the same mistake if we look at magic, or ritual, simply as an exercise in power-seeking – like examining the bodywork of a new car without bothering to look at the engine.

Magic and ritual are microcosmic expressions of the macrocosm: man's tiny torch of desire uplifted to the fire of the stars. We plug into the universe through the enactment of ritual – beginning, as we saw in volume one, with the propitiation of the elements and a desire to enter the womb of the world-mother. The Hermetic approach, as adopted by the magician, is more intellectually motivated, celestial rather than chthonic. The astrological calculations of 'star-led wizards' of Milton's *Ode on the Morning of Christ's Nativity* are a far cry from the instinctive actions of the tribal shaman – yet each in his way is motivated by the same needs and desires, only their methods have changed with the movement from tribal to individual consciousness.

There is no such thing as an archetypal magician, in any age, and to speak of his role with any certainty we are forced to generalize. If we look at some of the major figures who are classified as Magus or Wizard, we will see why this is so. We may also begin to notice certain points in common.

Let us look, for example, at Apollonius of Tyana, who flourished in the first century AD and was by some considered a god rather than a man. He was said to have been begotten by Proteus, god of the winds and patron of shape-shifters – an appropriate choice one might think, for the father of a magician – and to have possessed miraculous powers which enabled him, amongst other things to prophecy accurately the death of the Roman Emperor Domitian. He travelled extensively, performing feats which defied rational explanation, and vanished mysteriously after a long life. He frequently escaped death at the hands of the angry priesthoods of various cults with whom he came into conflict. He is also said to have visited Hades, to inquire of the god of the Underworld what was the purest philosophy then available to mankind. He emerged, five days later, with a bound copy of the precepts of Pythagoras, whose follower he afterwards became, observing a five-year vow of silence until his initiation was complete. Many of his contemporaries compared him with Christ and found him superior while others have regarded him as a figure of evil. (37) His *Letters*, which are all that remain of his once voluminous writings, are redolent with sound advice and mystical perception. To one neophyte he wrote:

> Listen well to me, my son, and I will reveal to you the mystery of wisdom, a mystery unintelligible, unknown and hidden for many, concerning the seasons and the times, the hours of day and of night, concerning their denomination and their influence and concerning the true wisdom hidden therein . . . (298)

He goes on to cite four books of his own 'more precious than golden jewelry and stones of great value' the fourth of which,

> noblest of all, contains powerful and terrible signs . . . that teach the first elements of the visible things created by God, so that he who reads this book may, if he chooses, be successful in realizing such wonders. (ibid.)

He speaks of methods of 'tying' and 'untying' the elements, through the pronouncement of the secret names of God – a method of magical practice which is fascinatingly like that of the Qabalistic magicians of a later age.

Here, then, is a magician who is able to exercise control over the different aspects of nature, and who has evolved or acquired a system with which he can relate magical activity to any hour, day, month or year. All of which, he claims, was taught him by God – an important point to which we shall return shortly.

Meanwhile, let us look at another magician-figure, somewhat more notorious than Apollonius, Simon the Magician, or as he is better known, Simon Magus.

Unlike Apollonius, whose claims he out-vaunted, Simon has come down to us as a picture of the failed magician. His famous contest with St Peter, in which he offered to take to the air like a bird to prove that Christianity was a false religion, ended in a plunge to the unyielding earth. Yet during his life Simon attracted a large following and showed himself by no means bereft of wisdom.

Having learned magic in Egypt he became the leader of a Gnostic cult after a spectacular magical battle with its former head. (37) His followers elevated him to the status of godhead, yet when his miracles were bettered by those of the disciple Philip he renounced his former beliefs for a time and was baptized a Christian. Later, however, he reneged on his conversion, when he unsuccessfully tried to purchase the power of the Holy Spirit with money. After this he became a deadly enemy of all Christians, contesting the miracles of the disciples at every turn until his fatal contest with Peter.

His innate Gnosticism can be recognized in the following passage from his writings:

I say what I say, and I write what I write. And the writing is this. In the universal Aeons there are two schools, without beginning or end, springing from one root, which is the power of invisible, inapprehensible silence. Of those shoots one is manifest above all, which is the Great Power, the Universal Mind ordering all things, male, and the other (is manifested) from below, the Great Thought, female, producing all things. Hence pairing with each other they unite and manifest the Middle Distance, incomprehensible Air, without beginning or end. In this is the Father who sustains all things, and nourishes those things which have a beginning and an end. (133)

We can see here the basis for a whole esoteric philosophy, a schema and structure of the cosmos which spans from before time and beyond it. Invisible, inapprehensible silence is the very stuff from which all things are generated: one feels that modern philosophers like Wittgenstein and Nietzsche would have approved of the nakedness of this idea.

But does it add to our conception of the magician? Simon Magus has come down to us as at best a victim of spiritual pride, and at worst a monster of depravity and a servant of evil – and the magician has taken colour from this ever since. Yet in his works (or whoever wrote the words attributed to him) are the seeds of a philosophical vision which still informs the work of the magician. Simon's 'universal mind' placed side by side with the 'I am Mind' of the *Poimandres*, parallels the evolution of consciousness argument advanced in volume one of the present work, and shows the magician becoming aware of the primal Light.

By comparison, the magicians of the Middle Ages seem positively backward in both their spiritual and philosophical motivations. This may be due to the influence of medieval Scholasticism, which could be described as the intellectual arm of the Church in Europe, since it governed the physical extent of knowledge – in the form of books, manuscripts and documents – under its scrutiny, and impressed upon them a wholly Christian view. In this the magician had no place, although it is ironic that the conventional stereotype of the magus as a celestially cloaked individual conjuring demons into a triangle from a safe distance, really originates from this time. We must consider that these demons were, in reality, *daemons*, spiritual helpers, esoterically akin to angels, who communicated the wisdom of higher worlds. Psychologically, we might observe that magicians who resorted to such methods of conjuration, were actually recognizing and integrating those aspects of their inner selves which communed with an Otherworld reality. To teat the helpful daemon as demon was to tussle with those inner aspects of the self which were as yet unbalanced or unintegrated. Bad individual aspects were demonic, whereas good aspects polarized as angelic; the unintegrated aspects remained so, bound in the triangle of conjuration forever.

But a far greater degree of curiosity existed during the medieval era than is generally understood. Alchemy flourished, admittedly under difficult conditions, as we shall see, and scientific investigation was a powerful force to be reckoned with, despite being curtailed severely by the control of Rome. Roger Bacon (*c.* 1214 – *c.* 1292) whom many consider the archetypal magician of the age, was in reality a proto-scientist, although he by no means excluded magic from his studies, allowing it to contain at least 'some truth.' 'Yet in regard those very truths are enveloped with a number of deceits, as it's not very easie to judge betwixt the truth and the falsehood.' (37) Yet Bacon certainly studied magic from the grimoires which were then available, and wrote a treatise called *The Mirror of Alchemy*, which contains much that is still valuable. (ibid.) Indeed he seems to have taken to heart words attributed to St Jerome by another medieval writer, Gerald of Wales: 'You will find many things quite incredible and beyond the bounds of probability which are true for all that. Nature never exceeds the limits set by God who created it.' (101) In his own cautious way Bacon was more of a magician than many of his more notorious fellows. He shares with the poet Virgil the doubtful honour of being called a worker of marvels after his death, being attributed with a magic mirror which enabled him to see what was happening anywhere in the world, and with the construction of a 'Brazen Head' which would answer faithfully any question put to it. In all probability, given Bacon's far-sighted genius, this is more likely to have been the world's first computer than a magical implement, although this is not to say that we should dismiss its creator from our list of magicians. There has always been a practical, inquisitive side to magic, which Bacon's lively mind represents as well as any.

Perhaps the most famous magician of all time is himself as much a product of the Middle Ages as any of the figures we have been examining. We refer to Merlin, and in the light of his extraordinary qualities and legendary status it is perhaps not surprising if he is found to embody within him the whole range of role-changes through which the magician has passed.

Beginning life as a shamanistic figure, living in the wilds with animals for company and prophesying the life and destiny of kings, Merlin develops rapidly through a succession of metamorphoses into the mage and wonder-worker of the Arthurian cycle. Cloaked in mystery, appearing and disappearing at will, moving in and out of the stories of Arthur and his fellowship in a completely unpredictable manner, he becomes the possessor of greater and greater powers. He can assume any shape at will, call forth whole pageants of imaginary beings from the air and dismiss them with consummate ease. He is, in fact, the pre-eminent power in the land during Arthur's reign, credited with orchestrating the mysteries of the Grail and of the various quests undertaken by the Round Table knights. (331)

He is thus, first and foremost in the consciousness of many, a literary figure, though he in fact stands for a great deal more. As in inner plane reality Merlin is one of the great masters who guide the steps of those travelling the Western Way. To quote the words of a modern magician, Gareth Knight, 'The importance of Merlin is his role as a way-shower to a new phase, or epoch, of conscious evolution.' (185) More than this,

> He represents a humanized Western form of the ancient gods of learning and civilization, such as the Greek Hermes or the Egyptian Thoth. He is furthermore, one of those, akin to Melchizadek in the Old Testament, 'without father or mother, without descent'. (ibid.)

To find Merlin compared with Hermes or Thoth should not surprise us: what is interesting is that it demonstrates his dual nature as a master of both Native and Hermetic traditions. As we said in the previous volume, he is more of a god than a human being, and as such represents the magician on a higher arc of evolution – as almost a summation of all that the worker with magic seeks to become.

If Merlin is an inner resonator who generated the literature which gathered about his name, then Dr John Dee must be considered almost his outer manifestation in the real world. He is probably the single most influential aspect of the magician ever to have lived and a worthy successor to the Arthurian mage. Though his abilities have often been called into question, his influence has continued to be felt right up to the present time.

Born in 1527 Dee rose from comparative obscurity to a position of power as adviser and court astrologer to Elizabeth I. He is considered to have been the foremost mathematician of his day, travelled widely, and left an abundance of writings, diaries and notebooks which testify to his largeness of spirit, depth of occult understanding and qualities of perception. Born while Henry VIII was still on the throne, he lived on into the age of James I, five reigns and five changes of religious allegiance in that troubled age. He died finally in 1608, all but forgotten by the world which he had subtly influenced for so long. During his long life he had synthesized much that has come to be accepted as an integral part of the Hermetic Tradition: Neo-Platonism and Pythagorianism, Qabala, Alchemical and Hermetic materials were moulded into his intricate system of correspondences – of which lengthy lists of angelic beings are a clear indication. His influence on Sir Philip Sidney and his circle, whom Shakespeare refers to as 'The School of Night', was considerable, and through him may well have come the cult of the Virgin Queen which became attached to Elizabeth.

In 1598 Dee visited Heinrich Khunrath in Germany, and may well have planted the seeds of what was to become Rosicrucianism. (364) Certainly his *Monas Hieroglyphica* (65) seems to have formed a basis for the *Consideratis Brevis* and the *Confessio Fraternitatis*, while the figure of the sleeping Venus in the *Chemical Wedding* (178) reflects the way in which Elizabeth was regarded by her courtiers through Dee's influence.

Dee is, then, a prime example of the magician in the political arena, transmitting Inner impulses to the Outer world – always, as we have said, the foremost task of the magus. But though he still moved in a twilight world of mystery and wonder, his work had begun to assume cosmic dimensions. He no longer worked solely with elementals or demons, but was seen to hold converse with spiritual entities of a higher order. Within the confines of his circle Dee could, like his fellow countryman, Owen Glyndwr, call up spirits from the vast deep, but they were of another order now, and the reasons for calling them had changed as well.

It will be seen from the above preamble that it is almost impossible to categorize the magician in any satisfactory way; as a character he eludes us with continual changes of shape and action, so that a modern day magus would find it hard to model himself on any single archetype. Fortunately for those who follow the way of the magus today, they are not called upon to do so. Their training, like that of any other initiate, comes as often from within – where like as not they will find themselves in direct contact with one of the great magicians of the past in their inner plane guise. It is still possible to be overshadowed by the spiritual form of Dee, or Michael Scott, or Roger Bacon, or Giordano Bruno, each one with their own wisdom to teach, their rich store of knowledge to impart.

Though the guise of the magician may have changed through the long ages since first he stepped upon the stage in the skin robe and antlered head-dress of the shaman, his aims have remained much the same. Contemporary magicians like Gareth Knight (179, 181) and W.G. Gray (114–16), follow the same path as Apollonius or Merlin or Dee, for all that their approach and many of their techniques have changed. Each still uses symbol-laden ritual and visualative techniques to focus their inner-guided intention to a point where it becomes actualized. Like the alchemist, striving to be born into the Inner realms, (cf. chapter 5) the magician, past and present, seeks to bring to birth the Inner impulse in the Outer world, acting as both parent and midwife.

That this role is also, to some degree, shared by the mystic, the saint, and the philosopher, accounts for the difficulty we experience when we try to assign the magician to any single heading. Like the 'shaman-in-civilization' with which we began, his function has become fragmented, held together only by the esoteric philosophy which underlies so much of the Western Way. To understand why this is so, we have to look more closely at that philosophical underpinning, and how it has helped shape the magical life.

EXPANDING THE UNIVERSE

The great traditionalist philosopher René Guénon first pointed out in his book *Crisis of the Modern World* (123) that with the dawn of philosophy in the Hellenic world, there came about a division within the mysteries between exoteric and esoteric. The former came to denote a radically realistic view of nature, argued from a purely logical point of view; the latter suggested an inner spirituality which was wholly transcendent. For philosophy as an abstract discipline to survive, it became necessary to concentrate on the exoteric to the exclusion of all else – and this the first philosophers did, creating in virtually a decade a wholly different way of looking at the universe.

Of course this was not the end of the mysteries, but it did cause a shift away from their open celebration towards a protective secrecy which has cloaked the magician and his magical activities ever since. It was secrecy of a new kind from that of the Mystery School – because, although the mysteries were kept secret by their initiates, they were still accessible to all. Those who followed the road of the magician had to move in a twilight world in order to survive.

This resulted in a curious state of things in which, despite the belief that the Greeks were anti-mystical and determined on a course of pure intellectualism, many openly continued as devoted servants of the gods at the same time as they were seeking to dispute them. Plato was a mystery school initiate who was several times attacked for revealing secret doctrines in public debate. Indeed the Platonic writings are to be read as part of mystery teaching, as is evidenced by their author's continued activity as an Inner plane teacher and initiator.

In fact Plato was a disciple of Pythagoras. Although best known as a philosopher Pythagoras was himself initiated into several schools – in Egypt, Greece and Babylon – where he undoubtedly picked up the basis for his numerical theories, as well as a cosmic attitude towards matters of the spirit. He was recognized in his own life-time as an avatar of Apollo – probably the Hyperborean aspect of the god if we are to credit the significance of his meeting with the Hyperborean priest Abaris (see chapter 4). He untypically initiated Abaris into his doctrines without the customary probation of five years silence and obedience, in all probability because he recognized the similarity between his own beliefs and those of the Druids, of whom Abaris was probably an initiate. Certainly there have been frequent claims ever since that the one system influenced or reflected the other.

Pythagoras' followers lived lives of strenuous abnegation – being both vegetarian and nomadic. Their master was virtually outcast from normal society because of these tendencies – so abhorrent to the Greeks – and it is interesting to note that the eremitical traditions within Christianity can probably be traced from Pythagorean inspiration.

Certainly the Essenes followed the Pythagorean mode in their life-style – with goods in common, sun worship and numerology playing a great part. They in turn influenced the development of the Desert Fathers in Egypt and Syria, elements of which could still be discerned in modern Ethiopia until recently.

But Pythagoras would not permit his disciples to speak about his doctrines, and those who broke their vow of secrecy were publicly mourned as though dead and cenotaphs erected to their memory. Because of this many garbled notions have been attributed to the movement and much of the core of Pythagoras' teaching still remains in darkness.

That these teachings became fused and confused with Platonism is little disputed. Plato drew upon the teachings of his master and reworked their mystical direction into a more general philosophy. Both Porphory (325) and Plotinus (268) were affected, and it is still difficult to know whether they ought to be classed as Neo-Pythagoreans or Neo-Platonists. But Pythagorean beliefs continued to be practised from the sixth century BC to the sixth century AD, when the Eastern Emperor Julian closed the Platonic Academy in Athens. After this the Pythagoreans exiled themselves to Persia, where they found a welcome and the recognition of many of their own doctrines in those of the East.

But by this time Pythagoras' teachings had deeply influenced the direction of both philosophy and magic, and had helped to preserve the mysteries far beyond the point at which they might otherwise have perished.

When the great Renaissance philosopher and magician Marsilio Ficino compiled a line of descent for the masters, he put both Pythagoras and Plato firmly amongst them:

> the first was Zoroaster, the chief of the Magi; the second Hermes Trismegistus, the head of the Egyptian Priesthood; Orpheus suceeded Hermes; Aglaophamus was initiated into the sacred mysteries of Orpheus; Pythagoras was initiated into the theology of Aglaophamus and Plato by Pythagoras. Plato summed up the whole of their wisdom in his letters. (227)

This was, of course, written with hindsight, but there is little reason to quarrel with the list, and it shows clearly the inheritance of the Western magician.

Platonism effectively stood things on their heads. Instead of following the direction of the mystery schools, which made the spirit prisoner of the body, it made *everything* in this world a shadowy copy of an original elsewhere – in a spiritual realm far removed from our own. Thus, while outwardly dealing with philosophical structures, the Platonic schools really fostered an esoteric system of thought which went straight back to mystery school teaching. Thus in Plato's 'Myth of Er' (266), as in Cicero's 'Dream of Scipio' (71) later on, the seeds of the greater mysteries were preserved. When Christianity was in the process of formulating its own doctrines, 'it denounced Platonism even as it confessed doctrines that it could not have formulated . . . without the illumination of Plato, thus speaking the language of Zion but with the unmistakable accents of the Academy'. (257)

Plotinus, Plato's chief disciple, forged the links with the magical teachings of the mystery schools even more solidly.

The primary purpose of his teaching was to lead men (those few who were capable of it) back to awareness of and eventual union with the source from which they and all things came – the 'One or Good, which in giving them being gave also the impulse to return'. (336)

Thus Plotinus came to see matter as a principle of evil because it was an absolute limit, the utter negativity and deficiency of being which marks the end of the descent from the Good through successive levels of reality. Yet he found the material universe good and beautiful as a living structure of forms and the best possible work of the Soul – unlike the Gnostic view of matter which he so utterly detested – and he sought ever more deeply to perceive the true nature of the puzzling world about him.

Thus Plotinus' system of Neo-Platonism connects both with magic and science, as well as philosophy, and relates all three to their most ancient roots. Born of humanity's striving to know about its origins, it parallels Christian theology sufficiently to be acceptable to later generations of thinkers as well as those following the inner way.

As we have already seen in chapter 6, there is little point in seeking the origins of Hermeticism. One can, indeed, look to Egypt for much of the material, and perhaps beyond catch glimpses of Chaldea. One can, as a recent commentator suggests, believe that the whole thing is a cultural projection of the Ptolomaic dynasty! (22). But in reality the nearest one can come to the beginning of the Hermetic impulse, and through it of magic, is the period when Christianity was establishing itself, both politically and sacerdotally, in the Roman world.

Here, in the seed-bed of the Graeco-Roman synthesis, as inheritors of Platonic wisdom and Pythagorean understanding, came into being not only what we now think of as the Hermetic mysteries, but Gnosticism and Alchemy also.

The climate of the times being largely unwelcoming for any such thing, the Hermetic mysteries went underground, assuming a desert burnouse under Islam – a cross-fertilization which was, some thousand years later, to return full circle to the West in the medieval mysteries of Alchemy, the Grail and Natural Magic. In this space of time Hermeticism gathered to itself not only the philosophies of Plato and Plotinus, but also the esoteric teachings of the Sufis, combining in a vast hotch-potch of mystical lore, magical system and esoteric philosophy, a brew of East-West mysteries.

Yet when Hermeticism returned to Europe, the reaction was at first one of shocked surprise, turning fast to hatred, at what was seen as a foreign invasion. Those who sought to oppress the Hermetic revival never realized that what they saw advancing towards them was an old and familiar figure, who had left their part of the world long ago and now returned wearing strange garments.

Magic was continually being redefined: in religious terms, as science, and as philosophy. Each person who took up the fragments of the magically-oriented past, impressed their own synthesis upon it, so that during the period referred to above magic went from a religious discipline to a philosophy, both of which approaches it continues to share. The figure of the magician, as we have seen, changed with it, mutating through several guises until what is presently understood by the name bears little or no relation to its origins. Strangely, because it was the age when all magical activity was likely to earn the ultimate penalty for those who were found to be practising it, it is the medieval image which has remained most firmly fixed in the consciousness. This strange figure, shambling through the darker pages of history with his robe of stars (actually a left-over from the Persian magi) his pointed hat and thick lenses (symbol of his proto-scientific attitude) is still a viable image. Yet it is figures like Roger Bacon who typify the medieval magician as he really was: scholar, cleric, seeker, probably in minor orders of the Church (the only way he could obtain the books he needed) and who are the real inheritors of the Classical tradition and the philosophies of Pythagoras and the Platonists.

In fact, the medieval magus would have been able to understand very little of the original matter of the mysteries; few remained in the West who could read the texts, or who, for that matter, even knew of their existence. Yet the 'hidden words' of Hermes did survive: fragments continued to filter through until, at the height of the Renaissance, the trickle became a flood. How this came about is a fascinating story in itself, though one which we can only touch upon here.

It is really due to the scholarship and devotion of one man, Michael Psellus (1018–78/9) who collected and codified many of the Hermetic texts, as well as those of Plato, Plotinus etc, that we still have their legacy today. As it was, the *Corpus Hermeticum* had to wait until 1463 before it found a translator, in the person of the great Renaissance philosopher and natural-magician Marsilio Ficino, who worked on the huge collection of manuscripts at the behest of his patron Cosimo di Medici. Significantly, Ficino was required to translate these before the works of Plato, because it was believed that the Hermetic texts originated in Egypt, which then, as in more recent times among the esoteric fraternities, was considered of far greater interest than Classical and neo-Classical Greece.

With the publication of the *Corpus Hermeticum* the Western world was once more tentatively in touch with the mysteries. We say tentatively, because the Renaissance Hermeticist had only texts, not living traditions, with which to perform his revival. He had to grope painfully towards an understanding of what had once been clearly comprehended and practised by the mystery-initiate, by means of translations of translations, pied scripts and tattered Classical references. It was a task of unimaginable difficulty, yet the Renaissance Hermeticist was equal to the task in enthusiasm if not in a full comprehension of its complexity.

The form of Hermetic gnosticism propounded by Ficino and his like really dates from Hellenic Egypt and not, as was generally held to be the case, from the time of the Pharoahs. But this misunderstanding enabled a kind of reconciliation between post-Christian and pre-Christian lore, giving the Renaissance thinkers an excuse to delve deeper. Thus a mistake in chronology permitted a new renaissance of magic to blossom and provided the foundation upon which the French magical revival of the eighteenth century could build. In this time, once again mistakenly, the literature of the earliest times was related to Biblical sources.

It is easy, with scholarly hindsight and in full possession of good translations, to condemn the medieval magician and the Renaissance investigator with their ragbag of Judaic and Babylonian spells and second-hand grimoires purloined from wandering Arab astrologers. But we forget the length of time and the cultural lacunae which lie between them and the richly syncretic mysteries of Classical Alexandria. In some ways the Renaissance Italy of Ficino and Pico della Mirandola reassembled Alexandria or the Greek Academy with more accuracy than the deeply-dyed ignorance prevailing in the rest of Europe.

In late medieval Europe the end-game of native spirituality and magic was being played out with the pieces of dynastic greed and clerical exactitude. Just as in the Chessboard Castle of Chrétien de Troyes' *Conte du Graal* (47), fantastic pieces were moving of their own volition across a landscape whose interior focus was forever shifting away from the shining turrets and splendid pavilions to a new Hermetic vision. The medieval blindfold was off and other rosy-coloured spectacles were donned in its place. (150)

The Renaissance produced many factors which brought about the death of the spiritual life of the Middle Ages. As Guénon has rightly pointed out, (123) the adoption of neo-Classicism only fostered that part of the Hellenic and Egyptian mysteries which had already been externalized sufficiently to make them acceptable and also less pure than in their original state. The loss was immeasurable and it meant that the Hermetic systems were from the start founded on insecure ground. They had lost touch with their original spark, and every step they took which was away from that point brought about a narrowing which excluded more and more of their old power. Even Renaissance adepts like Ficino, Bruno, Dee, or Francis Bacon, succeeded only partially in reconstructing the sources of their own speculations, and in disseminating some of their realizations into their own blend of Hermeticism. Perhaps they were too cautious; but their efforts became the foundation of modern Western esotericism, just as Hermeticism became, through them, part of the Renaissance as surely as it is a product of medieval and pre-medieval magic and religion.

Pagan, Christian, and Hermetic leftovers bobbed in the same melting pot. It was possible to revision archetypes, long outlawed except as educational paradigms, in the persons of the classical gods. Ficino, who was a Christian priest as well as a natural magician, wrote and sang hymns to Apollo; Bruno couched his philosophical speculations about the origin of the cosmos in dialogues between Jupiter and Mercury (33). Classical subjects began to replace the ubiquitous Christian Nativities and Depositions from the Cross; new passions and new nativities were depicted – The Flaying of Marsyas or the foam-born Aphrodite of Botticelli. Primavera decked in the garb of long-awaited Spring stepped from Attic to Tuscan forests. Everywhere the Classical heritage pervaded like the scent of crushed rosemary.

Here, the mysteries were secularized. The great thinkers and natural magicians were first and foremost Christian: other options were scarcely open to them. Yet here also were the old traditions: of Greece, Egypt, Persia. Their beliefs could not easily be discounted. And so there began slowly to emerge a new form of system *based* on the ancient mysteries, but seen as taking place within the framework of God's law. To be sure these were seen as heretical at the time – but those who practised them saw them differently. To them the deities were spirits of the air, angelic beings created, like humanity, to serve God and creation. Thus, while they became Christianized to a degree they lost none of their energy; they escaped being reduced to the fundamental levels reached, for example, by the 'mythology' of Christianity today. They kept their potency, but under a new guise.

Into this world stepped the figure of the Magician, fully fledged it seemed, escaped like Merlin from his hawthorn tower after a sleep of centuries. The riches of this heritage were as intoxicating as wine.

Hermetic texts, Qabalistic translations, scientific experimentation, the possibility of new interiors. Utopias: the City of the Sun, New Atlantis, ran from the urgent pens of Thomas More, Campanilla, and Francis Bacon, each one the vision of a perfect world, the product of a desire to have the microcosm reflect the macrocosm as perfectly as possible.

The Renaissance magician must often have wondered how really close to perdition he had been during the intervening centuries when esoteric pursuits of any kind had earned their inevitable stigma. Like the court Kapellemeister, whose music was sung at the mass, but who was expected to eat in the kitchen and enter by the back premises, the magician had been in his esoteric hutch ... a tame shaman to be chained in the King's cellars, a coiner of gold pieces, a demonic mascot against divine disfavour – sometimes pandering to the superstitious needs of the people, at others sailing among the stars with gods and angels at his side.

The gift of literacy, imbibed from the great medieval universities, was no longer solely in the hands of clerical academics. Had Roger Bacon still been living, he might have thrown off his Dominican habit and joined the throngs of alchemists and proto-scientists who not only loved God's but nature's mysteries also.

The Hermetic revival broke upon the world and woke it from sleep. Europe's gain was Byzantium's loss. The capture of Constantinople by the Turks in 1453 saw the dispersal of the Eastern Empire's wealth and learning: yet from this disaster the Hermetic texts were able to reappear in Europe, and while the *Corpus Hermeticum* had its effect on the esoteric revival, another tradition was suddenly made available to the West via the expedient of the Jewish expulsion from Spain in 1492 – the Qabala. The Qabala has altered the face of western esotericism and been central to the practice of ritual magic since the Renaissance, providing a fresh angelology, a language of exact macrocosmic correspondence and a ritual framework which has become the norm ever since.

As we have seen, Spain was the cradle of European Qabala. It fostered the great exponents such as Abraham Abulafia and Moses of Leon. It is often thought that Qabala was unknown among Gentiles until the Renaissance, but there is clear evidence that the Catalan philosopher, Ramon Lull (*c.* 1232–1316), was aware of its teachings to some degree. Lull was born one year before the publication of the *Zohar* – the major source for Spanish Qabala – and was contemporaneous with Abulafia, whose permutations of the Hebrew alphabet Lull in some measure imitates within his own system. The *Ars Raymundi*, as it was known to later esotericists, was a system of astral science, based on the Aristotelian elemental categories; it also combined the divine epithets (as they appear on the Tree of Life (fig 9) as they could be applied to all aspects of life from the mineral kingdom, right up the angelic hierarchies and beyond. Lull's aim was to provide a system which would harmonize all religions. He himself learned Arabic and saw his system as part of a missionary effort to convert Jews and Moslems. He was eventually martyred in Northern Africa.

Yet Lull's influence was considerable. Giovanni Pico della Mirandola (1463–94) who moved in the circle of the Medici court at the height of the Hermetic revival, recognized Lullism as a proto-Qabalist system. Pico had some knowledge of Hebrew and was able, prior to the Jewish expulsion from Spain, to obtain Qabalistic manuscripts which he translated and used as the foundation for his *Conclusions* by which he intended to confirm the Christian religion by means of Hebrew wisdom. These Conclusions were also drawn from other esoteric sources, notably Platonic, and neo-platonic texts, Orphic hymns and Chaldean oracles. Pico's philosophy is in many ways a restatement of Lull, but instead of going among Moslems and Jews to prove the truth of Christianity, he went to Rome in order to show how Christianity is a natural successor to these concepts. He was forced to make a formal apology in 1487 for his conclusions, such was the furore that broke out over him. (364) In his apology, Pico divided Qabala into two parts: the *ars combinandi* or the method of permuting Hebrew letters, and 'a way of capturing the powers of superior things', – the powers of angels and spirits. This was undoubtedly a magical rather than a theological conclusion! It is Pico who was responsible for assigning planetary ascriptions to each of the sephiroth, which leads the aspirant from the mineral and elemental kingdoms through to the planetary, angelic and divine realms which form the four worlds of the Jewish Qabala. In imitation of Lull's ambition to combine and reconcile the divided faiths, he was the first to make the link which welded Qabala to Christianity inexorably, sought to prove that by the addition of one letter, the Tetragrammaton – the Most Holy Name of God which is always left unpronounced by pious Jews, and is always substituted by a euphemism such as Adonai, Lord – could be turned into the Name of Jesus. The Tetragammaton is composed of four letters: Yod He Vav He or Yahweh. By the addition of a finial Shin,

YHVH becomes YHSHVH or Yeheshuah, Jesus. Such sloppy Christian gematra may seem insignificant in our day, but the effect of this conclusion was to have a widespread effect throughout Europe.

The synthesis began here. In the meantime, the Jewish expulsion from Spain meant the resettlement of Jews throughout Europe; a fresh meeting of minds such as took place in Alexandria occurred. Qabalistic manuscripts were discussed and translated. Johannes Reuchlin (1455–1522), a scholar of the German Renaissance, published his *De Verbo Mirifico* in 1494: following Pico's ideas, Reuchlin gives us a Platonic dialogue in which a Jew, a Greek and a Christian discuss the Qabalistic 'proof' of Jesus as Messiah. Other books followed this. The Franciscan, Francesco Giorgi (1466–1540), working from Venice, fully synthesized Qabala into Christianity, adding the neo-Platonic and Hermetic elements for good measure as part of a gnostic Christian system. (364)

Finally, Henry Cornelius Agrippa (1486–1535) brought Qabala into the form in which it is best known today – as a magical system. His *De Occulta Philosophia* (1533) presents a universe divided into three worlds: the elemental, celestial and intellectual worlds. This division naturally falls into a discussion of natural magic, celestial magic (following Ficino's model) and ceremonial magic which aims to influence the angelic world by means of Qabalistic magic.

Thus a Judaic mystical system became at one stroke the basis of a Christian gnosis and of a magical system. Qabala remains the lingua-franca of Western esotericism, although one which inevitably has its dialects of dissension. Thus Lull's vision of a reconciled and harmonized microcosm is partially fulfilled, in the way in which Gentile Qabala has evolved. It is ironic that Christianity, having rejected its own esoteric tradition, should have taken over and developed the esoteric system of a religion to which it owed its own existence! Yet, though the fathers of Jewish Qabala might quail at the thought of Christian Qabala, we see once more the subtle spread of esoteric concepts whose mysteries live to seed new traditions with old wisdom. The words of Isaac Luria still hold good for those who study Qabala, Jewish or Gentile.

> for every handsbreadth (of the mysteries) I reveal, I will hide a mile. With great difficulty, I will open the gates of holiness, making an opening like the eye of a needle, and let him who is worthy pass through it to enter the innermost chamber. (167)

The esoteric way is still a narrow one. Those who find their way easily and their passage unobstructed are likely to be travelling away from, not towards, the mysteries.

Unfortunately, there are no ethical standards approved by occult examining boards to which the aspirant can appeal. Those who dismiss the whole esoteric world as evil and misguided are fearful because of this very lack: nor should the esotericist be complacent on this score. If you have no teacher, no tradition behind you how can you be sure that your work is truly aligned with the Will of God, however you understand that term? As we have seen, such mystery and training schools as still exist often have extremely rigid standards to which students must adhere or leave. The same problems are now facing the medical world with the many practitioners of alternative therapies setting up in business. Some therapies as yet have no authorized body to ensure standards. The field is wide open to charlatans as well as to bone-fide practitioners who genuinely heal their patients.

While there is no 'Hippocratic oath' for esotericists, there is a tacit agreement upon standards between genuine practitioners of the magical arts. This may appear to outsiders as a kind of 'honour among thieves' arrangement. But the problem stands: the Western Way has become so fragmented, so distrustful of itself, that unless a more open and trustful exchange is arrived at soon, many important traditions will founder. We do not suggest that a central agency *should* be set up to arbitrate on such matters, but that we should always have recourse to the Inner, which is our only common ground, should we stand in need of verification.

THE DIVINE CHARIOT

Magic in the West has a long and sometimes ignoble history. This is partly due to the development of Christianity in the West which has excluded many practices fundamental to all religions in its simplification of local customs. All religion is a formalization of disparate beliefs: so is prayer the formalization of magic.

In his role as mediator the magician embodies the answer to this problem by becoming a co-worker in the progressive state of the cosmos – which should never be thought of as static or complete. Through ritual the inner impulse becomes externalized; the magician becomes the representative both of humanity and the orders of creation: his magic a visualized prayer technique. When it works, we can presume that dedication and commitment to the world's good bears it up. But magic is not foolproof – not the answer to every ill or want – as some think who rush into its practice without knowledge or understanding. It will not work on request, any more than prayer for a million pounds or miraculous healing necessarily works for a Christian. It will not turn aside the tide of events any more than lighting a candle will stop an earthquake.

Magicians, like believers, are not saints nor do they have super-human resources: they fail of their high purpose as do other human beings. Yet, while it is allowable for an ordinary mortal to fail, this is not allowed, it would seem, of the magician. If mediation is seriously considered, if either the ritual which bodies it forth or the mediation falls short of its purpose, then the consequences are serious. If this is due to some personal imbalance or pride, then the life of the operator will suffer.

In fact it is an occult truism that if the magic performed is not in accordance with God's will then the work will rebound on the sender; some say, threefold. Similarly we may pray God to send us a thousand pounds, and it may be that we get the money in terms of insurance after a seriously debilitating accident. We should be careful what we wish for, in all instances, for we will surely get it.

But the ethics of magic are nowhere clearly drawn: like other social understandings and rule-of-thumb moralities, magic has its own rules which need to be discovered by each individual experientially. The principle of operation is that no one is harmed – that nothing is unbalanced by the activity of the magician. Ahead is the beacon of the Great Work, the completion of a creative microcosm which perfectly mirrors the macrocosm of the Almighty.

> No magician could progress very far in his search for knowledge without coming to the point in which he realizes, at least tacitly, the unity of all things, and that realization nurtures compassion. Even the use of an effigy is a tacit recognition that the one is connected intimately with the other regardless of the vastness of time and space. (341)

The signature recognizable in everything, makes all matter interactive, in turn promoting the understanding that whatever is done has repercussions for the rest of creation. (ibid.) Compassion must inform the magician's work or it will be as naught. As St Paul says:

> If I speak in the tongues of men and angels, but

have not love, I am a noisy gong or a clanging cymbal.
And if I have prophetic powers, and understand all
mysteries and all knowledge, and if I have all faith,
so as to move mountains, but have not love, I am nothing.
(Corinthians I: 13)

Magic is not an exact science. The effects of working magically are subjective, like any art – clay holds within it many shapes, and words have a way of putting themselves together quite differently to the writer's original intention. Yet magic, like the science of engineering, can be used to build bridges and convey loads which would be impossible in terms of physical laws. The magician is himself a bridge between upper and lower realms. When he stands within the circle of the lodge or temple he steps outside time, to become a mote of dust in the light emanating from God. A mote which, nevertheless, has a causal effect vastly beyond his normal, human ability. Here, ritual becomes an enactment of inner reality in symbolic form. However the symbolism is transmitted, a direct link is formed with the Inner realms. How this happens we may see from the following paradigm:

When a sudden outrush of power from the Inner is experienced in the Outer, this may be picked up and interpreted differently by different people.

a) a magician will perceive this particular inrush as an Inner purgation which will have its effect on the Outer. He creates a ritual which will help syphon through the energy, in co-operation with God's will. His life will be made intolerable until this action is performed.

b) a seer/medium will receive the power and imagise it. A purgation of this type will often appear to the seer with disturbing clarity (cf. Jung's dream of the 1st World War).

c) a mystic will perceive God's Will – the forces of creation working to fulfil a divine purpose. Prayers for harmony within the universe will result, a greater unity with the will of God be sought for.

d) a poet will pick up the energy and transform it into verse, an artist will capture it on canvas or in a bronze cast, composers will introduce new harmonies into their instrumentation: all will seek ultimately to trace the energy to its source.

e) in countries and social groups the response will be less cohesive; if the force is purgative, as in this instance, civil unrest may be felt, wars or disturbances break out, until the inner force loses its cyclonic energy.

f) People may instinctively register the force which is communicating itself in ordinary Outer ways. Peace-movements will be strengthened or criminal activity increase; police vigilance will be prominent.

This is, of course, only a projected paradigm. The Inner forces can and do manifest in many other ways and are received and interpreted differently according to their strength and origin as well as those who feel their effect. When Inner forces of this kind are at work, all one can do is co-operate, help them pass, perhaps even feel their beneficent qualities.

Purgation is a mighty and terrible thing – but it is not evil in itself. The Inner activity is more often than not of a creative nature which will contribute a fresh impulse and vitality, helpful to all. Those who look for the Will of God in such cases, need not passively resign themselves to do nothing but rather actively take up their appointed tasks as they best can.

'For each of those who is allotted a place in the Divine Order finds his perfection in being uplifted, according to his capacity, towards the Divine Likeness; and what is still more divine, he becomes, as the Scriptures say, *a fellow-worker with God* and shows forth the Divine Activity revealed as far as possible in himself.' (70, our italics)

We are, in this, doing what all followers of the Western Way must do in the end – putting our interests aside to become workers in the great force of creation.

It is a theme we should be familiar with by now: the divine spark seeing its identity within the greater whole, the mystic seeking union with God.

The magician, then, places himself as close to the heart of creation as he can in order to work from and with it. He seeks to realize his potential within the framework of matter – becoming a priest in order to carry forward the work of the Inner realms, the Will of God. To be a magician is to be artificer, artist and priest in one. It is a noble art.

However, lest the foregoing picture should seem too attractive, let it also be said that the life of a magician is neither easy nor soft.

William G. Gray once remarked that there are no handouts in magic, only earnings collected when they fall due. This is as true today as it ever was, and is one of the first things we ought to remember before embarking on any esoteric work. It was the first precept of the magicians of the past, and to the degree which they either accepted or denied it were their work and lives full or empty, beneficial or harmful.

Magicians, are people too, and have ordinary lives, jobs and families. While they may be aware of other laws operative within these ordinary lives, they seldom or never engage in the kind of role-playing games described in occult pulp-fiction. Certain adepts who specialize in the kind of psychic first-aid work described by Dion Fortune in her Doctor Taverner stories (95) seem to bear out this fantastic image of the magician, yet there are few who regularly engage in this kind of work. It is specialist and responsible work dealing with the genuine disorders brought about through psychic imbalance, and is best dealt with by the adept who is experienced on multi-levels of reality, who is big enough to take the knocks which inevitably occur.

While on the subject of psychic attack it should be noted that the student is rarely aware of or troubled by such phenomena. It is a form of egoism to imagine that those responsible for sending out negative energies would be bothered with a mere minnow when the intended catch is a salmon. The worst a neophyte is likely to encounter are his or her own imbalances and their equilibration. Certain common-sense measures are always to be observed in esoteric work: seal off your aura, demark your psychic activities by clear opening and closing signs, keep alert on whatever level you operate, use your clan totem (see Vol I) as a shield. Murray Hope's excellent book on psychic self-defence (148) gives many practical means of coping with life in this seemingly unmapped area, while Dion Fortune's *Psychic Self Defence* has seldom been bettered.

The magical life is lived through the seasonal rituals which govern the tides of the year: the spring tide which runs from the Spring equinox and governs the tide of growth and inception of new projects or ideas; the summer tide, which runs from the Summer solstice and is concerned with consolidation and active working; the autumn tide of harvest, running from the Autumn equinox, when projects are brought into fruition and or maturity; and the winter tide of dissolution which runs from the Winter solstice wherein stale ideas and projects are cleared out.

Also to be taken into account are the monthly cycle of the moon, the weekly progression of the days, and the hourly microcosm of the day from dawn to noon, twilight to midnight. These minor cycles have the planetary and zodiacal patterns superimposed upon them, and all are recognized by the magician, who makes them a part of his inner and outer life. (182) He will take into account also, looking over periods of cosmic time, the greater pattern of the aeons – as in the Piscean and Aquarian ages which meet and change the flow of activity during our own lifetimes. Of course, it is by no means easy to correlate all these factors – hence the need for stringent training beforehand. Even the adept will find it difficult at times to adjust to these many combinations, but all ritual magic is at base a method of relating higher to lower, celestial to chthnoic, divine to temporal. The complex systems of inter-related powers taught by the mystery schools, the detailed tables of correspondences to be found in the grimoires of the Middle Ages and the Renaissance, and the techniques of Qabalistic training, all aim at the same target.

Thus the work of the magician is organized around great cyclic events which occur outside space and time: the recurring patterns which are the balancing act of the cosmos. They nova in his year, just as they feature in the dreams of the sensitive, and are reflected mundanely in the outer world. The magician may formulate these events into rituals in which the seasons and elements and the positions of the stars become an expression in the outer world of an inner reality, a sacramental encounter between the desires of humanity and the power and might of God.

Yet we must be careful of seeing the powers of creation as merely symbolic tools to work with but which have no ultimate reality. It is possible to evolve a theory of archetypes every bit as complex as anything to be found in the *Corpus Hermeticum*, but these are useless unless informed with practical application and realization. A grimoire is useless to someone who fails to understand its correspondences as keys to a larger reality. The would-be magician must learn to draw down the elemental powers into his own sphere of working, just as he must also elevate his human understanding to the point where he can appreciate the mysteries of creation and the presence of the divine principle within it.

Magic is the higher understanding of nature, a true vision of the universe as it whirls and roars around us. From ritual to Renaissance to the modern occult revival this has been the heart and centre of magical work. From the tribal shaman to the present day magus their work has arisen out of a fundamental belief in an ordered cosmos, that we are not simply born into the world for the sole purpose of providing amusement for some distant god or gods, nourishment for the soil, or blind animal existence. Rather, we should become part of the universal process of becoming.

> You must understand that this is the first path to felicity . . . the
> . . . theurgic gift . . . is called indeed the gate to the Demiurge of
> Wholes. . . . It possesses a power of purifying the soul and . . .
> produces a union with the gods . . . givers of every good. (152)

Magic as a branch of Hermeticism does not seem to concern itself with saving the soul. To the outsider it seems merely a way, a technique, a methodology. But to participate in magic is to be wound into the fabric of creation as a co-worker, to be purged and purified and made whole. This is to do the will of God in one's own life: it means living close to the wind, ready at all times to veer where it lists.

The qualifications of magical work such as we have discussed here should be written up large over the temple door of every individual who thinks they are ready to follow the life of the magician. Such a prescription might read: A sense of ritual, a sense of humour and common sense. With these three there is not far that you can go wrong.

Brethren should meet in harmony and depart in peace and silence, but this is not always the case. It is not often understood that the magical life imposes subtle pressures which can turn reasonable and pleasant people into aggressive and nit-picking individuals. Under pressure, human nature will out, and ritual work is highly pressured. It is the duty of the magister of the lodge to ensure this is understood and, if necessary, point this out to those concerned. Some ritual work can be quite disturbing, even to the experienced magician: if the quarter officers are mediating their roles properly, the risk of emotional aberration is substantially reduced among those participating. Minor irritations with fellow ritualists can grow from molehills into mountains very quickly, especially when the ritual has exaggerated any personal imbalance. These emotional reactions are usually quick to pass: if everyone remains objective about it, seeing it as a concomitant of the ritual, then there is no harm.

In a magical order each candidate is scrutinized and required to complete a questionnaire concerning their intentions and present mode of life. The imbalanced, the discontent, the ego-maniac, the depressed, the unhealthy, are all excluded for their own good. In magic, only the best is good enough – anything less than total commitment is a waste of energy and time. The dilettante approach to magic, instanced by many would-be Aleister Crowleys, is no better than Sabbath Christianity.

This may read strangely to those who consider magic as only black. Surely all this talk of 'world service' (20) and 'dedication' is merely a screen covering some ultimately evil intention? Despite what the papers say, this is not so. We have tried to show how throughout this book. But, just as there are unbalanced individuals in all walks of life, so there are in magical areas. These people are news, bad news. We must bear in mind that:

> Theurgy, or high magic, is the raising of consciousness to the appreciation of the powers and forces behind the external world in a pious intention of developing spiritual awareness and subsequently helping to bring to birth the divine plan of a restored earth. Thaumaturgy, or low magic . . . is the production of wonders by the use of little known powers of the mind. (180)

It was all summed up, long ago, by the Roman historian Dio Chrysostom, when he wrote that 'the magi . . . hold that the universe is steadily being drawn along a single road by a charioteer who is gifted with the greatest skill and power.' (227). The Magician does not seek to *become* the charioteer, only to prevent the chariot from running away with him and those of his fellows who journey at his side. The magical life is not usually commenced under the age of thirty, since the twenties are a time when the mundane life is being established as regards education and the beginning of a family. Responsibility is primarily to the family life – the path of the hearth-fire. When children are grown or sufficiently fledged to fend for themselves, the magical life can begin in earnest.

Such strictures do not normally apply within the Native Tradition, since its ways can be upheld and studied within the family unit very easily since they derive from tribal consciousness. The Hermetic Tradition imposes rather more rigorous standards on its followers. The way of involution must be followed until the candidate stands at the initiatory gates of life and starts the way of return on the evolutionary path. (184)

Yet magic is returning on all fronts in our own time – not always purely Hermetic or Native in its approach, but a mixture of old and new. The return of the magician is also the return of the shaman, and

Fig 11.   Isis, as described in Apuleius' Golden Ass *from Athan Sius Kircher's* Oedipus Aegyptiacus *c1652*

'shamanism is being reinvented in the West precisely because it is needed' (135). Its techniques, as well as those of the Hermetically-trained magus, point the way to the inner worlds, from where the long climb begins to the highest expression of both traditions: the mysteries and techniques of alchemy.

EXERCISE 4   THE HERMETIC WAY

The two texts which follow have been set aside from the main body of the book both to emphasize their importance and to enable them to be used as subjects for meditation. As a form of exercise which will illuminate much that has been discussed in earlier chapters, and which will prepare the way for succeeding exercises and techniques, it is suggested that they be read with attention over a period of two weeks, taking sections or sentences from each in turn and meditating upon them. Write down whatever realization comes to you. This should enable you to build up your own commentary on the Emerald Tablet and the extract from the *Corpus Hermeticum*. At the end of this period you might wish to engage upon a longer meditation (generally periods of from twenty to thirty minutes are sufficient) incorporating material from both texts and from your own notes. This should be seen as the beginning of a prolonged study and extended working with the Hermetic texts in general, which may become the framework for a lifetime's activity as well as deepening the awareness of the mysteries set forth in the remainder of this book.

The Emerald Tablet of Hermes Trismegistos

1 IN TRUTH CERTAINLY AND WITHOUT DOUBT, WHATEVER IS BELOW IS LIKE THAT WHICH IS ABOVE, AND WHATEVER IS ABOVE IS LIKE THAT WHICH IS BELOW, TO ACCOMPLISH THE MIRACLES OF ONE THING.
2 JUST AS ALL THINGS PROCEED FROM ONE ALONE BY MEDITATION ON ONE ALONE, SO ALSO THEY ARE BORN FROM THIS ONE THING BY ADAPTATION.
3 ITS FATHER IS THE SUN AND ITS MOTHER IS THE MOON. THE WIND HAS BORN IT IN ITS BODY. ITS NURSE IS THE EARTH.
4 IT IS THE FATHER OF EVERY MIRACULOUS WORK IN THE WHOLE WORLD.
5 ITS POWER IS PERFECT IF IT IS CONVERTED INTO EARTH.
6 SEPARATE THE EARTH FROM THE FIRE AND THE SUBTLE FROM THE GROSS, SOFTLY AND WITH GREAT PRUDENCE.
7 IT RISES FROM EARTH TO HEAVEN AND COMES DOWN AGAIN FROM HEAVEN TO EARTH, AND THUS ACQUIRES THE POWER OF THE REALITIES BELOW. IN THIS WAY YOU WILL ACQUIRE THE GLORY OF THE WHOLE WORLD, AND ALL DARKNESS WILL LEAVE YOU.
8 THIS IS THE POWER OF ALL POWERS, FOR IT CONQUERS EVERYTHING SUBTLE AND PENETRATES EVERYTHING SOLID.
9 THUS THE LITTLE WORLD IS CREATED ACCORDING TO THE PROTOTYPE OF THE GREAT WORLD.

10   FROM THIS AND IN THIS WAY, MARVELLOUS AP-
PLICATIONS ARE MADE.
11   FOR THIS REASON I AM CALLED HERMES TRISME-
GISTOS, FOR I POSSESS THE THREE PARTS OF WISDOM OF
THE WHOLE WORLD.
12   PERFECT IS WHAT I HAVE SAID OF THE WORK OF
THE SUN.

The Teaching of Hermes

IF THEN YOU DO NOT MAKE YOURSELF EQUAL TO
GOD, YOU CANNOT APPREHEND GOD; FOR LIKE IS
KNOWN BY LIKE. LEAP CLEAR OF ALL THAT IS COR-
POREAL, AND MAKE YOURSELF GROW TO A LIKE EX-
PANSE WITH THAT GREATNESS WHICH IS BEYOND
ALL MEASURE; RISE UP ABOVE ALL TIME, AND BE-
COME ETERNAL; THEN YOU WILL APPREHEND GOD.
THINK THAT FOR YOU TOO NOTHING IS IMPOSSIBLE;
DEEM THAT YOU TOO ARE IMMORTAL, AND THAT
YOU ARE ABLE TO GRASP ALL THINGS IN YOUR
THOUGHT, TO KNOW EVERY CRAFT AND EVERY SCI-
ENCE; FIND YOURSELF HOME IN THE HAUNTS OF
EVERY LIVING CREATURE; MAKE YOURSELF HIGHER
THAN ALL HEIGHTS, AND LOWER THAN ALL DEPTHS;
BRING TOGETHER IN YOURSELF ALL OPPOSITES OF
QUALITY, HEAT AND COLD, DRYNESS AND FLUIDITY;
THINK THAT YOU ARE EVERYWHERE AT ONCE, ON
LAND, AT SEA, IN HEAVEN; THINK THAT YOU ARE NOT
YET BEGOTTEN, THAT YOU ARE IN THE WOMB, THAT
YOU ARE YOUNG, THAT YOU ARE OLD, THAT YOU
HAVE DIED, THAT YOU ARE IN THE WORLD BEYOND
THE GRAVE: GRASP IN YOUR THOUGHT ALL THIS AT
ONCE, ALL TIMES AND PLACES, ALL SUBSTANCES AND
QUALITIES AND MAGNITUDES TOGETHER; THEN YOU
CAN APPREHEND GOD. BUT IF YOU SHUT UP YOUR
SOUL IN YOUR BODY, AND ABASE YOURSELF, AND
SAY, 'I KNOW NOTHING, I CAN DO NOTHING, I AM
AFRAID OF EARTH AND SEA, I CANNOT MOUNT TO
HEAVEN; I DO NOT KNOW WHAT I WAS, NOR WHAT I
SHALL BE'; THEN, WHAT HAVE YOU TO DO WITH
GOD? YOUR THOUGHT CAN GRASP NOTHING

BEAUTIFUL AND GOOD, IF YOU CLEAVE TO THE BODY,
AND ARE EVIL. FOR IT IS THE HEIGHT OF EVIL NOT TO
KNOW GOD; BUT TO BE CAPABLE OF KNOWING GOD,
AND TO WISH AND HOPE TO KNOW HIM, IS THE ROAD
WHICH LEADS STRAIGHT TO THE GOOD; AND IT IS AN
EASY ROAD TO TRAVEL.

CORPUS HERMETICUM : XI.ii. (302)

EXERCISE 5   THE FOUR-SQUARE CITADEL

The following exercise is worked in five parts and is a complete
initiatory system suitable for readers of any tradition. There is a
built-in fail-safe in that the four-square citadel can only be built from
your personal meditation: no one else can help you work this
exercise, nor will you find the answers in any books. The exercise is
based on a thorough knowledge of the elements and will only
succeed if you put in sufficient meditation upon each energy. In the
final, fifth part, you will be able to construct the four-square citadel
which forever afterwards will be your own personal temenos from
which you may meditate or work. It is ideal for those who have no
working-area specially designated in their home. Work each part
successfully before going on to the next; you may need several
sessions for each part. On no account attempt to work the whole
exercise in one go. At the beginning of each section state your
intention in these or your own words, thus:

e.g. I seek for the citadel with no foundations
Which lies within myself.

Adding for each quarter:

I seek the power of the East (or South/West/North):
The seed of power which lies within.

If you have difficulty realizing the Elemental qualities, *Magical
Ritual Methods* by William Gray (115), or *The Practice of Ritual
Magic* by Gareth Knight (182), give excellent pointers on how you
may come to experience them.

A) Sit in meditation with your chair in the middle of the floor, if you
have space: if you do not, then it does not matter. Visualize a circle
about you. If you have room, you may demark this circle on the floor
with wool or string. Face East and visualize the following scene

about you. The circle about you expands until it becomes the utmost limit of the earth from horizon to horizon, the edges of the world tilt away into infinity. You stand at the centre of the circled world: at the four quarters stand four figures of mighty power. They stand at the furthest point of four paths which start where you are standing, and where they have their crossroads. Each of the quarters is a different colour: the Eastern one is white, like crystal; the Southern one is red of transparent hue; the Western one is green as emerald; the Northern one is of opaque blackness. Each Power holds back the elemental forces from rushing into the centre of the circled world. Turn to face each power and sense the nature of the elemental energy which is being controlled.

In order to build your four-square citadel you have to enter into relationship with each Element by means of an initiatory meditation. Face East and meditate upon the Power of Air which is white as crystal. Consider the elemental quality of air from every level of your understanding. As you meditate, the whole Eastern quarter of the circled world is flooded with white light, as the power of the Eastern One builds up: the ground becomes white also, so that the white path disappears. You must journey along the invisible path towards the Eastern edge of the world and bring back the gift of the Eastern power. You journey blind across the whitened world. The snow is deep and cold, but you must travel on without stopping, Despite your uncertainty, tune into the Eastern power and feel it magnetically calling you. A white hare crosses your track and you understand that you are to follow it deeper into the snowscape. Wherever the hare runs, there a path opens up, and the ground is easy to travel. Elsewhere the ground is covered by such deep drifts that you cannot continue, so follow it onwards. You struggle onwards.

Suddenly the Hare stops and turns. It asks you:

'Where do you journey and what do you seek? You reply:
'I seek for the citadel with no foundations which lies within the East.' It asks:
'What are the powers of the Eastern One?'

You answer in your own words, drawing upon your own meditative realizations. If the Hare is satisfied with your answer you may proceed. If it is not, then the Hare vanishes and you must return to your starting place at the centre of the circled world. You may not continue for the path ends here, the winds blow and the snow deepens. If your answer is satisfactory the Hare will leap forward into the middle of the whiteness ahead, drawing you behind it until you stand at your journey's end. Before you is the Archon of the East, arrayed as a mighty power, in the mantle of the snows. In his right hand is a sword of adamant, and on his head burns a crystalline crown. His force and presence are overwhelmingly strong. Pay your respects to him and accept whatever gift he gives you as a token of your regency of the Eastern element. The gift will be an object which is easily held in the hand – only you know what it is: take the first thing that you see, however inappropriate your rational mind considers it – first impressions are generally correct. This is the first gift with which you will build the four-square citadel. Take your leave of the Archon of the East and depart. Swift as thought, you return to the centre of the circled world down the path which is now visible to you and easy to travel. Stand at the centre, face East once more, seeing the path before you and the Archon with his crown of white crystal standing at the furthest East of the world. Raise your gift in salutation and thanks, and set it down in the Eastern quarter of the circle.

As you work each quarter, lay each gift in its appropriate elemental quarter until you have worked all four. It is effective to draw the mandala of the circled world with coloured quarters on a sheet of card, placing each gift upon it, or, if you have a working-area, making a symbolic representation of each gift in the appropriate quarter of your room. However, these are your personal symbols and are not for display to others, because they are the keys to unlock your four-square citadel, so keep them safely.

B) Now face the South and establish the path to the furthest South of the circled world. At the end of it stands the mighty power of the South to whom you must journey. As before, meditate upon the Power of Fire which is transparently red like ruby. As the power builds up, the whole Southern quarter is flooded with light, obliterating the path before you. Again, proceed by instinct across the landscape which opens before you. The earth is red sand through which you trudge under the heat of an invisible sun. The sand is hot and hard to your feet, your throat and mouth are filled with its grittiness. Feel the power and orient yourself once more. Before you appears a sand-lizard, the same colour as the ground. Follow it and your path will be easier. Wherever it goes you can walk safely. It turns and asks you:

'Where do you journey and what do you seek?' You reply:

'I seek for the citadel with no foundations, which lies within the South.' It asks:
'What are the powers of the Southern One?'

You answer in your own words. If the Lizard is unsatisfied with your reply, you must return to the centre and travel this way another time. If your answer is satisfactory, the Lizard will shoot swiftly forward, taking you with it until you stand before the mighty Archon of the South. He is arrayed as mighty power, in a mantle of red glittering sand. In his right hand is a spear of adamant, and on his head burns a crown of ruby. His force and presence are overwhelming. Pay your respects to him and accept whatever gift can only be seen and known by you. Take your leave and depart. Swift as thought, you return to the centre of the circled world down the path which opens before you. Stand at the centre, facing South, and raise your gift in thanks to the Archon standing the farthest South of the path. Salute him and set down your gift in the Southern quarter.

C) Now face West and establish the path to the Westernmost quarter of the circled world. At the end of its stands the mighty power of Water, which is transparently green as emerald. Meditate upon the power of water. As the power builds up, the whole Western quarter is flooded with green light, obliterating the path before you. Again, proceed by instinct across the landscape which opens before you. Everything is green and damp. A jungle of plant-life and creeper surrounds you. The ground beneath your feet is moist and swampy, the atmosphere is hot and clammy. The way is difficult and winding, but ever seek the furthest West. As you struggle to break through the tangle of thick green growth about you, avoiding the swampy patches, a water-snake slithers across your path. Follow it and the way is instantly easier. It turns and asks you:

'Where do you journey and what do you seek? You reply:
'I seek the citadel with no foundations, which lies within the West.' It asks;
'What are the powers of the Western One?'

You answer in your own words. If your answer is unsatisfactory, the Snake will vanish and you must return to the centre of the circled world to attempt this journey again. If your answer is satisfactory, the Snake glides forward swiftly, drawing you with it, until you stand before the Archon of the West. He is arrayed as a mighty power, in a mantle of glimmering greenery. His force and presence are overwhelmingly strong. Pay your respects to him and accept whatever gift he gives you as a token of your regency over the powers of water. This is the third gift with which to build the four-square citadel. Take your leave and return, swift as thought along the path which is now open for you, to the centre of the circled world. Stand at the centre, facing West, and salute the Archon of the West, raising your gift in thanks. Set it down in the Western quarter.

D) Now face North and establish the path to the Northernmost quarter of the circled world. At the end of it stands the mighty Power of Earth, which is black as obsidian. Meditate upon the powers of earth. As the power builds the path is obliterated and flooded with blackness. Again, proceed instinctively through the landscape before you. This time, there is barely light to see by, only a thick gloaming in which you proceed mainly by touch. The ground beneath your feet is alternately hard as rock and shifting as sand: the loose earth has the consistency of gunpowder. Your way is hindered by the shifting ground and the darkness. But feel for true North. The air is cold and the wind is dry. Beneath your feet there is a scrabbling sound and a small furry creature brushes your feet. It is a mole with night-seeing eyes. It asks you:

'Where do your journey and what do you seek?' You reply:
'I seek the citadel with no foundations, which lies within the North.' It asks,
'What are the powers of the Northern One?'

Answer in your own words. If your answer is unsatisfactory, the Mole will disappear and you must return to the centre and travel this path again. If it is satisfactory, the Mole will scrabble into the darkness drawing you with it until you stand before the Archon of the North. He is arrayed as a mighty power, in a mantle of glittering blackness, outlined by silver light. In his right hand is a book of adamant, and on his head glints a crown of black diamonds. His force and presence are overwhelmingly strong. Pay your respects to him and accept whatever gift he gives you as a token of your regency over the powers of earth. This is the final gift with which to build the four-square tower. Take your leave and return, swift as thought to the centre of the circled world, along the path which is now open to you, with light enough to see by. Stand at the centre facing North and salute the Archon, raising your gift in thanks, and lay it down in the quarter before you.

E) It may have taken you many sessions and months of meditation to reach this point, but you have persevered. This last section may also take longer than one session. We will now proceed to build the four-square citadel.

Set your four gifts in their appropriate quarters around your feet, in meditation, where you stand at the centre of the circled world. Slowly circle, regarding each of the paths in turn: East, South, West, North. All paths lead to your feet. The gifts at your feet are your instruments with which to build the four-square citadel – these and no other. Meditate upon their meanings, which are applicable only to yourself and your own theory of correspondences. Here there are no right answers. If you have trouble realizing their meanings, then look along the path of the quarter from which they came and ask the creature of that quarter questions until you are clear. When each gift is activated by your understanding, power will rise from them in a clockwise spiralling movement from the ground upwards. The walls of your citadel rise around you: do not fear that you will be trapped inside, for each side has a door. There are five levels to it altogether, with a connecting staircase which spirals up the centre of the structure. In each level are set four windows which look out on each of the quarters. Each level corresponds from the ground upwards to the room of earth, the room of water, the room of fire and the room of air, respectively. There is a topmost level which has another function. See below.

This is your four-square citadel where you can observe the motions of the inner world. Go to the topmost level and look out over each quarter in turn. As you circle the horizon you can see that where the Archons stood is a tower in each quarter – these are the Watch-towers of the circled world: they are in communication with your own tower. You will come to this level when you wish to communicate with the four watch-towers and their guardians.

Now look over the land through which you travelled so laboriously through the initiations of the elements. In the East, the snow is beginning to melt: the thaw of early Spring breaks over the land and the ground is covered with young plants and green shoots. Only the Eastern Tower is still white. In the South, the endless sandy desert gives way to a land where the Summer's heat is tempered by lakes and rivers, and where trees give shelter from the noonday sun. Only the Southern Tower is still red. To the West, the rain-forests and swampy terrain are tempered by the gentle coolness of Autumn. There are red and brown leaves upon some of the trees, relieving the endless greenness. The ground settles into the splendour of Autumn.

The Western Tower is still green. To the North, the black rocks and barren soil give way to fallow wakefulness and Winter. There are evergreens growing and though the earth looks bleak, it harbours the hope of Spring. The light is the clear brightness of the North. Only the Northern Tower remains deepest black.

There is much work which you can effect in this your citadel. In the rooms of earth, water, fire and air you can work rituals and meditations proper to these elements, furnishing each room according to your preference, but observing the conventions of each element. But you can also balance the elements: for instance, the room of earth has four windows each looking over the four quarters, giving you the following combinations – air of earth, fire of earth, water of earth and earth of earth. These can give you months of meditative activity.

Normally you work with the creatures of the quarters, rather than the Archons of the Elements themselves. The creatures are messengers and intermediaries and are easier to work with than the raw powers themselves. However, if you find it difficult to work with animal forms, you may request each of the beasts to transform into anthropomorphic forms. If you wish to work with the Archons themselves, this is best done by means of the symbols of adamant.

Their symbols are:

East – Sword of Adamant
South – Spear of Adamant
West – Cup of Adamant
North – Book or Tablet of Adamant

(Adamant is a legendary substance of great durability: you may visualize each symbol as made of diamond-like stone, in the appropriate quarter colour.) The topmost level of the citadel can become the Chamber of Adamant where the symbols can be displayed on the appropriate wall of their quarter. To acquire the symbols, work a ritual appropriate to the quarter and request the Archons, by means of their messengers, that you may obtain the symbol you require. You may find that the structure of obtaining the four gifts may be used in a slightly adapted form. The original symbol always remains with the Archon – you are given an authorized copy which is the same in all respects. The Archons and their servants are at liberty to refuse you, until you are worthy of obtaining each symbol. These are powerful tools which should be considered archetypes of any actual weapon or object which you may make in the future.

To enter and leave the citadel, you need only envisage your four gifts again. To form it, set them down and meditate on their qualities and feel the tower rising round you in a clockwise spiral. To leave it, go to the lowest level room and dissolve the citadel in an anti-clockwise spiral until all you are left with are your gifts. Evidently, no one else can have access to your citadel, because everyone's gifts are different. They are your keys and can be personalized symbols of the elements which you can meditate upon when you need the help of a particular elemental energy.

Always close carefully after each session and beware of any imbalances which may arise from working with the Elemental energies: work the Self-Clarification exercise (vol. I) if necessary.

Figure 12:   Four Square Citadel

The Archons of the Elements are the Elemental kings. Some readers will recognize Enochian undertones in this initiatory system. To those who can read the clues, a very interesting game of Enochian chess can be played in a three-dimensional meditation. (Cf. Regardie (283) and Casaubon (43).)

CHAPTER 4
Through the Inner Door

Understand that you are a second world in miniature, and the
sun and moon are within you, as are the stars.

Origen: *Homiliae Leviticium*

All have their keys, and set ascents: but man
Though he knows these, and hath more of his own,
Sleeps at the ladder's foot.

Henry Vaughan: *The Tempest*

CELESTIAL MEMORIES

If the inner resonance of the Native Tradition is the Under or
Other-world, then the inner resonance of the Hermetic Tradition is a
Celestial one. We speak not, of course, of an outer location but of a
working-metaphor, a world-model. These antiphonal inner realities
polarize the two streams of the Western Way in a distinct manner,
but we must beware of ascribing all the devils to a Native underworld and all the angels to a Hermetic heaven, for such is the way in
which symbologies and world-models have been wielded as sticks
with which to beat ideological antagonists in the past. In this chapter
you will find no dogmatic presentations of the cosmos: there are
many maps, drawn from different perspectives, that is all. Each
initiate proceeds according to his or her own lights. The macrocosm,
like the microcosm, is an evolving entity, not a static phenomenon
(90) so we should not try to confine it within half-guessed definitions.

The medieval world inherited the Hellenic cosmos consisting of
the earth, the seven planets, the fixed stars, the zodiac, extending in
spherical progression, beyond which lay the Empyrean. Through
these spheres filtered the power of God by means of the angelic
hierarchies as defined by Dionysius the Areopagite, about whom
more later. This hypostasis of the cosmos is now lost to us – the

Fig. 13   The Hierarchy of Creation

moon is a dead piece of rock, the planets do not behave as Ptolemy believed, the earth is not the centre of the Universe any more than it is the centre of our solar system. Yet, 'those who travel externally to these heavenly bodies will only find empty planets. The real cosmic universe is an interior one.' (304) Our concern is to establish how the celestial world-model has faded from scientific importance yet remained central to hermeticism.

Up until the Renaissance humanity believed itself to be, not at the top of a Darwinian evolutionary ladder, but at the bottom of a vast celestial hierarchy and cosmology – this resulted in a very proper humility. The revision of the Ptolemaic world-model in favour of the Copernican system at the Renaissance resulted in a radical disassociation with the macrocosm, producing an existentialist or, as the medievals would say, a melancholic state of consciousness, in which humanity was prey to being morose and solitary. This disconnectedness with the macrocosm has been partially remedied in our own times where the interdependence of man and animal, tree and river, rock and star are being realized (fig. 13). This lack of a central world-model is reflected by a fearful attitude, expressed in mockery, towards the metaphysical or the spiritual in general. Those who mock have grown up in an era where many current world-models are outmoded or eroded, yet they have nothing with which to replace them.

C.S. Lewis suggests (193) that 'you must go out on a starry night and walk about for half an hour trying to see the sky in terms of the old cosmology' – a sky which was closer than is now scientifically understood, one in which the moon represented an unpassable boundary, the sublunary realm in which Nature alone held sway, beyond which the stars rotated in their fixed courses, represented by a treasury of corresponding imagery.

The Ptolemaic system of cosmology – whereby the earth was the centre of the universe – has remained the *metaphysical* inner world-model of the macrocosm among hermeticists. This is not to say that they reject the Copernican and post-Copernican heliocentric cosmology of the physical cosmos. Adam McLean instances the way in which Robert Fludd was alert to the importance of the Ptolemaic system in the way that it underpinned the hermetic concept of *inner* space, yet he was scientifically aware of the Copernican system at the same time. (211) His work, *Utriusque Cosmi Historia* (The History of Both Worlds, 1617–1621) was a defence of the old world-model. He retained it because he understood how, if the Copernican system was once established in the Hermetic realm of thought, it 'would give rise to a non-spiritual picture of the Cosmos' (ibid). Our sense of cosmic unity was on the line.

The Ptolemaic cosmology saw the world in relationship to humanity: a system of steps up the ladder of the cosmos by which micro- and macrocosm were reflected and interrelated. Fludd's book presents us with the old cosmology, not in terms of astronomical understanding, but as a valid spiritual philosophy for the hermeticist. He follows the emanatory movement of spirit into matter in much the same way that Qabalists saw the prismation of God's glory through the sephirotic vessels. McLean points out that Fludd's system of spiritual evolution was established three centuries before either Steiner or Blavatsky presented their theory deriving from Eastern sources. Fludd's emblems, which illustrate his work, are still the clearest expressions of this cosmic understanding, and reward meditation upon their principles. (105) They are the Western mandalas of the inner spaces, emblems of the soul.

Another factor which contributed to the medieval world-model was Plato's *Timaeus*. (267) This alone of Plato's works was known to the medieval world through a Latin translation by Chalcidius, so that Plato was not known so much as the founder of a philosophy but seen as 'next to Moses, the great monotheistic cosmogonist, the philosopher of creation.' (193) The *Timaeus* presents a benevolent Demiurge (unlike the Gnostic Demiurge who enslaves the spirit in matter). The celestial hierarchies of such cosmologies and their inhabitants are very much the concern of the hermeticist who uses their archetypes in his or her work, often unknowingly. Dionysius the Areopagite (*c*. AD 500), the mystical theologian, supplied both the Christian and esoteric corpus with the authoritative work on angels in his *Mystical Theology and the Celestial Hierarchies* (70). This book deals with the interrelatedness of the divine intelligences who stand, each according to his sphere, receiving power from the order of beings above and passing it to the order below. This lyrical study stresses that only by poetic and symbolic means are such high mysteries to be understood, not in mundane language. Dionysius' angels perhaps originate from the Iranian *spentas* (cf. chapter 1) or from Babylonian guardians where they filter through Judaism into Christian teaching. Yet the divine intelligences who govern the celestial hierarchies have not always been seen as benefincent beings. The Gnostics held that the rulers or archons of each successive level of their complex cosmology were the servants of the evil Demiurge. Each archon governed one of planetary spheres. (cf. Fig 6) Yet, short of worshipping these, the Gnostics believed that after death they would have to encounter and overcome these dread instruments of Fate. A number of interior journeys through the spheres of the archons was necessary to reach the point of no further incarnation: a notion also held by the Orphites. Certain of the Elect (the pneumatics) were believed to have reached this goal, such as Enoch (31), Baruch and Ezra. To this end a series of psalms and invocations were conned so that the Gnostic, after death, might overcome the power of the archons. The Mandaens had the largest literature on this subject, with detailed instructions on how to render up the body to the elements, and the vices assigned to each of the planetary archons who ruled each zone. They form, in effect, a Gnostic 'Book of the Dead' similar to both the Egyptian and Tibetan kind. Says the Naasene Psalm: 'all the worlds shall I journey through, all the mysteries unlock.' (350, 291)

We have only to consider Dante's *Divine Comedy* (61) as a 'Book of the Dead' in the same manner as these Gnostic narratives to see how widely held and practically understood were these complex world-views. Dante travels through 'all the worlds,' through many levels, through Hell, Purgatory and Heaven to gain his initiatory experience. Of course, as for Dante, there are guardians upon the way who guide the traveller through the worlds: we shall be considering these later in this chapter. Enoch (31) travels through the halls of heaven, as well as through the realms of earth and of the Hebraic underworld, Sheol, accompanied by similar visions of apocalyptic terror, as does the Qabalist who explores the interlinking worlds of the Tree of Life.

The shattering of the vessels is yet another statement of inner cosmology whereby each of the sephiroth experiences the emanations of God as a progressive prismation of white light into colour. Here the initiate can follow the path of the great ones who prayed appropriately at each gate linking the Four Worlds of the Tree, reciting the unifications through which the light of God was restored. (168)

The esoteric world is not without its own cosmologies written in our own times. Blavatsky presented an Eastern-influenced world-model which has subtly invaded many levels of consciousness. Rudolph Steiner, rejecting her Theosophical outline, visioned an Anthroposophist cosmology whose complexity and detail is positively Gnostic. (317) Dion Fortune's received text, *The Cosmic Doctrine*, is favoured as a cosmological paradigm by many followers of the Western Way, although its style is dry and its concepts, though concisely logical, lack sufficient illustration. (90) Truly there is no lack of world-models with which to experiment and explore.

These celestial memories are attempts to comprehend the macrocosm, to order it according to human understanding. In the works of Plato and Pythagoras we see an attempt to order the inner world-model by means of music. In *The Myth of Er* (266) we meet the Spindle of Necessity which stands for the cosmic system of stars and planets rotating about the axis of the universe. (cf. fig. 14) On each whorl of the Spindle sits a siren singing a single note. Pythagoras' cosmic ship of music (107) is a similar theme: it sails through the heavens emitting *rhoizimata* or rushing sounds. The Music of the Spheres gives us an insight into the cosmic order which is far more than mere planetary correspondence. If we skilfully strike the seven-stringed lyre of our beings, we resonate with the Music of the Spheres so that microcosm and macrocosm sound in harmony.

'Were it not for the orders of music hidden we should be claimed by the preponderant void', writes Ronald Duncan (121). The seven strings of the lyre correspond indeed to the seven planets known to the Classical world, and gave order to it. A hypothetical 'eighth sphere' was envisaged to correspond to the octave whereby the scale of creation is closed. Robert Fludd invented an instrument which would express this very theory: the monochord's strings could be divided and subdivided, in the manner of a musical abacus, to produce intervals or fractions of the original note. (105) Thus the original note sounded at the creation could be refracted, like sephirotic divisions upon the Tree of Life.

> From harmony, from heavenly harmony
> This universal frame began:
> From harmony to harmony
> Through all the compass the notes it ran,
> The diapason closing full in man.

wrote John Dryden, in his poem 'A Song for St Cecilia's Day'. As alchemy deals with the nature of matter and its transmutation, so music deals with the correspondence of note and planetary archetypes. 'There is another music of the soul and of the spheres which gives to actual music that is sung by voices and played on instruments its reason for existence.' (103) Combinations of notes such as major and minor thirds can be heard as syzygies of harmony, while other, discordant, intervals sound like the warring and irreconcilable archons. Sophia falls from the higher to the lower octave and, with humanity, strives towards union with her syzygy-octave through the scale until they are joined in the apocatastasis of music, through natural harmonic progression.

Music justly deserves its primacy among the arts. Its immediacy transcends the necessity of language or translation of idiom. Music is aural light, pouring inspiration through the prism of the ear, informing us of archetypal natures, of Platonic forms. From the aulos and lyre celebrating the mysteries of Apollo, to the hymns to Orpheus sung by Ficino, music has been one of the hermetic arts. Ficino hymned not just the deity but also its planetary ascriptions and correspondences in a talismanic way. Even the birth of opera can be seen as a development of the Renaissance preoccupation with mythology. Masques enabled monarchs to participate in 'mystery dramas' attired as gods. Modern stagings of operas are the nearest many of us come to experiencing the mysteries which were once staged in the amphitheatres of Greece: in them the archetypal forms are presented by means of light, music, colour and highly choreographed movement. At the end of this book we have appended a discography of evocative music. Through its appreciation we come to understand what Plotinus meant when he wrote:

> We are like a company of singing dancers who may turn their gaze outward and away notwithstanding they have the choirmaster for centre; but when they are turned towards him then they sing true and are truly centred upon him. Even so we encircle the Supreme always; but our eyes are not at all times fixed upon the centre. Yet in the vision thereof lie our attainment and our repose and the end of all discord: God in his dancers and God the true centre of the dance. (269)

If music is a remembrancer of interior states of being, then what of the correspondences and richly freighted lodes of symbolism with which hermeticism is associated? Symbolism is the language of the Inner and its laws are those of the Emerald Tablet. Though the exoteric world is no longer symbolically literate, the vestigial traces of planetary correspondences remain in its fascination with astrology and divination. Yet these half-understood sciences are but two strands in the fabric of correspondences and signatures. In a world which is closely linked by television, radio and telex through the physical means of satellite, we should be prepared to consider the communication network of the Inner which is linked, in an incredibly sensitive manner, by means of symbolism. 'The lower must symbolise the higher, but the opposite is impossible,' writes the philosopher, René Guénon. (124) Yet from the standpoint of a material world, it is hard to realize this fully. The archetypal forms of the macrocosm are no longer potent realities from which the formation of our own microcosm stems: they are remnants of a rejected world-model, archaic ghosts echoing in the windy streets of common man. If the hermeticist clings somewhat superstitiously to the resonant correspondences of ancient worlds, it is in order to have some equipment by which to steer. Just as the archetypes of the Native Tradition have faded, only to appear afresh in our own times, so the Hermetic Tradition needs to revision its own symbologies and estimate their value. Not every word in a dictionary is consistently used in everyday speech, for instance, yet obstruse words remain exact indicators for what is meant: they cannot be discarded because they are used less often.

In volume one we spoke about the pied language of the Celtic poets in whose riddling dialogues and boasting pronouncements were hidden the mystery teachings of the tribe. Such teachings have been hidden not only in language but in number, colour, music, sign, symbol, smell, dress and god-form. These correspondences, like the sum of the notes upon the Spindle of Necessity, harmonized by the aid of one faculty – the gift of the muse, Mnemosyne – memory. The oral traditions of earlier times were upheld under the Hermetic dispensation by means of memory-systems. Memory is part and parcel of the law of correspondences, provoking, as it were, a Pavlovian response to the macrocosmic transmission. Analogous signs, symbols and mnenomics encapsulate certain meanings. Memory is the nervous system of Adam Kadmon, connecting microcosm with macrocosm.

'Individual souls,' said Henry More, the neo-Platonist, echoing Plotinus, 'proceed from the universal soul; hence that ability to reason, remember and initiate action'. Francis Yates in her exhaustive work upon the Theatre of Memory has shown that memory-systems were obsessively employed from earliest Classical times right up until the Renaissance and beyond as a feature of basic education. After widespread literacy prevailed, such systems became the preserve of Hermeticists. (362) The Theatre of Memory was an imaginative device whereby sets of facts were associated with locations. One could, for example, 'store' the titles of the Biblical books by associating them visually with the rooms of one's house. It is a clumsy system, but it gives an insight into the methods of imaginative visualization employed by Renaissance Hermeticists.

The emblematic conceits of alchemical and Rosicrucian books were pictorial initiations which used images to trigger Inner remembrance. All mediums and psychics who are in touch with the Inner use the screen of their Inner vision to receive impressions in this way. Contrary to popular expectation, Inner visions do not physically manifest three-dimensionally in one's living room, but are of an *interior* order. 'Reading the akasha', as it called in esoteric parlance, is merely a method of cosmic picture-reception; not everyone has the skill to pick up these transmissions. Those who can are the prophets of our age. Divination is really of this order, or should be. The scryer sees – not what will be – but a 'Platonic' hologram of past, present and future resonances which form a totality never to be manifest in one particular time-scale. Such work needs the dedicated exactitude of only the most patient esotericist, one who is unlikely to take credit

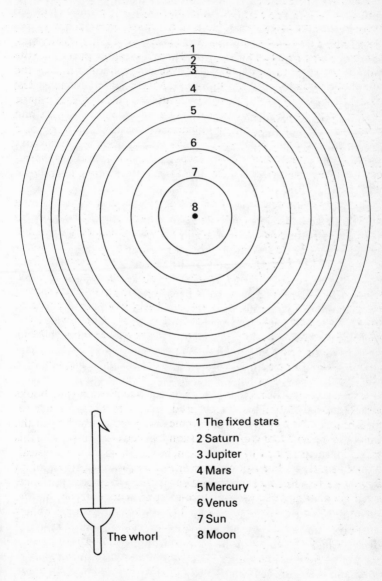

1 The fixed stars
2 Saturn
3 Jupiter
4 Mars
5 Mercury
6 Venus
7 Sun
The whorl   8 Moon

Figure 14:   The Spindle of Necessity

for what he or she visions and who will guide the seeker to self-understanding rather than arid prognostication of events. Memory of Inner things requires a trance of concentration which can be triggered by use of suitable correspondences. The prophet Elisha required to have music, in order that his psychic faculties might be roused: ' "Let the harper be brought," said the prophet. And while the harper played behold the hand of the God was upon Elisha' (II Kings 3, 15).

There have been many exponents of the doctrine of signatures, the greatest of whom is undoubtedly Paracelsus, the hermetic physician, alchemist and philosopher. Everything appearing in nature was a sign of an inner reality: 'you can discern man's immortal part of his visible, innate, characteristic signs, and you can know him even by his appearance; for the outer reveals the inner.' (134) Paracelsus did not only preach but also practised this doctrine in his work of healing. Hacob Boehme's doctrines were structured within as complex a cosmology, as we have discussed, and his theories underlie not only Steiner's work but also that of Blavatsky. Along with many Gnostic features such as Sophia, and the androgynous Adam, he strove to realize the macrocosmic signatures within man the microcosm.

Hermetic correspondences have been rendered unwieldy due to the accumulations of symbolism. It is axiomatic to cite Venus' day as Friday, her metal as copper, her perfume as rose, and her colour as emerald, for instance: the list could be prolonged indefinitely and argued over by different practitioners for an eternity. The planetary and other significances of archetypes stretch from Sumerian practice down to Ficino's day with great consistency. Add to this the imagery with which Christian Qabalists have laden the Tree of Life which stands like an overburdened Christmas tree in some textbooks on Qabalistic practice, and finish with Aleister Crowley's book of correspondences, 777, and you have an ill-assorted relish-tray to choose from. (58)

Symbol-systems are the memory of a tradition and require a minimum of application if we are to learn the language. The ritual use of some god-names is now questionable on the grounds that if you don't know the meaning and therefore the correspondence of the name pronounced, you cannot ensure results. The Chaldean Oracles advise, 'Change nothing in the barbarous names of evocation, for they are titles of divine things energized by the devotion of multitudes, and their power is ineffable.' (367) At the other extreme we must also beware of the shifting metaphors which contemporary society provides us with in these matters. The use by certain psychological schools of hermetic and other symbolisms may lead to a degradation of the traditions represented by these images and archetypes, as well as being a dangerous practice in that it involves the non-integrated use of great Inner energies. The current semantic gap in psychic matters is often bridged by the use of psychological language – again, a misleading and inexact terminology. Modern physics has also sought to employ the language of spiritual disciplines to physical phenomena which cannot be scientifically encapsulated: here there is a venerable tradition in that the medieval and Classical proto-scientists, who were often also philosophers – metaphysicians as well as physicians – used a common spiritual semantic for describing phenomena in either world. We are driven to make our own correspondences, our own metaphors and models and if, for convenience's sake, we seize upon earlier esoteric models, let us be aware that these are metaphors, *not the thing itself*.

It is always important to bear in mind that there are levels of meaning in symbolism: we may not perceive all of them concurrently, and we should always be prepared to explore deep before discarding an image. We should beware of allowing the symbol to *usurp* the Inner reality. For instance, it was a symbolic convention to symbolize God the Father in the Middle Ages as a hoary, bearded patriarch. This symbolism eventually took over until God is now almost totally identified with this imagery in most people's minds. Yet God is neither father nor mother, male nor female, but pure spirit. Despite this, God still lurks in the consciousness of many as a retributive patriarch, ready to strike the sinful dead with his thunderbolts. If such symbolism evokes fear and suspicion, it is void, and other possibilities should be investigated. Levels of meaning are easily muddled by those unused to thinking metaphysically. This is why we need the poet, the lucid mystic and the pragmatic esotericist who can operate objectively in the worlds of symbolism and interpret them to the metaphysically confused.

Yet it remains that correspondences are the essence of the magical art and no hard and fast rules can be applied. The individual practitioner must make his or her own lists: too often Crowley's 777 is referred to by students in search of a quick way into a magical system. (58) Create your own correspondences and then experiment cautiously with their working possibilities – if they don't work, then change them.

How should one go about selecting a list of correspondences? It will of course be dictated by the spiritual system or mythology which you work with. The normal seven planet system is a useful coat-hanger on which to drape your magical garments. The normal ascriptions of the Greek and Roman pantheon need not necessarily be employed: any set of archetypes drawn from either Native or Hermetic sources can be used. Celtic, American Indian, Egyptian, Platonic, Christian or Qabalistic archetypes and their correspond-ences can be selected. The only criterion is that they should be personally sought, selected and worked with. We give below a few suggestions merely as examples.

PLANETS	ANGELS	SAINTS	EGYPTIAN
Sun	Metatron	St John the Baptist	Re
Moon	Gabriel	St Joseph	Khonsu
Mars	Michael	St Barbara	Sekmet
Mercury	Raphael	St Christopher	Thoth
Jupiter	Tzadkiel	St Gregory	Ptah
Venus	Haniel	St Mary Magdalene	Isis
Saturn	Uriel	St Jerome	Osiris

If the planetary system does not appeal to you, then use another symbol system such as the tarot or the Qabala. Fig. 17 gives further suggestions on working with the Tree of Life. But such schemes cannot be pursued without the help of the inhabitants of the Inner realms. Plotinus says:

'Even the Celestials, the Daimones, are not on their unreasoning side immune; there is nothing against ascribing acts of memory and experiences of sense to them, in supposing them to accept the traction of methods laid up in the natural order, and to give hearing to petitioners: this is especially true of those of them that are closest to this sphere, and in the degree of their concern about it.' (268)

These 'celestials' are those very Lordly Ones we encountered in volume one of *Western Way* who stand midway between our world and the spiritual realms whose cosmologies we have read of. It is important to know who they are and how they function upon the Inner. This we can know only through the great scriptures of mystical traditions and the subjective experience of those who have journeyed in these worlds. Before we set foot through the inner door ourselves, let us meet the guardians who will guide our way.

HIDDEN MASTERS: SECRET SIBYLS

In volume one we spoke extensively about the Otherworld and its inhabitants. Both are based on the ancestral Underworld and the wisdom of tribal progenitors: the archetypes are localized expressions of principles which transcend merely Native experience. The Hermetic Tradition, as might be expected, has its own inner correlatives some of which transpose directly, with little or no change, from the Native Tradition, while others originate solely in the Hermetic reality. Some appear from the ranks of the great dead, the ancestors, like Elijah, or from the realms of the gods, like Osiris and Isis. Some arise from hero-saga or other literary sources, Christian Rosenkreutz or Perceval. The tribe sees its ancestors and is comforted: the shaman sees greater beings, but is not disquieted. Likewise the Hermeticist visions the inhabitants of the Inner, who may appear not only in local dress but in the guise of different cultural traditions. It is possible to 'pick up' contacts from the Inner as though they were transmissions of radio channels: the adept can 'tune in' to the appropriate 'station' when necessary. On p. 164 we give a brief list of 'tuning-frequencies' which can be contacted. But we must establish two vitally important principles straight away: the Inner inhabitants, which we can call *contacts*, have many means of appearing to our consciousness and although they are co-workers on the spiritual plane, they are not God.

Yet the question will be asked: where do contacts come from, do they exist and what are they good for? Hidden Masters, Lost Continents, and Otherworldly Visitants – it does not matter whether they ever really existed: what matters is that people behave *as though* they were real. This suspension of belief is not self-delusive, despite appearances, or the lack of them. (Contacts, like God, are not capable of ontological proof.) As any novelist will attest, the creation of archetypes is practically impossible: whatever is thought about has already existed in the timeless dimensions of the infinite. That expression 'as though' is an important one: if it is one which offends anyone's reality then consider the use of the *x* within algebra. If our knowledge of Inner Worlds is sketchy, we are reduced to this kind of algebraic formula in order to proceed with our researches. We take a lot on trust, but we always refer to our known experience in these matters. And this is something which everyone can do.

The implantation of heroic and other archetypes can be traced to childhood and young adulthood; these remain with the individual long after earth-shattering intellectual realizations have ceased to matter. The human psyche is a plastic substance, allowing itself to be moulded, wrapping itself willingly around a desired image. But there is no abiding in this realm: the images fade, leaving only their effect behind. The Prospero in us conjures up inner archetypes with whom to play in imagination, only to banish them when a more exciting newcomer arrives on the scene. We manipulate our inner lives and are manipulated by them too. As to the existence of contacts: there are more existences than the merely physical one. As to the work of contacts, such as the Masters, we will discuss this shortly. But our contacts, and everyone has his or her own, act as way-showers and companions on our way to inner understanding.

The multiplicity of forms and images is perhaps at the root of the differences within the Western Way. There has been little or no attempt to codify levels, methods and messages of the Inner on a purely esoteric basis. If a Martian landed in Piccadilly Circus or Times Square, the first man and woman met would perhaps be representative of the human species, but not of its infinite variety. Likewise, the teeming variety of hierarchical entities, angels, saints, prophets, masters, Indian chiefs and Tibetan doctors which are 'transmitted' to many levels of esotericists make it difficult to generalize about the Inner. So often a medium is contacted by or contacts one entity and then bases a 'world-message' on the results without 'testing the spirits to see if they be of God': the result is a worthless stream of loquacious aphorisms – analogous to the willing babble which might be recorded on our hypothetical Martian's tape-recorder if you or I were asked to 'say a few words' as a representative of earth to the entire Martian race. Discrimination is vital. On the Inner, every level of disincarnate entity may be encountered from atavistic demons to archangels: it is necessary then, to work through approved channels and with tested contacts. Just as we judge what is appropriate to our lives in this world, so we must realize that not everything on the Inner is for us – as those who run thither in an access of psychic enthusiasm find to their cost. The work of the Inner is not to mislead or endanger people and this is why certain high-powered contacts are hard both to establish and maintain.

The concept of Hidden Masters is one which is closer to the Middle East than to the Western Tradition, but the West has not been without its Inner guardians. In modern esotericism the term first appears within the German order known as The Golden and Rosy Cross Brotherhood which was operational in the eighteenth century. This had a line of 'secret chiefs' – a term which was to be bandied about a good deal in both Theosophy and the Golden Dawn. This is the theme of Edward Bulwer-Lytton's novel, *Zanoni* (1862) which had considerable effect upon many esoteric innovators. (207) The vexed question of the Masters continued into our own time. Madame Blavatsky's statements about her Tibetan masters seemed to clarify the situation, but the pale oleographs of turbaned divines which peer from theosophical walls are far from the reality: they are merely the clothing of deeper archetypes which lie beyond expression. Each age pictures them differently, each individual clothes their archetypal forces in suitably arcane robes so that Dr Dee, Merlin and scores of reverend gentlemen appear to fit the bill. Personality cults of the Masters are misleading and unnecessary as we can understand if we refer to Dion Fortune's *The Cosmic Doctrine* (90):

> The Masters as you picture them are all 'imagination'. Note well that I did not say that the Masters *were* imagination . . . (they are contacted) through your imagination, and although your mental picture is not real or actual, the *results* of it are real and actual.

This book, together with Gareth Knight's essay 'The Work of the Inner Plane Adepti', cuts through the swathe of 'bunkum and informed superstition' which surrounds those known as the Masters. (9)

So, what are the Masters? 'Human beings like yourselves, but older. They are not Gods, nor Angels, nor Elementals but are those individuals who have achieved and completed the same task as you have set yourselves.' (90) The Masters are to be understood as those adepts who are not presently incarnate, but who mediate from the Inner those energies with which the earth meshes its microcosm with the macrocosm.

Mystery schools and esoteric movements have been quick to claim as past-masters of their orders those famous in history for their cultural and philosophical achievements: comparison of a handful of such schools yields a remarkably similar list of personages – Socrates, Francis Bacon and Hypatia, for instance. The inner understanding has led to an exoteric confusion when such lists are produced. For, although the mystical hierarchies of ancient streams of wisdom establish an inner chain of initiates, this does not necessarily imply an apostolic succession of famous incarnate initiates. As we indicated in volume one, knowledge is not necessarily handed on from person to person unbroken through the generations, but is fragmented, hidden and rediscovered in other ways. Julius Sperber, a German Rosicrucian, writes of the wisdom of Christian Rosenkreutz as an inheritance from Adam, who retained some knowledge of paradise after the Fall – this passed into many traditions, including Zoroastrianism, Chaldean, Persian, Egyptian and Qabalistic streams and was fulfilled in Christ, passing in turn to the Christian theurgists of the Renaissance and thence to Sperber's own tradition. (207) Thus do many mystery schools speak of their own tradition, but this should not be confused with a blood-lineage.

The generations of humanity are usually reckoned from Cain, yet the mystical remnant are the descendants of Seth. This tradition of 'inner family' permeates the whole of Judaic and Islamic mysticism, and was once present in Gnosticism as a Christian understanding. The inheritance of Adam's wisdom passes to Seth and this is symbolized mystically as 'the seed of Seth' which passes, by means of *inner* generation to successive initiates. Bound up with this concept is the understanding of the encoding of life, the spiritual DNA or spark, which is transmitted via the seed or pearl. (72) This mystical symbol has often been applied in an exoteric and literal way. Recent suggestions that Jesus' bloodline succeeded via his offspring begotten of Mary Magdalene are but modern proof of this idea's survival. (18) The bloodline of Christ is indeed extant, but it is the mystical body of Christ made up of communicants, not the royal family of the Hapsburgs that we must look to. Similarly, the Magdalene may be viewed as a spiritual Mother: one who announced the Resurrection and who, in Gnostic tradition, was privy to Christ's most secret teachings. (239)

These extensive examples reveal just how carefully we must mark our levels in Inner matters. Language, which is based in material expression fumbles at metaphysical concepts. Even symbolism and imaginative use of image can go part of the way when it comes to explaining inner dimensions, and even this can fall foul of fundamental acceptance at face value. The language of the Inner is that spoken by the prophets and sibyls: Elijah, Isaiah, St Hildegard of Bingen, (143) Joachim de Fiore (9), St John – these all speak with the fiery tongue of revelation, from the standpoint outside of time, breathing apocalypse and new hope. Like poetry, prophecy is eclectic: certain images are programmed to trigger response in the heart of the initiate which will remain enigmatic to those who would only be fearful if they understood the inner language. The Masters speak in this manner but, as we shall see, according to the individual understanding and capacity of the pupil.

This brings us to another vexed question. It is often argued that the guardians of tradition, whether incarnate or disincarnate, are male. Truly, there seems to be a superabundance of Masters. One might enquire, where are the Mistresses of tradition?

> 'Why is it that women do not manifest themselves as Masters and Adepti on the inner planes, or indeed on the outer? In the very early days they did so manifest but the dividing line between positive and negative was then very subtle. In the future they will again and even now there are certain adepti in female bodies who have definite inner plane missions and who are genuine adepts.' (91)

This script, emanating from the Master who stands behind the Society of Inner Light, is frustratingly elusive on the subject. In the Western Way there is a tradition that the prophet and sibyl sustain a joint guardianship: they are the Hermetic equivalent of the Native Tradition's shaman and shamanka, and are roles which can be found on both Inner and Outer planes. Theirs are the voices of the Underworld and of the Stars, sending out the antiphonal song, weaving the mediations of the microcosm and macrocosm. If contact is made with this ancient tradition, then the initiate is privileged to be a part of their work. In many ways, the archetype of the sibyl comes from deeper or earlier levels of cognisance than that of the prophet. But, though we can polarize sibyl with the Native and prophet with the Hermetic tradition, we must not be dogmatic on this point: we speak in symbols. The prophets are nearer to our own consciousness and cultural conditioning and have therefore accumulated personae by which they are known to us. The sibyls back onto a phase of consciousness which is outside modern understanding, although this is beginning to resonate once again. The Muses of Classical mythology, the Mountain-Mothers and Cailleachs of Native Tradition, the sisterhoods of sibyls and priestesses of ancient times are comprised within the sibylline tradition. They come from such deep levels that they often appear as a collective rather than an individual entity.

The sibyls usually work chthonically, from the earth, in antiphonal exchange with the prophets, who work from the heavens. Their inter-polarization can be the subject of intense contemplation. (Lest there should be any confusion of levels, we stress again that this complex concept is an Inner one.) The sibyl receives and synthesizes the impulse mediated by the prophets: the prophet receives and synthesizes the impulse of the sibyls. Thus each informs and is incomplete without, the other. This is not to make any statement about the role of women or men. As we wrote in volume one, the levels between sexual polarity and magical polarity are clearly distinguished. The gender of magical polarities is used powerfully as well as symbolically in this paradigm:

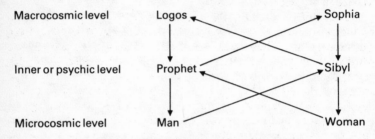

Figure 15:   Diagram of Polarities

Just as there can be a relationship between man and woman, so there can be a relationship between man and sibyl, or woman with prophet. Each male or female operator stands directly under both the Inner level archetype and the macrocosmic archetype, with whom a relationship may also be established. We have used the terms Logos and Sophia to indicate the Divine Male and Female principles, but god and goddess can be substituted, as could any other suitable image. This system of relationships is, *per se*, supraphysical, but of great importance for an understanding of magical working. The Inner Level on which prophet and sibyl stand, is the creative and inspirational one. Thus various schools of thought have typified this function variously as anima and animus, daimon and muse, or, negatively speaking, as incubus and succubus. To find and interrelate with the source of one's inner wisdom is of paramount importance to the walker-between-the-worlds. Although no specific exercise is here suggested, the reader is invited to meditate upon these things. If any symbols are required for meditation, the cards of the High Priestess and the Hierophant from the Tarot bring awareness of the sibyl and prophet polarity.

The shuttle of their song interweaves microcosmic and macrocosmic levels. The sibyls and prophets are the Just men and women made perfect, who hear our despair and pain, who understand our dedication to the Great Work, and who inspire us secretly within our souls. One might think of them as a celestial and chthonic system of communication cables who can put us in touch with any part of the cosmos – past, present or to come. Any contact we have with them is tenuous, and cannot be long sustained. Like the Mighty Ones, spoken of in volume one, the sibyls and prophets are impersonal, yet their hearts are set on the will of God. A greater understanding of their role might well help revision the rather out-dated concept of the Master in Western esotericism.

Certain adepts already perform the role of sibyl or prophet while yet incarnate among us. These, like the saints, live in obscurity, rarely teaching openly. They are known, after their death, through the work of their disciples. Such adepts are the real hidden ones who perform the work of mediation on behalf of the microcosm. Some are guardians of the ancestral land, others sing the song of paradise: these marginal shamans are indeed the Just Ones – a quorum of which is traditionally believed to sustain the world from destruction. Positively, their work synthesizes 'whatsoever things are good, acceptable and perfect.' (Romans 12,[2])

The concept of an inner communicator is comprehended within the word *maggid* or inner teacher (130), who accompanied the Qabalistic adept. This could be a past-master or expositor of Qabalistic lore, such as Isaac Luria or Abraham Abulafia, or one of the prophets – Abraham or Elijah. We shall be going on to speak more about such teachers, but let us consider that guide which is nearest to us and with whom we established rapport in exercise 7 of volume one; our inner guardian, our angel. 'When a person keeps a commandment, he earns an Advocate' (angel), (168) we are told. This idea of a heavenly 'other' or guardian angel has become rather thinly strained from Jewish into Christian tradition – the Church seems to have become embarassed about its heavenly hierarchies, and rarely alludes to the positive work of angels, despite Dionysius the Areopagite's codifications of inner inhabitants. The popular view of angels is not much better and even that great angelologist, Dr Dee himself was not immune from the narrow view of his own age when he was confronted by an angel in female shape. This meeting, recorded in Casaubon's *A True and Faithful Relation of What Passed for Many Years Between Dr John Dee and Some Spirits* (43), was Dee's first encounter, through the mediumship of Edward Kelly, of a spirit. He asks, rather indignantly, how she can appear thus. She replies:

> 'Angels (I say) of themselves neither are man nor woman; therefore they do take formes not according to any proportion in imagination, but according to the discreet and appliable will both of (God) and of the thing wherein they are Administrators.'

Both Jacob Boehme and Emmanuel Swedenbourg enjoyed such angelic conversations as Dee's. Inspirational writers of all kinds attest to angelic assistance. To cultivate the knowledge and conversation of one's Holy Guardian Angel was, of course, one of the aims of the medieval magician: but let that not limit your own appreciation of your angel.

Angels, unlike the Masters, are not nor have they ever been human. They are an order apart. There are angels not only of individuals, but of countries. They are the watchers and intelligences of God. G. Davidson's *A Dictionary of Angels* is recommended for those who wish to read further, (63) as well as Peter Lamborn Wilson's *Angels*. (360)

Where and how are the Masters to be found? This is a question which has been asked since the Rosicrucian manifestos first made their impact upon early seventeenth-century Europe. (cf. chapter 1) The invisibility of the Masters, of Lost Worlds and other curious phenomena is frankly inexplicable to some occult enthusiasts: they cover this rather grey area by rationalizations and crank literature. The truth is much simpler, and involves a clear perception of levels once again.

The Mirror of Wisdom by Theophilus Schweighardt (301) surely scotches the question of an earthly location for the Masters. He writes:

> that according to the announcement of the brethren although the incorporated gathering of all Rosicrucians does not take place in one particular place, nevertheless a true-hearted, devout and upright man can easily and without great trouble come to speak with one of the brethren.

He proceeds to give clues as to their location and advises the reader to turn 'towards the sunrise, noon and evening and finally towards midnight,' if they wish to seek the College of Rosicrucian adepts. This reads like a mystery instruction which tells the seeker to look within, not without. The keys of the four-square watch-tower of the day are precisely noted. More openly he says, 'Thou seest that the Collegium hangs in the air, where God wills, he can direct it. It is moveable and immovable, constant and inconstant . . . and thou must undergo . . . examination.' He is telling us that the College of Masters is contactable through the common means at our disposal – meditation, prayer, a good life – the very boring commonplaces which hide the mystery so effectively that few realize their value. Those seekers whose inner sight and senses are roused will find a master:

> I assure thee that a brother will appear in person to thee. It seems wonderfully incredible, but . . . I assure thee, thou shalt find the Art and Collegium, and thus is the only way, for else there is no avail to seek the place, for it is not and yet it is.' (ibid.)

Beginners in the mysteries are often driven to their wits end by this sort of calm assurance, that 'when the seeker is ready, a master will appear.' What does it *mean*, they ask? What are the proper channels for approaching them? So many great promises seem to be made within mystery orders that we may do well to look closely at the kind of answers one of these gives:

> If a man sets out to look for the Path he evinces a desire. That desire is noted by those who watch on the Inner Places and he will be 'assigned to a class' according to his temperament. After he has gone a certain way under that tuition he will be put in the care of what is called a 'guide': . . . (who) will try to impress the teaching he wishes to convey on the soul of his pupil by telepathy, and the pupil must try to catch what is 'said'. Later the pupil will be put into touch with one of the Lesser Masters and be one of a number of pupils for whom that Master is responsible. A guide has only one pupil at a time, but a Master has many. As the pupil advances further he will be passed to Masters of higher grade. His problem will always be to catch what his Master says. (90).

This neat hierarchical system coincides with that of both the Theosophical and Alice Bailey Schools: it is, in fact, from *The Cosmic Doctrine* by Dion Fortune, the founder of the Society of the Inner Light. We would say, from our own experience, that things are not always so neat and tidy, that progression is not assured. There is, in effect, no merit system of an earthly kind. Some esotericists form lasting attachments with their Inner Teachers and progress as described, but most attend different seminars in the College of the Masters and learn a balanced curriculum, specializing only later on in their experience.

Gaining a contact is something which normally occurs consciously only later: it is not something a student will be either aware of or feel the need of – it is enough to learn the basics at the outset. Yet, even in the early stages of training, one should be alert for the contacts which perhaps have already laid their foundations.

The choice of a magical name very often reveals one's secret affiliations with the Inner in this regard. Members of the Golden Dawn took Latin tags as their names, often using the acrostic formed from it, such as W.B. Yeats took: Deus est Demon Inversus or DEDI (dedicated). Dion Fortune (Violet Firth) took as her own name a contraction of Deo Non Fortuna. Not all initiates choose names or affiliations in this way. Very often the candidate places him or herself under the patronage of a past traveller of the Western Way. This may well be a case of an overshadowing teacher, as described above, or it may be a case of 'soul-likeness.'

Soul-likeness is sometimes misunderstood as reincarnational memory but as one modern occultist has remarked, 'Yes, I remember some incarnations, but are they *mine?*' This is a valid question which the reader should ever bear in mind: those who are sensitive to the workings of the Inner have at their disposal a great deal of information. Just because your psyche has keyed into the Egyptian Book of the Dead does not necessarily make you a priest or priestess of Maat in a past incarnation. Soul-likeness is the immediate recognition between the worlds which we sometimes experience with people and places in our everyday life. It is possible that both genetic and inner memory are at play here. In the cycles of occurence it is inevitable that there should be an overlay of worlds when we, as it were, see down a corridor of time. The trainee pathwalker will use these opportunities wisely and not discuss them publicly.

Isaac Luria, the Qabalist of Safed, 'could look at a person and tell him how he was connected to the Supernal Man, and how he was related to Adam'. (168) Not all of us are so discerning, and even those in the position of teacher would be chary of finding such relationships for their students. Such correspondences can be fraught with danger, as a visit to any mental home will reveal. When you are operating between the worlds, never confuse yourself with any Inner role or entity: always seal off one operation from another so that

Merlin or Morgan le Fay is not in the driving seat of John or Ann Smith, when you return to everyday life. Mental homes are full of Napoleons and Mary Queen of Scots — weak personalities submerged in stronger ones.

A real Inner Teacher will not seek to dominate a relationship with a student; indeed he or she will develop the strong and strengthen the weak aspects of the student's personality, nurturing the student's essential self without imposing an exclusive imprint. Of course, great teachers leave their mark upon good students: we have only to listen to some of the most accomplished musicians of our time to hear the unmistakable technique and discipline learned in the master-class of a past virtuoso of that instrument. Learning from one's contacts is like that.

It is often asked, 'how will I know when I've made a contact?' or 'how do I know that my Inner Teacher is reliable?' To the first question we would say that we all make contacts throughout our lives. Whenever our hearts go out to distant friends or when our imaginations are engaged in a gripping book, we are using the same facility to 'contact' something which is not present. These subtle influences shape our lives and are, to all intents and purposes, the contacts which we all experience.

An Inner Teacher is something else. It is unlikely that one will be acquired without a good deal of basic training, usually of a formal mystery school nature. If one follows a tradition, an Inner Teacher will be standing ready on the periphery of that tradition to help those students who seek the esoteric depths. (cf. exercise 3) As to the Inner Teacher's reliability, we refer the reader to volume one of *Western Way* and to Isaac Luria's advice: 'It must certainly speak the truth, motivate one to do good deeds, and not err in a single prediction.' (168) We judge by results, or by our intuitive rightness in this matter. Contacts and one's own wishes are easily confused, unfortunately, and it is hard to tell when one is merely using the rationale of the Inner's influence to smooth one's own way. Wayward mediums have been known to insist that a holiday in the Bahamas is what the Masters have ordered, when they want to get away from things themselves. Inner maturity is a hard thing for anyone to learn: the Inner Teacher will not spare your finer feelings when it comes to showing up your own imbalances: the only way is to be humble and take advice. The preceding remarks assume that the reader is not in receipt of any training but, of course, the dangers of going through the Inner Door are considerably lessened by the tuition of an Outer Teacher.

Such warnings sound dire enough, but there are benefits also. Service to the Inner, to the will of God – as mystics would term it – is rendered with love and there is a reciprocating love which more than balances our service. (cf. chapter 3) This does not mean that money and all good things will necessarily shower upon you, but that spiritual gifts are given to the co-workers with God. Love is the ultimate discrimination in this field of operation: if your work promotes your ego and polishes spiritual pride, ask your angel for clarification of yourself and your motives. You cannot weave microcosm and macrocosm together at the cost of your pearl – the divine spark.

The pressures of inner work are immense. Esotericists have jobs like other people, and have to cope with children, bills and overcrowded housing. Conditions are tough and only the resilient survive the pace. There is no ideal hermetic existence in a country retreat where dedicated disciples do your living for you, while you meditate in blissful quietude. The brief solitude of the study and meditation period must be managed so as to provide a daily temenos and refreshment of the spirit, from which one may emerge to face one's daily life. The increasing 'impatience' of the Inner to bring through certain teachings sets grindingly hard conditions upon sensitives who undertake to mediate these into the outer world. Yet this mediatory work is of such importance that many make the sacrifice of time and effort to ensure its proper grounding. At this point, we can see that the work of prayer and mediation are substantially the same: the mystic and the esotericist, who can work at this level of awareness, have a reciprocal function.

Mediating the impulse of the Inner is a matter of timing and rhythm. Great store is currently set by many ordinary citizens by their biorhythms – calculated charts of emotional, mental and mundane potential for the month: the esotericist already knows his or her biorhythm and aligns the personal pattern with the macrocosmic one. All esoteric work is done according to prevailing Inner currents, tides and influences. These are measured by means of moon phases, astronomical alignment and conjunction, the flow of seasonal tides. Time and time again, synchronistic events prove that rhythm is of the essence on the Inner, especially when it is aligned with purpose, pattern and power. Certain Inner alignments come round, rather like stellar alignments, once in a millennium whereby the resonance of one historical time-scale is available to us centuries later. This, as we have already described, is happening now with the rediscovery of the Native Tradition. Certain aspects of the Hermetic Tradition are not 'in phase' at this time. We have striven in this book to deal with those which underlie many contemporary concerns: resonances which will shortly be making their presence felt in common consciousness.

The resonances of the Inner are mediated to us via the Hidden Masters and Secret Sibyls but that does not make us merely passive receivers. After an apprenticeship serving the Inner, the student is given the means to become a journeyman. Esoteric books often speak of this process as 'the foundation of a magical personality', which sounds grandiose but is no more than the assumption of suitable travelling garments for work on the Inner. The Magical Personality is the *real* robe of the magician. It is acquired by a long process involving a deep knowledge of the self, an integration of one's imbalances, a strengthening of one's potentialities until the working image of the self – the Body of Light – can be constructed. This is not an exalted self-image or egocentric idealization of the self, but a vehicle of the higher self – the *merkabah* or chariot by which one makes the ascents. Rather than being the assumption of a mask-like persona, the magical personality is an identification with the Holy Guardian Angel, the Otherworld guide. This stage is accomplished when the student has served his or her apprenticeship in the Great Work, when the student pays homage to no one under God, but is prepared to get on with the work of his or her destiny as a trusted co-operator of the Inner. The student becomes, at length, a teacher of others.

It is often asked how one goes about this process: by faithful practice of daily meditation, by continual awareness of the tides of one's own life, by observation of the shifting pattern of Inner and Outer tides, by dedication to the Great Work, by working harmoniously with one's contacts. Only so will the work of integration be achieved.

Adepthood is the adulthood of the Inner – the inner maturity to work between the many levels of life effectively and responsibly, without inflicting one's imbalances on others. To be adept means to be skilled, to be master of one's craft. An adept is no more than this.

The Magical Personality sounds an awesome thing but we should be aware it is liable to become as static as the psyche of an analysand who boasts of being 'individuated'. There is no such thing as final enlightenment: the cyclic nature of human life renders us all liable to forgetfulness as well as to awareness. We spend our lives striving to establish the ever-shifting parallels by which the Inner can be perceived and mediated, discovering new possibilities, alert to the dangers of self-deception or self-complacence. Yet once the magical identification of self with teacher occurs, things can never be the same again. The period of overshadowing and then of integration occur at different rates, according to individual experience, but there is a deeper comprehension of both Inner and Outer events because the life-experience of the teacher becomes part of the adept's consciousness. This subtle process does not make the adept into Superman. In fact, the further the adept travels into and co-operates with the Inner, the less noteworthy he or she becomes in Outer matters. Personality is not melted down or dissolved, nor does it become part of a uniform expression: personal identity is, rather, made the spearpoint of Inner mediation. Here, we reach the limits of descriptive language, where personal experience alone can explain.

It may be that you have already started your apprenticeship in the College of Masters, that you have a set of working contacts and that you travel often through the inner door. In the next two sections, those who have not begun their exploration, may find a few indicators of how they might start. There are many ways into the Hermetic Landscape, and many guardians.

GUIDES AND GUARDIANS

'These great ideas (archetypes) are not at all sterile, they multiply their likenesses throughout the universe', (68) so wrote Marcilio Ficino. Some archetypes which appeal to national consciousness rarely cross their localized frontiers, but, mythologically speaking, many do emigrate from their native traditions because their archetypal energies are universally acceptable. Thus, Hermes appears locally in almost every culture, under a different name: Merlin and Thoth are well-known resonances, as we have seen.

We spoke in volume one about the regeneration of forms. It is the task of each generation to localize the formalizations of the forces it intends to work with: if these forms are inappropriate for that time, then they must be regenerated by means of practical work, so that the synthesis of energies can mesh. For instance, one may decide to use a little-known Sumerian deity in one's ritual. If the form, whose energy you require to co-operate with, has been unused for many centuries, then one works up to the ritual by first meditating on every known aspect of that deity in great detail and then earths the principles behind the outer form by mediating them cautiously. If there are any unbalanced results from this method, then the form has not been regenerated. This applies in the Hermetic Tradition as well as in the Native Tradition, where extremes of atavistic reversion are often encountered. If you desire to drive along a motorway, a hansom-cab or a Celtic war-chariot are equally inappropriate vehicles, for instance. There is no point in working with any energy, however it is imaged, if you have no personal rapport with it. The rhythmic Inner alignments we spoke about above, must be carefully scanned for suitable resonances which overlap with one's own inner work.

The following list is made up of archetypes which can be contacted, as well as concepts which permeate the Hermetic Tradition which can be utilized as symbolic meditation subjects. If you intend to work with any of the characters or concepts mentioned, then be sure that you find out as much as possible, if you are unfamiliar with these archetypes: the entries are considerably contracted due to exigencies of space. Most of us are woefully ignorant about the stories which inform our culture. Many of these archetypes are now only known through folk-story, mythological cycles or psychoanalytic commentary, where they can be safely ignored as fit for children and madmen. This objective distancing of ourselves from the living essence of Inner life has done more than anything to erode our spiritual tradition. A religious tradition is, after all, nothing other than a story to live by – and there are as many stories as there are human lives.

> We must learn God's story, our tradition. It is one of our worries today that so many young people do not know elementary concepts and language and even personalities that characterize our tradition. Knowing God's story is a prerequisite for knowing our own. (25)

Many of the archetypes are as the masks of God and have been so used in our own age by the exponents of Jung. The neo-Gnostic nature of Jung's work has enabled us to use and discuss the archetypes which until recently were subsumed in saints, angels and literary figures. However, there arises the question that each archetype is an energy of great power and cannot be used in psychological 'ritual workshops' with impunity. To work with these figures you must *know* them. The archetype which *you* experience as a friendly guardian under the form of Anubis, will not necessarily so appear to someone else of your acquaintance. If you intend to use these, or indeed, any other archetypes as a basis for ritual work with others, make sure that everyone present is experienced in mediating that degree of energy.

Which leads us to the question of respect:

Angels won't be invoked
Ancient folios are not Yellow Pages (229)

is good advice. One does not command the appearance of any energy on the Inner, one *requests*. Further, if you construct a ritual working from the results of your experience, don't mix systems. Celtic and Enochian systems won't necessarily mix, neither will Gnostic and Native systems. Isis and Demeter should not appear in the same ritual – one is an aspect of the other, but from a different mythos. Gentile Qabala has successfully combined both Jewish and Christian aspects; Gnostic and alchemical systems have much in common, but don't push the correspondences too far.

Use this section imaginatively, add your own examples and work with whichever excites you. It may be that one of these archetypes carries the key to your own spiritual heritage. If you find a particular preference for a tradition arising as a result of this experience, you might well combine this with exercise 3.

Abaris.   Master of the Hyperborean mysteries which are based in North-West Europe, some say in the region of the British Isles. Abaris was a servant of Hyperborean Apollo. He lived without food and travelled on a golden arrow (which was the symbol of Apollo). He is said to have been initiated into the Pythagorean mysteries. His fragmentary mythos bears a similar ring to that of *Bladdud*, the legendary founder of the pre-Roman city of Bath: he also had the ability to fly, and instituted the temple and worship of the goddess Sulis – later to become Sulis-Minerva, under the Romans. If Bladdud visited Greece as legend credits, and was initiated into the mysteries, it is possible that the two myths have become identified with each other. Abaris links the Celtic Native Tradition with that of the early Hermetic Tradition. The Hyperborean mysteries, of which he is master, are safer to work with than those of Atlantis.

REFERENCES: Stewart (323), Chapman (45), Lievegoed (195).

Adam and Eve.   Our primal parents. They can be understood, mythologically, as every man and woman. Sibyl and prophet are their inner resonance, just as Logos and Sophia (q.v) are their cosmic and ultimate reality. Their Fall and expulsion from the garden, however interpreted, is representative of a loss of the perfect state. Their prayer of return to that state can also be ours:

> O precious Paradise, unsurpassed in beauty, Tabernacle built by God, unending gladness and delight . . . with the sound of the leaves pray to the Maker of all: may He open unto me the gates which I closed by my transgression, and may He count me worthy to partake of the Tree of Life and of the joy which was mine when I dwelt in thee before. (191)

The Orthodox icon of the Descent into Hell, shows the glorified Christ extending either hand to Adam and Eve; he stands upon the bridge of the Cross, and the unregenerate ancestral forces, depicted as locks and bolts, are broken asunder.

REFERENCES: Graves (110, 112), Every (78), Apocryphal New Testament (10)

Adam Kadmon/Anthropos.   Common to many traditions, the concept of the Hidden Adam or macrocosmic man, finds its fullest expression in the Qabalistic Adam Kadmon whose body is seen as a cosmic glyph of the Tree of Life itself: all ten emanations (sephiroth) of the Tree of Life are superimposed upon Adam Kadmon's Body of Light. The original stature of Adam was that of the cosmos itself but, as in the Orphite belief in the apportioning of the deity into men by Titans, the Body of Light is scattered. However, Adam Kadmon, made in the image of God, *is* the Universe in its totality 'The body of Adam is the body of the world, and the soul of Adam is the totality of the souls.' The concept of Anthropos is a Hermetic resonance of the Qabalistic one: 'but All-Father Mind, being Life and Light, did bring forth Man (Anthropos) co-equal to Himself.' Exercise 6 provides a method for experiencing this energy. Any extensive work with Qabala will put the reader directly in touch with this archetype.

REFERENCES: Halevi (127), Mead (227), Rudolph (291) Drower (72).

Aeon/Aion.   The Aeon is seen as the coming age in which a saviour-figure will come to restore all things to their proper order. Many

speak of the Aquarian Age as a fulfilment of their hope. The child of
the Aeon is Horus/Harpocrates (q.v.). Aion, the god of time, was
associated with the cult of Kore at Alexandria. His birth was
celebrated on the night of 5 January, which is now the eve of the
Epiphany of Showing of Christ, which strengthens the connections
of the Aeon with Aion. Latterly, Aion was identified with Mithras as
god of time. A statue from the Mithraeum at Ostia, shows him as a
lion-headed man, a serpent girdling his body six times; in his hands
are a key and sceptre. He has wings with symbols of the seasons on
his back, a thunderbolt on his breast, and at his feet are the hammer
and tongs of Hephaistos (representative of the alchemist), the pine
and tongs of Aesclepios, (representative of the healer) and the
caduceus of Hermes (representing the Hermetic Tradition. (cf. fig. 1)
He is often fused with Agathodaimon (q.v.)

REFERENCES: Guénon (124), Godwin (104), Lindsay (197).

Agathodaimon.   His name means 'Good spirit'. Porphyry tells us
that he was represented among the Egyptians as anthropomorphic,
with blue-black skin, with a girdle about his waist, carrying a
sceptre, and wearing a winged crown. He is the first aspect of
Hermes Trismegistos, identifiable with the Anthropos (q.v.) or
Cosmic Man of Light, 'who has heaven for head, aether for body,
earth for feet and for the water round (him) the ocean's depths.' He is
perhaps identifiable also with Kneph-Kamephis or Lord of the
Perfect Black, who teaches Isis the mysteries of alchemy. Agathodaimon is the shepherd and guardian of all initiates who invoke him
thus:

> O mayest thou come into my mind and heart for all the length of
> my life's days, and bring unto accomplishment all things my
> soul desires . . . come unto me, Good, altogether good . . . thou
> whom no magic can enchant, no magic can control, who givest
> me good health, security, good store, good fame, victory and
> strength, and cheerful countenance.

REFERENCES: Denning and Phillips (68), Lindsay (197), Mead
(227).

Akashic Records.   Although there is no Western name equivalent to
this concept, the concept itself is discernible within the Western Way.
The Akashic Records are a vast computer-bank of the Inner, whose

guardians are the recording gods, Thoth and Hermes. In earlier times, this role was held by Mnemosyne and the Muses (q.v.) who are the guardians of the Well of Memory which the initiate drinks (cf. exercise 2, vol.I). The Hermeticist's task, like that of the shaman, is to tap this memory-system of Hermes and retrieve information not currently available by other means.

Angels. These are the inner protectors of humankind and the helpers of God. They are beings who have never been incarnate, like humanity, and therefore, cannot attain to the perfection of perfected man. They are common to the Middle Eastern mysteries from Sumer onwards. The archangels Raphael, Michael, Gabriel and Uriel are still invoked to protect the ritual temenos of the magician, just as the evangelists, Matthew, Mark, Luke and John are still invoked to guard the beds of sleeping children. The Hebrew version of this protection is given on p. 95. All have their origin in the Babylonian invocation: 'Shamash (sun god) before me, behind me Sin (moon god), Nergal (Underworld god) at my right', Ninil (earth goddess) at my left.' Such invocations are lorica-prayers (breastplates) and are often found in Celtic tradition, notably St Patrick's Breastplate. Dr Dee and Edward Kelly worked out a complex angelic system. Qabala has its own angels and archangels. Exercise 5 will give the beginner a taste of the archangelic qualities as represented by their elements.

REFERENCES: Davidson (63), Dionysius the Areopagite (70), Oxford Dictionary of Nursery Rhymes (252), Wilson (360).

Anima Mundi is the world-soul, the planetary angel or mediator. In Plato's *Timaeus*, she is described as the animating principle of creation. She can be visualized as an angelic figure or as a caring mother who holds her mantle of mercy around the totality of the globe. Christians may wish to visualize her as *Mater Misericordia*, Mother of Mercy, sheltering all human souls under her cloak. Her imagery is closely associated with that of the Shekhina (q.v.) and Sophia (q.v.). Ecologically-minded readers will find that this archetype can be worked with in meditation for the healing of the earth on more than a physical level.

REFERENCES: Plato (265).

Anubis. Son of Nephthys (q.v.) and Osiris (q.v.). He is a form of chthonic Hermes, guardian of the dead, a guide to initiates and to all lonely travellers. He is depicted as a black-skinned man with a jackal's head.

REFERENCES: Hope (147), Lurker (203).

Apocatastasis means the reestablishment or restoration of all things to their primal unity. It was used by the theologian Origen to denote the return of all created things to God, including that which was considered Fallen. The Gnostics saw it as the end of the Aeon when the Logos (q.v.) and Sophia (q.v.) would celebrate their nuptials in the Wedding Chamber of the Pleroma. This concept is found in many traditions within the Western Way. The Zoroastrians call it the *Frasokereti* or 'the making-wonderful' when a saviour would be born of a virgin from the seed of a prophet, and grow up to combat evil and bring an end to the world. Christians understand this as the Day of Judgement when every creature will be judged and either enter heaven or become one with the damned. (Yet 'Christ is risen and there is none dead in the tomb') Qabalists have seen it as the *Tikkun* wherein the breaking of the vessels will be rectified. The final redemption in Judaism is described as the *Tzaftzaf*, or 'breaking-forth', which is referred to as 'spiritual pressure, where one breaks through to a higher level, sensed by the mind.' This concept is closely associated with the partnership of the Syzygies (q.v.)

REFERENCES: Kaplan (167), Origen (246), Rudolph (291) Lossky 200).

Apollo.   His name is said to mean 'appleman' or 'destroyer'. He is closely associated with Mabon (cf.vol.I) in his role as Hyperborean Apollo. For his complex mythos, see Graves (111). He is the son of Zeus and Leto, a daughter of the Titans. His symbol of the lyre was invented by Hermes who gave it to him in return for Apollo's caduceus. Apollo, like Zeus (qv.) is closely associated with the Muses (q.v.). Because he is such an old archetype, his mythos reflects the many changes it has undergone. Hermetically, Apollo is seen with his lyre of seven strings – one who has perceived and represented the keynotes of the seven planets.

REFERENCES: Graves (111), Kerenyi (171).

Asclepios.   The son of Apollo and Coronis, he is the god of healing. He had sanctuaries or Asclepeia at Tricca, Epidaurus, Cos and Pergamus where the patient slept, either on the skin of a sacrificed animal, or near a statue of the god. He appeared to counsel patients in dreams which were subsequently interpreted by an hereditary priestly family. This form of temple sleep can still be performed under Asclepios' aegis either in a consecrated circle or in bed, after having invoked the healing power of sleep. He is shown as a mature bearded man, leaning upon a staff or tree trunk around which winds a serpent. His symbols are the pine-cone, cock and caduceus of healing. He is sometimes shown accompanied by a child in a hooded cloak known as Telesphoros – 'finisher or healer.' Asclepios heals on all levels.

REFERENCES: Kerenyi (172).

Christian Rosenkreutz is the hero of the *Chymical Wedding* and of the Rosicrucian manifesto the *Fama Fraternitatis*. He is the initiate who has entered the Hermetic chamber of the Rosicrucian vault for this time and who has made a compendium of ancient wisdom which all pathwalkers upon the Western Way can utilize. His life, told in the *Fama* relates a parallel one to that of Christ: he travels in the East and is acclaimed by sages; he returns to contact the wisdom of the West and founds the Fraternity of the Rose Cross. The members of the brotherhood travel into many countries, pursuing their various arts, agreeing to meet yearly. The discovery of the Vault or tomb of Rosenkreutz is told in the *Fama*: it is a text of great implication for the hermeticist. Rosenkreutz appears either as a venerable man, in his guise as Master of the Rosicrucian tradition, or else, in the guise of a candidate to the mysteries, as a young man or youth, in simple clothes with crossed red-bands over his shoulders – a similar figure to that of the Fool in the Tarot.

REFERENCES: Allen (6), Knight (178, 184), McLean (208).

Cundrie is the Grail messenger in *Parzival*. She is analogous to the figure of Sovereignty (cf. vol.I, chapter 1) and appears as the Loathly Lady of Celtic tradition. She is the personification of the Waste Land, yet is closely associated with the Shekhina and Sophia (q.v.). In *Parzival* she admonishes King Arthur, saying that his kingship and the fame of the Round Table have been diminished by the behaviour of Parzival who has neglected to ask the Grail Question by which the Wounded King and the Waste Land would be healed. She laments and demands that a champion ride to right this wrong. In the event, Parzival succeeds in his quest, but only at her urging. Cundrie later brings news of the redemptive hope of the Grail's achieving to the Templeisen, as von Eschenbach calls his Grail company. She appears to them dressed in a white wimple, covered by a black hood which is embroidered with golden Turtle-Doves – the sign of the Holy Spirit, of the Divine Feminine principle and of the Grail itself. Her cloak of black can be visualized as having an emerald silk lining, indicative of the emerald stone itself – the Grail. (q.v.) Cundrie is of hideous aspect – a woman of disfigured beauty, lined by grief, yet she is the guardian of the Grail-quest who will accompany the initiate path-walker, and advise him or her. She is a fund of wisdom. Her beauty is restored when the Grail is achieved – although this is not stated within von Eschenbach's story.

REFERENCES: Matthews C. (219), von Eschenbach (344).

Dante.   As Virgil conducted Dante through two of the three regions of existence by virtue of his shamanic experience as poet and underworld-commentator, so Dante may act for our age. A meditative reading of the *Divine Comedy* will give the reader many insights into these realms of states of being. Dante's historical appearance – a scholar's gown with tightly-buttoned sleeves and black hood – are appropriate for visualization purposes.

REFERENCES: Dante (61), Jackson-Knight (153)

Daimon.   The daimon is the inner entity or guardian who guides our steps or inspires us. (In this volume we have discussed the daimon in a particular sense as pertaining to the inner masculine quality which Jungians call the *animus*, but here we consider it in its general sense.) Much like the angel, the daimon is the psychopompos of the soul and the mouthpiece of the inspiring god. Orpheus may be seen as a type of daimon, or the Agathodaimon (q.v.) who, like the Good Shepherd, leads the soul through the tangled paths of the worlds. Plato's daimon is discussed by Plutarch. In Roman myth every man had his *genius* and every woman her *Juno*: a concept similar to the Jungian anima and animus. The character of the daimon is as the inner helper for the hermeticist. The Tibetan concept of the personal inner deity or *yidam* is the Eastern equivalent of the daimon.

The word daimon is often confused with *demon*, which is, indeed, a diminishment of the archetype by those who make the gods into the demons of succeeding generations. The concept of the medieval magician who conjures demons to do his will is a faint memory of an adept working in close harmony with the daimon.

REFERENCES: St Augustine (14), Plato (265), Plutarch (271).

Demeter/Cybele/Rhea. The name of Demeter means 'mother', and she mediates the initiatory sacrifice of motherhood to the initiate. Her mythos was taken and amalgamated with that of Isis so that there are many resonances between the two stories. She is the bountiful earth. With Kore and Hecate, she forms a powerful triplicity of goddessly energies. Her search and mourning over the lost Kore is at the core of the Eleusinian mysteries which she instigated during her exilic wandering. She strove to make an immortal out of Triptolemus, the child of her host, but initiated him instead into the mysteries of agriculture, by which the barren earth is rendered fruitful by good husbandry. In her sorrowful aspect she appears as the Black Demeter of Phygala, and is thus closely associated with the goddesses Cybele and Rhea. Rhea was the Titaness married to Cronos (cf. vol. I). She alone, with Metis, escaped the banishment of the Titans when Zeus her son contended with them. She, like her Asiatic counterpart, Cybele, is a mountain-mother, a wielder of Titanic force, like the Celtic Cailleach Beare (vol. I). Cybele's mythos deals with an earlier resonance of Demeter's sacrificial motherhood and is not as suitably regenerate as hers. Hecate seems to have taken over the more terrifying aspects of Cybele and Rhea as a goddess of the cross-roads and of wild beasts. Demeter appears as a mother with barley-sheaves, usually accompanied by Kore and Hecate. Rhea is a massive, seated figure of hieratic power. Cybele appears in a chariot drawn by lions. The image of the Tarot Empress is an objective form for beginners to work with.

REFERENCES: Graves (111), Pausanius (256), Vermaseren (339), Lucian (202)

Demiurge. In Plato, the demiurge or creator had none of the malefic overtones associated with the Gnostic demiurge or false god. He was seen as a benign creator in the *Timaeus*. The Christian image of God the Father has been much devalued because of its association with a white-bearded patriarch who has become a tetchy demiurge after the Gnostic model, akin to William Blake's Old Nobodaddy. However, the reader can initiate a rerouting of this false image by meditation, if he or she considers the statue from Chartres Cathedral showing God lovingly creating Adam from the dust: or a reading of Proverbs 8 will provide the image of God creating the world with the help of the Shekhina/Sophia (q.v.) who is described as 'master-workman' delighting in creation. Hermeticists who are non-Christian might wish to consider working with the Egyptian forms, *Khnum or Ptah*.

Khnum created children upon his potter's wheel and implanted the seed in the mother's belly. He was called 'Father of father and mother of mothers.' He is depicted as a ram-headed god. Ptah was the 'master of gold smelters and goldsmiths.' His temple was called the goldsmithy and his priest had names like, 'the Great Wielder of the Hammer' or 'he who knows the Secrets of the Goldsmiths.' Ptah is the craftsman-god who appears as a closely-wrapped figure, with a tightly-fitting cap, carrying a sceptre with the *djed* or sacred-tree symbol on it.

The images of God as Creator have received the fearful projections of many ages and this archetype stands in need of much positive meditation if the true energy of creation is to flow smoothly. The Gnostic demiurge is analogous to Satan or the Devil in Christian terminology: it is terrible that a misapplication of symbolism should confuse God and God's antagonist. Contrary to popular belief, pathwalkers of the Western Way do not pray to or invoke the devil. The dualism of God and Devil has severely hampered the Christian tradition: the problems of good and evil are best considered within a reading of the book of Job.

REFERENCES: Blake (27), Lurker (203), Plato (267), Rudolph (291).

Dionysius.   As Dionysius Sabazius, he is the breaker-in-pieces, the Western equivalent of Shiva. Yet he is himself rent in pieces by the Titans. This was a feature of his mysteries where a bull-calf (some say a child) was torn apart, and eaten raw. His devotees were the Maenads, frenzied, inspired women whose rites good citizens took care to avoid. Dionysius has the chaotic power of Cybele (q.v.) and should be invoked cautiously. His appearance may be as a rather dark man with long hair and beard, with richly embroided robes, in his Underworld aspect, enthroned with his consort Ariadne, whom he raised to immortality as his bride. He also appears as the young lord of the hunt, his nakedness casually draped with a panther-skin, in his hand a thrysos or pine-cone tipped wand. He is also called the 'child of the double door' signifying his joint birth from the womb of Semele, his mother, and from the thigh of Zeus (q.v.) his father. Yet this title also denotes the two births of the initiate: the physical and initiatory births.

REFERENCES: Danielou (60), Graves (111), Otto (248).

Elijah Enoch Metatron. Elijah is the great wonder-working prophet of Jewish tradition. (I Kings 17ff) He ascends to heaven in a fiery chariot and passes his succession to his disciple, Elisha, who prays for a double share of his master's spirit. Elijah then enters the seventh hall of God and perceives the divine will. From then onwards he is a master or prophetic guardian of tradition. He appears in times of danger to comfort and lead the way to justice. As a co-worker with God, he helps all who call on his name. With Enoch he guards the seventh level of paradise. At the seder table (the Jewish passover supper) Elijah is invited to join the guests: 'Elijah opens up for us the realm of mystery and wonder. Let us now open the door for Elijah.' He anounces the Messianic promise to creation. He can be envisaged as a prophet in desert dress, venerable and bearded, yet not aged. His oracular bird is the raven. His Islamic name, Khidir, means Green One. He is 'the psychopomp whose duty is to stand at the crossways of Paradise and guide the pious to their appointed places.' He has been identified with the archangel Metatron (q.v.)

Enoch, who guards the gates of paradise with Elijah is called Idris in Islam. His name means 'dedicated or initiated'. He never tasted death. He oversees and instructs the world and is identified with the archangel Metatron. His journey through the regions of the inner and outer worlds is found in the apocryphal *Book of Enoch*, which has awesome prophecies regarding the end of the world. Enoch is known among the Mandaens as Anosh.

Metatron is the greatest of the archangels. His stature is 'equal to the breadth of the whole world,' – which was the stature of Adam (q.v.) before the Fall. Clearly, Metatron is identifiable with the Body of Light. He stands at the gate of Kether on the Tree of Life and can be visualized as a shining angelic form with many wings.

REFERENCES: Bronstein (32), Davidson (63), Book of Enoch (31), Halevi (129).

Fisher King/Wounded King. The wounded king of the Grail cycle. All partake of the Grail mystery but he – his suffering suspends him between the worlds. He is at once identifiable with the wounded land, with the Grail guardian and with Christ. The *Corpus Christi Carol* is sung of him. He usually appears as an ancient, wasted figure, lying on a bed. To offer the cup of healing to him is to work for the mending of all riven things. He is the wound in creation, which only the highest form of self-sacrifice can restore. He cannot relinquish his role as Grail Guardian until the Grail-achiever comes to take his place.

REFERENCES: Matthews (219), Stewart (322).

Four Holy Living Creatures/Elemental Guardians. These mighty correspondences are best understood as guardians of the cosmic year. They are applied in many traditions, as below. They appear in Ezekiel's vision, and then are applied to the Four Evangelists in Christian tradition.

Vision of Ezekiel	Evangelist	Qabalistic World	Element	Fixed Zodiacal Sign
Man	St Matthew	Aziluth	Fire	Aquarius
Lion	St Mark	Yetzirah	Water	Leo
Bull	St Luke	Assiah	Earth	Taurus
Eagle	St John	Briah	Air	Scorpio

REFERENCES: Halevi (129), Knight (182)

Grail. The vessel of redemption, knowledge and fulfilment. It is sought everywhere on quest, but achieved by few. It is not a physical object, although real cups, chalices and cauldrons partake of its virtues as the inner symbol superimposes over them by means of worship or cult focus. It is a powerful resource for meditation and many pathworkings can be made from the texts available. It is important to followers of the Western Way because it unites Native with Hermetic traditions in its forms as cauldron and alchemical stone. It represents a passing forward into other realms and gives direct access to the Higher Mysteries.

REFERENCES: Jung. E. and von Franz (166), Knight (185), Malory (216) Matthews J. (220, 221,) Matthews. J. and Green (222), Quest of the Holy Grail (277), Perlesvaus (258).

Hermaphrodite.   The perfected Great Work is symbolized by this figure, sometimes also called the Rebus or Androgyne. Rather than being seen as a blatantly sexual anomaly, the ancients realized the hermaphrodite as the summation of perfection. Exercise 8 gives a meditative use of this figure. The word is a conflation of the god Hermes with the goddess Aphrodite, and can be considered as the symbol of the yin-yang in the West.

REFERENCES: Fabricus (79)

Hermes is the messenger of the gods, the guardian of travellers and imparter of wisdom. He invented the lyre and exchanged it for the caduceus of Apollo, with which he cared for the celestial herds. He can be visualized as Roman Mercury, with winged sandals, cap and caduceus, or as Agathodaimon (q.v.). He lays his staff upon the eyes of the dead and is sometimes called 'the whisperer'. As chthonic Hermes he is the keeper of wisdom and ancient knowledge, coming in dreams and meditation to impart his secrets. As *Thoth-Tehuti*, he is seen as the inventor of the Egyptian system of hieroglyphs and the keeper of the book of initiation. Hermetically, he can be seen as on the famous pavement at Siena; a mature figure in heavy robes, with a high pointed cap.

REFERENCES: Graves (111), Kerenyi (176), Mead (227).

Horus/Harpocrates.   Horus is the child of the Aeon (q.v.), the son of Isis and Osiris, from a union effected by Isis after Osiris' death and dismemberment. Horus' symbols are the two eyes of moon and sun, or he is seen as a hawk-headed man. As a child he appears seated in a lotus, with his finger to his lip, signifying silence. He shares the symbolisms of Apollo and Mabon. (vol I)

REFERENCES: Hope (147), Lurker (203).

Isis.   Isis is the divine saviour goddess, her power alone brought together the scattered fragments of her brother/husband's body, emblematic of the unification of the Body of Light. Her cult spread throughout the Roman world as far as Britain. Like the Lady Mary, she subsumes all lesser manifestations of the Divine Feminine Principle under her cloak. She is a particularly relevant archetype for the present age, being a comprehensive manifestation of the Goddess. Her influence continues to the present day. The Fellowship of Isis, a world-wide network of all pathwalkers who acknowledge the Divine Feminine, was founded in Ireland in the 1970s. Isis appears dressed in white robes with rainbow-like translucence, with an ankh or systrum in her hand. Her girdle is knotted in a distinctive way, making the shape of an ankh-shaped loop. A beautiful invocation to Isis and her many aspects can be read in Apuleius. (cf. fig. 11)

REFERENCES: Apuleius (11), Hope (147), Plutarch (270), Witt (361).

Joseph of Arimathea. The wise Jew who gave Christ burial in his own tomb, and who provided the shroud. He also collected the blood and water from the side of Christ at the Deposition from the Cross, in two cruets – the earliest form of the Christian Grail. After the crucifixion, Joseph was imprisoned for many years and kept alive only by the Grail which he had with him. He was instructed secretly by Christ during his captivity, and fled to Europe with his family to found a line of Grail guardians. He is said variously to have landed in France or, more usually, come to Glastonbury where he founded the first Christian church, in honour of the Lady Mary (q.v.). He is the contact for Grail wisdom.

REFERENCES: de Borron (64), Matthews, J. (221) Apocryphal New Testament (10)

Just Ones/Sibyls/Prophets. The 'Lamed-Vau' or thirty-six hidden saints are those for whom the world exists, according to Jewish tradition. They reveal themselves in times of danger. They keep the world in balance, as mediators between the worlds. Like the angels, the sibyls and prophets can be seen as totally Inner figures, but their role is also a grade of inner-working which those still incarnate may attain to. Like the Just Ones, they are as the hidden inspirers and sustainers of the earth. (cf. 153) They can be visulized as a double choir who sing the song of creation antiphonally. Jan van Eyck's picture of *The Adoration of the Lamb*, may serve as an inspiration for this visualization, or they can be seen after a more Classical Greek mode as a chorus of men and women who chant the mighty themes of the story.

REFERENCES: Schwartz-Bart (300)

Logos.   The Logos is the word of God, just as Sophia (q.v.) is the wisdom of God. Gnostics, Platonists and Christians have all used this concept. St John's Gospel (chapter 1) will give much for meditation. For practical purposes, the Logos can be visualized as Christ the King – crowned, robed in glory and standing triumphant upon the cross, or as Christ Pantocrator, Lord of the Earth, with an open book. The Logos comes to ransom the soul in order that he may unite with his syzygy: gnostically, with Sophia; or, in the Christian tradition, with the individual souls of the created faithful in the person of Lady Mary. His energy is that of God the Son and Wayshower. The following chant is his promise:

> Send me, O Father!
> Seals in my hands, I will descend;
> Through Aeons universal will I make a Path;
> Through Mysteries all I'll open up a way!
> And Forms of Gods will I display;
> The secrets of the Holy Paths I will hand on,
> And call them Gnosis.

REFERENCES: Mead (227), Rudolph (291).

Mary, Lady: The Blessed Virgin. Just as Isis subsumes all earlier goddesses under her aegis, so Mary comprehends all the goddessly aspects of the Divine Feminine throughout the world. Wherever a Goddess shrine was located, under the Christian dispensation the shrine's original focus is remembered by Our Lady of (that place). She shows us God as Mother. Although orthodox theology does not admit her a goddess and accords her honours such as are shown to angels and saints, Lady Mary is enshrined in the hearts of the faithful with a special love because she shows them the face of their first homely Mother. She can be visualized in either of three aspects which correspond to the three mysteries of the Rosary: as a young maiden dressed in white with a blue cloak; as the sorrowing mother in black, at the foot of the cross; or as the Woman Clothed with the Sun (Revelations 12).

Mary Magdalene.   One of the female disciples of Jesus who discovered his Resurrection and declared it to the disciples hiding in the Upper Room. The loyalty and special place of Mary Magdalene is of so impressive a character that it has passed into folklore – often to the extent of making her Christ's physical consort. She shares the virtues of Sophia (q.v.) and of Cundrie (q.v.). She knows Christ's inner teachings and is trusted with them by him, although the other disciples complain that she is only a woman. Her reputation of a reformed prostitute is due to her identification with the Penitent woman in St Mark 14. She and Lady Mary, the Virgin, are the female pillars flanking the Incarnation of Christ, just as the two Josephs – Lady Mary's husband and of Arimathea, are the male pillars. Mary can be visualized as a woman of mature beauty, with long unbound hair, and a green cloak.

REFERENCES: Baigent (18), Bible (26), Rudolph (291) Nag Hammadi (239)

Melchizedek was the priest-king who came to welcome Abraham after his victory over the Kings of Edom, with gifts of bread and wine. This is seen as a type of the Eucharist and of the Eternal High priesthood of Christ. Melchizedek is hermetically considered to be an inner master because he had neither 'beginning of days nor end of life.' He is regarded to have come from the planet Venus bringing honey and asbestos. His motif is woven into the Grail legends. His is a strong and high contact which will bring the reader into the presence of eternal things. He can be seen as in the statue outside Chartres Cathedral, bearing a cup in which can be seen a stone or piece of bread, and crowned as a king.

REFERENCES: Bible (26), Matthews (221), Fortune (96)

Merlin.   The archetypal magus of the Western Way, he is the genius of Britain and guide to many inner realms. He can appear as a white-bearded sage, a beautiful youth or as a savage wildman. His contact can be productive of prophetic insight and he is especially important to the Western Way because he stands behind the Native mystery impulse and yet has strong affinities to the Hermetic path. His origins are obscure, but his name means 'from the sea' and he has been identified with an Atlantean master.

Fig. 16   Orpheus and the Nine Muses

REFERENCES: Knight (185), Tolstoy (331).

Mithras.   God of creativity and light, he bears a strong resembl-
ance, in his mythos, to Christ as Divine Child born at the Winter
Solstice. As a slain god his symbol is that of the bull, the raven and Sol
Invictus (the Triumphant Sun). His cult was very much a male-
oriented one which had a series of initiatory grades: the Crow, the
Secret, the Soldier, the Lion, the Persian, the Runner-of-the-Sun, the
Father and the Father of Fathers. Mithras usually appears as a youth,

dressed in Phrygian cap and short tunic: he is an excellent overseer of esoteric training, upon which his followers set great store.

REFERENCES: Godwin (104), Cumont (59), Vermaseren (340), Mead (225)

Mnemosyne and the Muses.   Zeus lay with Mnemosyne for nine nights and she later gave birth to the nine muses (cf. fig. 15). She is 'memory as the cosmic ground of self-recalling.' Her dual role is of memory and of forgetfulness (Lethe). These aspects are combined in exercise 2 of volume I. The Muses do the work of the sibyls. When they all sing, sky, stars, seas and rivers stand still to listen. They can appear in bird-shape or as imaged in the Mantegna tarot. Their names, patronage and symbolic representations are given below. Their energies have been greatly neglected since the Hermetic revival of the Renaissance, but there appear no subsequent forms or symbolic representations which can replace these:

MUSE	PATRON OF	SYMBOLS
Clio (giver of fame)	History	heroic trumpet and waterclock
Euterpe (giver of joy)	Flute-Playing	flute
Thalia (festive)	Comedy	shepherd's crook and comic mask
Melpomene (the singer)	Tragedy	Tragic mask and Hercules' club
Terpsicore (she who dances)	Lyric Poetry and dance	cithara
Erato (awakener of desire)	Love poetry	tambourine
Polyhymnia (she of many hymns)	Storytelling and heroic hymns	lyre or portative organ
Urania (the heavenly)	Astronomy	celestial globe and compasses
Calliope (of the beautiful voice)	Epic poetry	stylus and tablets

References: Kerenyi (173), McLean (209).

Nephthys.   the sister of Isis. Her function, like that of St Brigid (vol. I) to the Virgin, is to be the midwife and guardian of the Holy Child. She has the ability to be a revealer of hidden things, according to Hope. She appears as the supporter of Isis, her arms protectively raised: her head-dress has the basket of offering upon it, which is her symbol. She can be seen as an inner guardian of Isis' veiled role as Mistress of the Mysteries.

REFERENCES: Hope (147)

Orpheus.   His early beginnings bear traces of the Thracian shaman. Ovid's *Metamorphoses* gives a romantic story of his descent to Hades to reclaim his wife Eurydice. Like Hermes and Thoth, he often appears as a spokesman for the gods. His reappearance in medieval times as Sir or King Orpheo established him in Native Tradition as a harrower of the underworld, a visitant to Faery. The Orpheus of the Renaissance is the spirit of music incarnate, the master of the muses. Tamino, in Mozart's *The Magic Flute* is based on Orpheus: he wins through the tangled webs of the Queen of Night in order to rescue Pamina. Orpheus is an oracular god, after the manner of Bran the Blessed (cf. vol I). His dismemberment and beheading make him one with Osiris and others (q.v.). Ficino restores Orpheus as psychopompos, divine intermediary and celestial musician. He appears very like Apollo, of whom he is a close resonance. Traditionally he is depicted as singing in the wilderness, surrounded by enthralled beasts, or, as in fig. 16, with the muses.

REFERENCES: Warden (353), Ovid (249), Orphic Hymns (247).

Osiris.   The brother and consort of Isis, Osiris is one of many verdant gods who is cut down. His mythos is in Plutarch. His appearance as a green-skinned figure in white wrappings reminds us of his nature, as does his symbol of the *djed* or Tree, in which, according to some legends, he is shut. Like John Barleycorn and others, he is 'the grain of wheat' which must fall into the earth in order to bear seed.

REFERENCES: Budge (34), Hope (147), Plutarch (270)

Persephone.   is the Underworld name of the Kore (which means maiden). She descends to the Underworld, abducted by Hades, the

King of that realm. She changes her nature rapidly from that of maiden to chthonic hag, and while she is under the earth, Demeter mourns and winter reigns. But she is the merciful maiden and is hospitable to the initiate who takes the Underworld journey. Her appearance can be as a Spring Maiden of hieratic stillness and simplicity, or else as a heavily robed queen with black glittering diadem upon her head; her unbraided hair frozen into lines of icy water. Her Underworld aspect should not be shunned, since the initiate must go the way of the White Cypress to the Well of Memory within Persephone's realm or turn back from the mysteries.

REFERENCES: Graves (111), Matthews, C. (218), Stewart (322), Fortune (93, 94)

Prester John.   The mysterious Christian king of the East. He is the son of Parzival's half-brother, Feirfiz and Repanse de Schoye. A description of his kingdom and its strange inhabitants (the phoenix and unicorn) show it to have been a type of Paradise. The Grail is sometimes described as being kept there in a great temple, and Prester John is considered by some to be the Grail-guardian for our own age. Sometimes he appears as a glorious king in rich robes and with a triple crown, but more usually as a young man in a plain white robe whose features have a slight Middle-Eastern cast. He holds the keys to several inner landscapes including that of the Eastern Grail and the paradisal home.

REFERENCES: Matthews. J. (220, 221), Silverberg (308).

Prometheus brought fire from heaven. He is considered to be the Titan who created humanity and who resisted their planned destruction by Zeus (q.v.) The sufferings of the world were visited upon him because of his championship of the earth's inhabitants: he was chained to a pillar where a vulture tore out his liver all day throughout eternity, although every night the liver would grow again. With the exiled Shekhina (q.v.) he represents the pain of incarnation but he is ever hopeful of humanity's potential. He is a mighty man and a rugged wielder of the earth's elements. He stole fire from heaven to give to man in a hollow fennel stalk. This symbol of the upheld stalk has been reversed to become the symbol of nuclear disarmament, whether consciously or not. It might well serve as a useful symbol of meditation.

REFERENCES: Kerenyi (173), Graves (111).

Psyche.   The story of Cupid and Psyche is told in Apuleius, where it may be meditated upon. Beautiful Psyche is a type of the soul, which is what her name signifies. She marries the god Cupid, but lies with him in darkness. Her sisters suggest that she is wed to a monster and at their bidding she secretes a lamp to reveal the beautiful god sleeping. She incurs the jealousy of Venus, Cupid's mother and, as in the folkstory the world over, she has to perform impossible tasks. She achieves these with Cupid's help and is made immortal. The story has been retold by C.S. Lewis in a way which points many features concerning the interrelationship of the Goddess's light and dark aspects.

REFERENCES: Apuleius (11), Lewis (194), Knight (184)

Saints.   St Paul calls them 'a great cloud of witnesses'. In the early Church, all Christians were saints, but the title was latterly reserved to those who merited honour by their holy lives. All manner of humanity is represented by the saints. Most people in the Christian West are given the names of saints to be their Inner world patrons. Many energies are represented under the patronage of saints which would once have been associated with gods: their patronage can be invoked still by prayer and meditation, and they can serve as guardians for the pathwalker. They can be seen as facets of a mighty crystal which is the Body of Christ.

Seth.   As the inheritor of Adam's paradisal experience, Seth has been a figure of redemptive hope to many traditions: his descendants, both earthly and spiritual, partake of the Gnosis of life. Among the Mandaens, Seth is called Shitil and at death, the soul must outweigh his purity if it is to enter into the kingdom of light. He can be envisaged as a tall, strong man whose form is almost angelic. His head is intelligent and between his brow is a flame of light, representing his state of inner illumination. He is one of the guardians of Gnosis.

REFERENCES: Nag Hammadi (239), Quinn (278), Rudolph (291).

Shekhina is the Jewish figure of wisdom. She 'brings the gift of the queen to them that wander with her in exile.' (121) She is God as

Spirit, the co-worker at Creation. (Proverbs 8) She represents the emanatory presence of God among created life, and so is closely associated with both Sophia (q.v.) and Anima Mundi. Her symbolism bears traces of earlier Goddess cults. She is the Pillar of Cloud by day and a Pillar of Fire by night which accompanied the Ark of the Covenant in the desert. She is the cloud on the sanctuary in the temple of Solomon. She is best visualized in these images, or as a mighty pair of wings which are outstretched over one's head. (cf. prayer on p. 95). However she is also seen as a sorrowful widow who walks the road in exile, like Isis or Demeter (q.v.).

REFERENCES: Patai (255)

Sophia.   Divine Wisdom herself and syzygy of the Logos (q.v.), Sophia can be found, under many forms, throughout the world. Iconographically she is represented as a winged angelic figure dressed in red and gold, with a diadem on her head, and with the world at her feet. The Temple of Wisdom, Exercise 3, will give the reader a direct contact with her. She 'dwells with all flesh' according to the gift of God and therefore can be the possession and heritage of all living things.

REFERENCES: Nag Hammadi (239), Rudolph (291), Bible (26).

Syzygies are divine partners or consorts, according to the Gnostics. Sophia and Logos are the prime syzygies (q.v.) but Solomon and Sheba can be seen as a type of this concept, representing the union of knowledge with wisdom. William Blake's theory of emanations, which was probably derived ultimately from Eastern sources, represents a Western view of the Shiva/Shakti union in his *Jerusalem* poem which shows a system of deities and their consorts. In alchemy, the union of the syzygies is shown in the image of the *coniunctio* or the *hieros gamos*, the holy wedding.

REFERENCES: Blake (27), Rudolph (291).

Zeus, who subdued his father Uranos by castrating him, seems to have taken on the mantle of the evil demiurge. Yet he is aptly named *Pantomorphos* – of many forms. Like Math and Gwydion (cf. vol. I) Zeus is a shape-shifter. His many amours and unions should not be seen in a fundamental light, but as reflecting the divine union with all life. As a type of the Norse god Odin, Zeus lies with Mnemosyne (q.v.) for nine nights, just as Odin hangs on the windy Tree for nine days and nights: both are initiates of the mystery knowledge. Zeus is married to divine female representations of the three Native levels of existence: the Underworld – Persephone; the earth – Maia; and of heaven – Hera, and so he has knowledge of the three realms like the shamanic Odin who comprehends the three levels of the World Tree, Yggdrasil. Zeus may appear in any form, as stated, but his symbol of the thunderbolt suggests his power. He can be visualized as the Emperor card of the Tarot.

REFERENCES: Graves (111), Kore Kosmou (186), Kerenyi (173).

THE HERMETIC LANDSCAPE

Everyone has an inner landscape: 'the way to this place – and the place itself – have been unknown for a long time, and it is hidden from the greatest part of the world. But notwithstanding that it be difficult and laborious to discover this way and place, yet the place should be sought after,' wrote Thomas Vaughan in his *Lumen de Lumine* (338). If you have already attempted the Two Trees Meditation in volume one you will have begun to see certain facets of the Otherwordly landscape which is the inner reality of the Native Tradition. Such mapping can take many years until real familiarity is achieved. You may perhaps have noticed how certain locations appear over the years in your dreams – these represent the personal landscape which may impinge upon the greater archetypal reality of a tradition.

Just as the Native Tradition has its Otherworld, so the Hermetic Tradition has its own landscape. But whereas the Otherworld is rarely depicted, the Hermetic landscape has frequently made its appearance within the emblematic designs of both magical and alchemical texts. If we return for a short while to the Otherworld, we will remember that one of the aspects of the Native Tradition's inner reality is that of the island-paradise or garden. Aspects of this can be seen within medieval illuminations: angels sporting in paradise, fantastic beasts prancing in the Garden of Earthly Delights as in Bosch's picture. The image of the garden is common to both Native and Hermetic Traditions, and here we can step from one reality into another. The fusion of otherworlds is achieved by the connecting impulse of Rosicrucian and alchemical imagery which used earlier symbologies on which to base their own inner explorations. The result is a compelling mixture of the two.

The key image of this mixture keeps its perfume:

> O no man knows
> Through what wild centuries
> Roves back the rose. (347)

The rose is a signature of the tranquil continuity of the esoteric tradition: wherever it grows, there the tradition flourishes. Esoteric knowledge has been personified as a beautiful veiled maiden who must be sought by the lover of wisdom. This identification has made it possible to address the Virgin as 'rosa mystica', or, in the words of the Song of Songs: 'a garden locked is my sister, my bride.' There is no way into the *hortus conclusus* save by love, by desire to find the hidden rose which grows within. That which is spoken by 'sub rosa' is 'under the rose' – the knowledge which is transmitted only within the hidden garden itself, the wisdom which is freely given by the beloved to the lover. In alchemy the rose symbolizes this wisdom and the *rosarium* – the rose garden – symbolizes the Great Work itself. The symbol of the Rosicrucians is the Rose-Cross: the rose of the spirit blooming upon the cross of the elements – a symbol also of the marriage between pagan and Christian streams. Before the rosa mystica became the symbol of the Ever-Virgin Mother, it was the Lady Venus' sign. (217)

The garden makes its easy transition as an inner landscape for both Native and Hermetic traditions through the medium of not only pictorial representation, but also through the works of poets and mystics. From the medieval allegory of *La Romaunt de la Rose*, where the poet's quest is for the rose itself, down to Edmund Spenser's *Fairy Queen*, the Otherworldly paradise slowly becomes transformed. Enclosed within the intricate knot-gardens of sixteenth- and seventeenth-century Europe the spiritual journey is enacted by Christian in Bunyan's *Pilgrim's Progress* and by Christian Rosenkreutz in *The Chymical Wedding* (178). The esotericist makes his or her way along the ceremonial mazes, planted in mimicry of spiritual progresses. Trees, arbours and herbs are planted according to planetary correspondences, so that the microcosmic *hortus conclusus* mirrors the macrocosmic garden of the heavens.

Within the landscape are the hermit's oratory, the alchemist's laboratory, the astrological tower from which planetary movements are observed and computed. There are lakes, streams and cunning displays of water which fountain from Classical water deities and from creatures of the deep. Sometimes the overtly Hermetic nature of the garden is apparent as at Edzell Castle, Angus, Scotland, where a garden of the planets can still be seen (212), or as in the now desolate gardens devised by Salomon De Caus for the Elector Palatine at Heidelberg. (210)

Beyond the places of habitation, in the wilder and inaccessible regions stands the Mountain of Initiation – sometimes called Mount Abiegnus or the Invisible Magic Mountain, where the initiate stakes his or her adepthood in pilgrimage and discovery. As in the Kingdom of Prester John, here, too, the traveller encounters beasts which seem proper to the pages of heraldic and alchemical scrolls – the green lion, the crow, the unicorn and the phoenix. Here sits the pelican in her piety and there soars the crowned eagle. Each beast symbolizes a secret process to be undergone. The traveller finds the way by means of sigils graven in the rock which indicate some part of the way. The totemic symbols of the Hermetic Tradition are as powerful and elusive as those ancestral totems which we sought in volume one.

These are but some of the aspects of the Hermetic landscape, waiting to be discovered. Just as Books of Hours presented Biblical scenes with glowing intensity for the active participation of the faithful in the Middle Ages, so do the emblem books of Hermetic allegory reveal a rich mine for our own meditation. *The Western Mandala*, by Adam McLean, (213) is a particularly good starting point for the apprentice Hermeticist, but more and more alchemical texts complete with their illustrations are being made available. Imaginative work with some of these will present further opportunities to enter the Hermetic landscape and explore deeper. The means of entry can be the black and white pillars of the Tree of Life, which can be visualized as a gateway before you. Your guide should be a personage appropriate to the scene to be contemplated: Hermes or Christian Rosenkreutz, for instance.

But the emblem books are not the only sources to which we can go for inspiration. The Tarot, which is now interpreted in the light of modern consciousness, is really a book of medieval emblems which embody important aspects of the esoteric world-model: the grim reaper of death, the rota of Fortune's Wheel, the savage, sublunary world of the Moon card. The four suits represent the four elements. In stylized forms they give us a glimpse into another part of the Hermetic landscape. The origins of the Tarot have been a vexed

question in esoteric circles. The argument that they derive from
Egyptian sources can be traced to the rediscovery of things Egyptian
which motivated the French esoteric world at the time of Napoleon's
Egyptian campaign, when the Rosetta Stone was deciphered. This,
like the translation of the Corpus Hermeticum in the fifteenth
century, led to a series of revivalist inventions (cf. chapter 1). Paul
Christian (48) gives a splendid pathworking in his *History of Magic*
in which the reader is asked to imagine the initiation of a candidate
within the Great Pyramid wherein all the images of the Major
Trumps are operative. The initiate goes along a route, rather like a
man in a Ghost-Train, meeting frightful, fearful and tempting images
which he overcomes by means of the Major Trumps – failing only if
he cannot comprehend the lesson of each trump. A similar pathworking, along Gypsy-lines appears in Basil Rakoczi's book *Fortune
Telling*, wherein the reader goes through the three caverns of initiation. (281)

Adam McLean has suggested an alternative source for the development of European tarot – one which is essentially Western in
origin. (209) His study of the Mantegna tarot (c.1465) is persuasive.
These cards, which number fifty in total, emanate from the School of
Ferrara and are based upon the Platonic academies of the mid-
fifteenth century Renaissance. The cards are split into five decades,
representing a) the conditions of life from beggar to pope; b) the nine
muses and Apollo; c) the seven liberal arts, including philosophy,
poetry and theology; d) the seven cardinal virtues, with the spirits of
astronomy, chronology and cosmology; and e) the celestial hierarchy
of the seven planets together with the eighth sphere, the primum
mobile and the First Cause. Despite the different entitling of the
cards, their symbology is remarkably similar to traditional packs.
The card representing Mars in the fifth decade, for instance, is
identical to the Chariot; Jupiter stands in a mandorla, like the World.
Obvious qualities like Justice and Strength are almost identical.
Whereas the conditions of life decade give us the Fool from the
beggar, and the Magician, who is like the artisan with his table and
tools of the trade. The squire and knight pass into the minor trumps.

Although there are fragmentary tarot packs dating from before
this time which follow the traditional schema, it is interesting to
conjecture just what kind of symbolism is common to both. The
Mantegna tarot shows the basic virtues, qualities, cosmologies,
abilities and conditions of human life which were the unwritten
norms of medieval life. These images were familiar to all, even the

unlettered. Look through your own tarot pack with new eyes: just what kind of symbolism and culture created this book of wisdom, which its numerous archetypes? With the key of the Mantegna tarot we can unlock many of these mysteries for our own time. Few modern tarots have succeeded in replacing the old symbolism with one which is efficient in our own age. The mighty archetypes behind the major trumps are now commercially mangled in the mouths of latter-day tarot-readers who, in striving to bring the cosmic message to their clients, reduce even the microcosmic message of the tarot to a handful of glib material applications. It is possible to enter each card as though it were a picture, explore the scene and speak with the archetype. In this way, the tarot can become an initiatory system. (120)

As with the Tarot, so with the Qabala. To the uninitiated, the Tree of Life appears like an underground map – a two-dimensional set of blobs connected by lines. But each of the sephiroth is a multi-dimensional place and is as real a destination as Oxford Circus or Île de la Cité. In a book of this size it is imposible to indicate the possibilities of exploring such a complex glyph as the Tree of Life. The reader is referred to *A Practical Guide to Qabalistic Symbolism* by Gareth Knight (183), where the correspondences and inner symbolism may be more readily explored. Here is a vast field of exploration indeed, which has occupied both Hebrew and Gentile Qabalists for centuries. There is no one method of applying correspondences – you find some of your own, but here the way-showers have been many and the multiplicity of signposts may prove confusing. The Qabala gives a unique method of exploring the Hermetic landscape in that its system is also a way of life, for those who can realize its possibilties.

The Tree of Life is a depiction of the Man of Light, Adam Kadmon, in whom the ten prime attributes of God are manifest. (127) These may also be seen as the emanations for the many archetypes which are used in magical workings (cf. figs 3 and 7). The Middle Pillar of the Tree is the spine of Adam Kadmon upon which the Western equivalent of the chakras are to be found. The side pillars of Mercy and Severity, the white and black pillars, are the right and left sides of Adam Kadmon. The totality of the Tree of Life is a macrocosmic Body of Light. Any exploration which we make within this wondrous universal glyph is a discovery of ourselves also.

There are many more systems and symbolic paradigms in the Hermetic Tradition, which the reader can explore in similar ways.

CHART OF CORRESPONDENCES UPON THE TREE OF LIFE

no of sephira	planetary image	virtue	vice	magical image
1. Kether	Primum Mobile	attainment of the Great Work	none	An ancient bearded king in profile
2. Chokmah	The Zodiac	devotion	none	A bearded man, a father
3. Binah	Saturn	silence	avarice	A mature woman, a mother
X. Daath	Sirius	selfless perception	spiritual pride	A head with a male and female countenance facing in either direction
4. Chesed	Jupiter	obedience	bigotry, tyranny	A strong king, crowned, seated on a throne
5. Geburah	Mars	courage	cruelty	A warrior in a chariot
6. Tiphareth	The Sun	devotion to the Great Work	pride	A child, king or sacrificed god
7. Netzach	Venus	unselfishness	lust	A beautiful naked woman
8. Hod	Mercury	truthfulness	dishonesty	A hermaphrodite
9. Yesod	The Moon	independence	idleness	A beautiful naked man of strength
10. Malkuth	The Earth	discrimination	inertia	A young woman, crowned, seated on a throne

Chart of correspondences upon the Tree of Life

No. of sephira:	Planetary image:	Virtue:	Vice:	Magical image:
1 Kether	Primum mobile	attainment of the great work	none	An ancient bearded king in profile
2 Chokmah	The zodiac	devotion	none	A bearded man, a father
3 Binah	Saturn	silence	avarice	A mature woman, a mother
X Daath	Sirius	selfless perfection	spiritual pride	A head with a male and female countenance facing in either direction
4 Chesed	Jupiter	obedience	bigotry tyranny	A strong king, crowned, seated on a throne
5 Geburah	Mars	courage	cruelty	A warrior in a chariot
6 Tiphareth	The sun	devotion to the great work	pride	A child, king or sacrificed god
7 Netzach	Venus	unselfishness	lust	A beautiful naked woman
8 Hod	Mercury	truthfulness	dishonesty	A hermaphrodite
9 Yesod	The moon	independence	idleness	A beautiful naked man of strength
10 Malkuth	The earth	discrimination	inertia	A young woman, crowned, seated on a throne

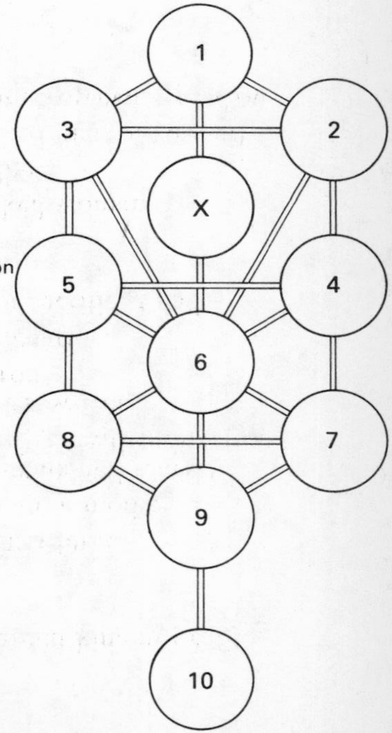

Figure 17: Chart of Correspondences upon the Tree of Life

Ultimately, the systems and symbols do not matter – it is what they stand for that we should be concerned with. Symbols are power-houses which should be used with care. The celestial hierarchies, angels, and evolutionary beings are metaphors of our own condition: realizations of what we may be.

> Apart from the constant circulation through his astral body of planetary and solar and cosmic energies, every human being has appropriated, out of the greater Whole, enough of the astral energy wherewith to construct his own individual and separate astral body, responsive to his peculiar note, coloured by his peculiar quality, and limiting him or not according to his point on the ladder of evolution. (21)

We take what we need from these symbol systems, learning our theory of levels, which is the work of a lifetime. Their cumulative effect is to tune us, prepare us for the Great Work itself. We have looked outwards at the heavens, the time has come to look within, to find the balanced point, to fashion the Stone.

> The pupil who receives force from his Master on a higher plane for the purpose of transmission to the physical plane must be prepared to effect the transmutation of the corresponding amount of force in his own nature from a lower place to a higher in order to preserve the necessary balance. (90)

This is the work of the alchemist who, in pursuit of the Great Work of transmutation, does not retain the inner force and impression, but in order to transmit it to the mundane world, transmutes that part of himself in a reciprocal exchange: matter for spirit.

EXERCISE 6 THE CADUCEUS OF HERMES

'It is taught that there is a single Light, in the form of a Man, which radiates through all the four universes, *Atzilut, Beryah, Yetzirah* and *Asiyah*, reaching down to the physical elements. This Light is bound to the Lights of the Supernal Man, which are called the ten *sefirot*. These are clothed in this Light, which is called the "Light of the Quarry of Souls" and in it are included all souls below'. This description of Adam Kadmon is at the same time a description of the Tree of Life which forms the basis for this exercise. Our purpose here is to create an affinity with the macrocosmic body of the universe, to heal those souls who are included within it, and to maintain our unity within the Body of Light. It is not necessary to have any knowledge of the Qabala in order to perform this exercise, although if you are well-read and practised in the subject you will be able to utilize it in more sophisticated ways.

First of all, sit in an upright chair, or stand, weight balanced equally on either foot. Then make a cross of light in the following manner. This action seals the aura and stabilizes the subtle bodies. Say:

Between heights,	(Touch top of forehead with the middle and index fingers of the right hand)
And depths,	(Touch solar plexus)
Between justice,	(Touch right shoulder)
And mercy,	(Touch left shoulder)
I am centred.	(Cross hands over the breast.)

As you perform this, visualize white light which comes from above your head, descending into the earth, beneath your feet. The cross is completed by a bar of white light from shoulder to shoulder, extending beyond your actual body. If you wish to put yourself under the protection of God with your own form of words, do this also. Establish your auric field by a steady circulation of breath: visualize your breathing as a double band of light which outlines your body from left ear to left foot and back over the head, and from forehead to feet, from feet to back of the head. There is no need to maintain this visualization after a while, once the pattern is established.

Your feet are upon the physical earth of this world, but your body is going to stretch through the worlds of inner space. Visualize the earth beneath you as it is seen from space: a planet with land-masses and seas. Here you are firmly established. Your body is stretching up through inner space, until the moon is at the level of your genitals: visualize it as the moon you know in the night sky. Stretching further you travel onwards until the sun is at your heart. Sirius at the level of your throat – a needle-bright star – and above your head is the primum mobile itself – which can be visualized as a whirling white nebula, the centre where creation is endlessly effected. It is very important that you do not equate these positions exactly with the subtle centres of your etheric body. See the planets as aligned vertically in front of you. When you have completed the stretching, visualize the spheres before you. You are now indeed a giant. Your body and that of Adam Kadmon are aligned over each other. For the first time you perform this exercise, do nothing other than this. Quietly establish a steady rhythm of breathing, and very slowly reverse the instructions, coming gently back down to your own size and to your own place. Seal off by the formula given above, write down any realizations and then eat and drink to ensure that you are well-earthed.

Once you have taken this part of the exercise in your stride, it is time to build the next part, which continues from where you have aligned all five positions before you. Your visualization should be aligned to *inner* and not outer space. If you experience any dizziness or disorientation, make sure you reverse the procedure slowly and seal off completely. This time, feel two great forces of polarized intensity – like two great poles of electrical current – rise from the earth beneath your feet, either side of your body. Breathe evenly and slowly. The energies weave and grow – positive and negative forces about each of the spheres, until they stop just below the primum mobile, at the level of your ears (see fig. 18). Remember, the energy interweaves the spheres, *not around your own body*. You have now built the Caduceus of Hermes upon the body of Adam Kadmon. As you meditate, you will notice an exchange of energies between the two currents of the wand. Be aware of the cosmic unity of all life, of your own vocation as an instrument of the Inner. Be especially aware that the wand which you have built is also the symbol of Asclepios, the god of healing, as well as the staff of Hermes. It can bring healing to all who need it: every divine spark within every human body goes to comprise the Body of Light. Do not hold this visualization very long, the first time. Do not attempt it if you are emotionally unbalanced or unstable on any level. If commonsense measures are observed, this exercise is cosmically beneficial, but it is a powerful one and should not be attempted often. NOTE: the positive and negative streams of energy on the caduceus should *not* be taken to denote good and evil influence, but reciprocal flows of energy which each have a necessary function. (179)

EXERCISE 7 OTHERWORLD GATEWAYS AND SYMBOLS

Working with symbol systems is a basic skill which needs to be acquired by all who follow the Western Way. There are, as we saw in

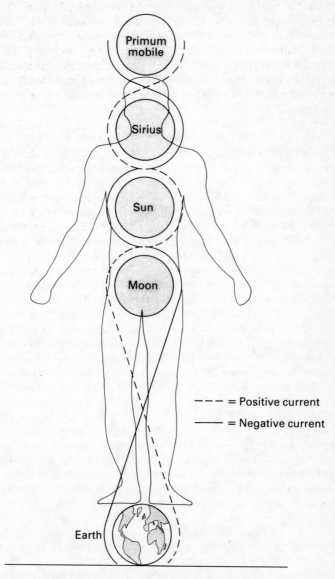

Figure 18:   The Caduceus of Hermes

volume I, many gateways to the otherworld, or to other dimensions of existence. Those who follow the Hermetic path should not necessarily need to visit actual sites – though these can sometimes serve as lenses to magnify and concentrate the will of the operator. For most the skill and building power of the imagination should be enough. A visionary glimpse of the Pylon Gate or the Cave of the Sibyl, to name only two of the many hundreds of entrance glyphs, should enable the proficient operator to project themselves into the realms of the infinite.

Symbols in themselves hold no reality; they are constructs made up of the collective belief of those who work with them. Magically speaking, the esotericist takes these symbols, and having externalized them, makes of them gateways to an inner reality totally different from the outer reality in which he or she may be standing in contemplation of the image. Thus infused with power, the symbol becomes a focal point for the operator's whole being, and as such can be imbued with a kind of external reality which can be experienced. Thus the guardian angel or elemental contact, which may have no *concrete* reality (at least not in our dimension) assumes a *symbolic* reality – initially in the consciousness of the operative, but latterly exterior to that consciousness. Thus the angelic archetypes of the kind often mediated in Qabalistic magic, may build up in pillars of textured colour rather than anthropomorphically, until it is possible to almost taste and feel the colours, which have received the impress of a reality outside our normal understanding.

The whole question of what we actually understand as real comes into question here. It has been said that we spend a great deal of time and energy establishing perimeters of reality and in reaffirming them daily in order to protect ourselves from the madness which would result in the apprehension of *too much* reality. In this instance we may see the work of the esotericist as establishing a bridgehead between two kinds of reality: inner and outer, enabling others to pass from one to the other without fear. It should not be difficult to envisage invisible lines of force in the air about us – even, perhaps, with geometric precision. Most of the time we remain unaware of the existence of these vital links with the infinite, though they are really no different from the shining paths which connect the stone circles and standing hills of the Native tradition. When we draw upon the air a great symbol of power, representing some age-old truth, we are locking our own sigil into the web of invisible force which surrounds us.

Such an understanding requires a radical alteration of our daily consciousness, and for this reason we use symbols and signs as visual keys. To the ancient mind signs were of the greatest importance: they were efficacious representations of things which could not be seen with the naked eye but which could nonetheless be understood by the inner optive: 'all things which the eye can see are mere phantoms and insubstantial outlines; but the things which the eye cannot see are the realities. . .' (22) This is to posit a different order of reality; it harks back to the *synthemata* of Iamblichus (152) or forward to the efficacy of signs discussed by the artist David Jones. (158)

An example of the kind of thing we are speaking of might be the drawing or making of a three-dimensional pyramid. The four faces of this figure can represent a number of things: North, South, East or West; a god form, a colour, name or archetype. These can then be seen as meeting at the apex of the pyramid, which becomes the point where the powers interact and are balanced to produce an effect such as a flash of visionary insight or an opening of an entry-port upon another dimension.

Meditation upon such figures can bring much into focus which before seemed hazy or insubstantial. All traditional figures of this kind are the product of inner teaching. The Grail, drawn as a cup, takes on the form of inverted pyramids, and is particularly effective as a glyph of upward aspiration and downward energizing:

Here the nexus point stands for the position of the operator, in which the initiate (lower pyramid) receives and transmits the downward flowing energy of the gods meeting his own upward mounting aspiration (upper pyramid).

Or take the star, five pointed or otherwise. This may be seen as the endless knot or pentacle with each point representing a different aspect of deity, or a symbol of force (one of the aspects of the Grail for example). Draw this out and try different combinations of symbology until you feel you have arrived at a workable system, then use it for meditation for several days or even weeks depending on the results you receive. This can also relate to the positioning of sacred objects in the temple or working-area, or indeed to the places taken by participants in any ritual performed under the aegis of this system. It can equally well be related to star-alignments or ley-line points, cardinal positions in the ritual temenos, or aspects of deity assumed by the operators.

With these few examples, and others which are readily available in the writings of Regardie, Gray and Knight (see bibliography) it should be possible, in a comparatively short space of time, to build up a thorough working system of 'telesmic' imagery which will be of considerable help in any magical work undertaken either singly or in a group. Do not be concerned, however, if you get little immediate response; some are better equipped to work with symbols than others. If more effort is required, longer periods of study and meditation, it is well worthwhile pursuing the elusive moment when a chosen symbol will 'click' into place in your consciousness. Once this step has been achieved you will find that the rest follows naturally.

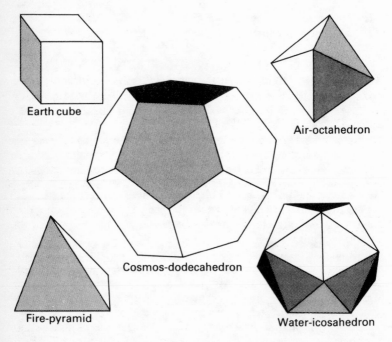

Earth cube

Air-octahedron

Cosmos-dodecahedron

Fire-pyramid

Water-icosahedron

Figure 19:   Platonic Solids

CHAPTER 5
Alchemy: The Fire-tried Stone

You should understand that alchemy is nothing but the art which makes the impure into the pure through fire.

Paracelsus

Matter is the last step on the path to God.

Rudolph Hauschka: *The Nature of Substance*

THE HUNTING OF THE GREEN LION

'Matter cannot be created or destroyed,' says the scientific law of conservation: 'But, it can be transformed', replies the alchemist. God's Great Work is the creation itself in which are set the signatures and correspondences by which it may evolve. Everything created has life: not *human* life, but a life according to its proper nature, and an inner corrollative analogous to the Platonic forms. Science scoffs at the idea of matter being alive, as is evident from its disregard of the integral ecology of the natural world. Alchemy has ever treated matter as its *prima materia*, from which the divine spark can be kindled into awareness of its potential. The alchemical process concentrates upon isolating the *prima materia* of creation in order that the evolution of matter might ensue. And, as with matter, so with humanity: the whole chain of creation releasing its divine sparks, rising through the planes of existence in a joyful return to the primal unity – such is the vision of alchemy.

If the search of the philosophers is for Wisdom, then the quest of the alchemists is for the philosopher's stone – the keystone of the earth's structure itself – the *lapsit exillas* which fell from heaven and from which all matter is formed. In this stone is encoded the cipher of life's mysteries – the male and female components which, in the outer world are divided, but which, on the Inner, are conjoined. In the pied language of alchemy both Wisdom and the Philosopher's stone are described as 'a gift and sacrament of God and a divine matter, which deeply and in diverse manners was veiled in images by the wise.' (15) If such language seems unduly veiled, we must consider that our very existence is due to a genetic process of alchemical complexity. What is hidden under the sign of emblem and glyph with alchemy, is scientifically discernable under the microscope as the genes and chromosomes, the individual DNA of human consistency. The real *prima materia* of humanity is the flesh wherein we are incarnate: the way in which our bodies develop is partly encoded into us already at birth, partly attributable to the physical conditions in which we grow up. The potential of every human being resides within the genes, and within the spiral of DNA: a strange alchemy dictates our transmutation from the fusion of ovum and sperm, through the cyclic metabolic renewal of our cell-structure, to our eventual demise when our flesh joins the chain of matter. Physics had sought to comprehend this mystery; medical science is now striving to recreate the conditions in which the mystery of life can be transmitted and genetically altered, with who knows what eugenic possibilities? The fact remains – though science may be able to produce crude DNA spirals and graft one life upon another, it has not discovered the hiding place of the spirit.

> I behold how all things in the
> aether are mixed with pneuma.
> I see in spirit how all things
> are sustained by pneuma:
> Flesh hangs itself upon soul,
> Soul is upborne by air,
> Air hangs itself upon aether.
> Fruits rise up from the depth,
> A child is lifted from the womb. (15)

The spirit is the inner corollative of the flesh, and no life can be reproduced upon earth without a corresponding ensoulment upon the Inner.

The conception of a child is the most mighty alchemy, but while the birth of a child necessitates its taking one or other gender as a requirement for earthly life, so the work of the alchemist, which is an attempt to be born upon the Inner, necessitates the reconciliation of opposites within the finding of the Philosopher's Stone. The true secret of alchemy is that the operator *becomes* the Stone.

But what is this Stone and how do we become it? Its beginnings are obscure, black like the rich soil of the Nile Delta which gave its name to alchemy. (Egyptian, *keme* = black earth.) The Greeks, who understood the symbology of colour, knew that the inner tincture of black was really gold (197) so, although Apollo was pictorially depicted with black hair, his hair was symbolically golden. This mystery was also seen in the cult of Isis: the Hermetic document, the *Kore Kosmou* (197 or The Universal Maiden, tells how Isis was given the secrets of alchemy which were to be transmitted only to her son, Horus. She is given 'the gift of the Perfect Black' – who, in the context of the text, we must see as Osiris himself – the consort with whom she is united, in alchemical union. Yet she herself is the black earth, and the pupil of the eye of Osiris: (227) she is the veiled mystery who appears outwardly as Black Isis, but whose inner reality is the Bright Isis of the Stars.

Here is the kernel of the mystery which assigns feminine symbolism to matter and masculine symbolism to spirit, Isis and Osiris, Sophia and Logos, White Queen and Red King, are syzygies whose union can only be achieved by the levels of the alchemical process. Nowhere is it stated or implied that matter = woman, spirit = man – nor should we seek to impose these meanings upon our understanding. This union of complementary opposites: matter and spirit, queen and king is the subject of this chapter.

But surely alchemy is merely the foundation upon which chemistry was established, many object? Indeed, alchemy includes proto-scientists and chemists within its history as well as mystics and magicians. It is not easy to reconcile the application of both physics and meta-physics within one discipline if one sees science from a contemporary standpoint.

This book has been much taken up with the nature of the spirit: for only by understanding things eternal will we begin to perceive the things temporal, and for this reason, we have left a discussion of matter to last. We cannot look upon matter with the fundamentalism of rational science, nor with the disdain of the Manichaen, when we approach it with the compassionate perception of inner awareness and eternal correspondence. 'Aristotle wrote of the *prima materia*, Plato of the *hyle*, Hermes of the *umbra horrenda*, Pythagoras of the "Symbolical Unity", and Hippocrates of the deformed chaos,' says Robert Fludd (307) showing how crucial matter was in relation to esoteric philosophy. The language of metaphysics was applied continuously to the realm of physics throughout the Western world up until the Enlightenment (that much-misapplied term). Now the New Physics has come full circle in its self-understanding of science by its use of Eastern spiritual terminology: that which is inexplicable in mundane scientific language can be encapsulated within cosmic conceptualizations. This ironic turn of fate, whereby the once-despised mythological paradigms have become the new currency of physics, should be cautiously heralded. The spiritual symbolism of mythology, which has become the stock in trade of the psychologist, may become the banner of the New Physics with as little justification and sense of guardianship. When the alchemists spoke in symbolic language they, at least, knew the interior reality of the symbol. This is the difference between the shaman and the psychologist, or between the alchemist and scientist, let us be clear on that score.

Alchemy is spiritual chemistry for, although it is said to have developed from physical experimentation to 'soul-alchemy', it has ever been concerned with the reconciliation of opposites, as described in the Emerald Tablet. We have already seen how planetary correspondences were observed in all the manifestations of nature in chapter 4: the colours, shapes, sounds, smells and tastes by which our senses tell us the story of any created thing became the palette and keyboard of chemistry. These subtle correspondences were the first study of alchemy, beginning with base matter – the metals, minerals and compounds of matter which were the foundation of the hierarchical chain of being itself. If a metal could be transmuted then the chain of existence was affected. The creation of gold from lead can be looked upon as the Hermetic equivalent of bringing back faery gold from the Otherworld: a transference of energy from the Inner to the Outer. Alchemists 'understood that what they were working with was not so much the actual substances as spiritual properties concealed in the metals.' (273) We might say, they attempted to bring out the inner potential, the divine spark within the metal. 'Lead is gold fallen sick' (232): the metal of Saturn/Cronos no longer has the lustre it once had in the Goldern Age.

The alchemist stands in direct succession to the Smith of the Native Tradition – he who forged the first tools from the ores of the earth itself and who was held in superstitious regard as the guardian of a great mystery. The Smith is the weapon-maker of the Gods: Govannon, Wayland, Hephaistos – the blackened, lame one.

The alchemist seems to have shared the almost universal distrust which is meted out to all metal-workers, tinkers, and miners from the time of Prometheus onwards. The miner burrows into the womb of the earth herself, careful to propiate her – as we see from the finds excavated from the Neolithic mine, at Grime's Graves in Norfolk. The metal-worker knows the mystery of fire-transmutation. The tinker and jobbing blacksmith knows the mystery of metal and has the horseman's word – the means of controlling animals, the lingua franca or *shelta* of all smiths. And as such people were anciently under the patronage of the goddess Brigid, so the alchemist pays careful attention to the service of the Anima Mundi of Our Lady Earth.

The Alchemist was the midwife and priest of transmutation: 'metals and minerals were born, grew, married, copulated, gave birth and died. Rocks and stones had bodies, souls, emotions and wants'. (55) Entering into a real relationship with the metals and elements in his or her charge, the alchemist administered alchemical sacraments to these living children of the earth. Like the real midwife and priest, continence, sobriety, watchfulness were neces- sary in the lying-in chamber – the laboratory – a word in which the Benedictine motto, 'laborare est orare' (to work is to pray) was made manifest.

We can see within alchemy the descent of the Western Way, in microcosm: it arises in the cosmological speculations of Native Tradition, receives the tributaries of philosophy, Gnosticism, Qabala, magic and Rosicrucianism, finally splitting off into a complex meander of chemistry and psychology within our own time – the studies of the physical and psychic constituents of creation, of which we are still amazingly ignorant. The Hermetic texts drew upon knowledge of Egyptian alchemical techniques as well as upon Hellenic scientific thought which subsequently informed both Platonic and Neo-Platonic philosophy. The insights of Gnosticism, themselves derived from multifarious Middle Eastern sources, fructified the symbology of alchemy – as we shall go on to see. By the time Qabalistic magic and Rosicrucian elements fed into this ever-powerful stream, the Western Way had received all the necessary nutrients to help it survive. Alchemy virtually became the equivalent of the Tantric and Varjayana path of the West.

The transmission of this powerful path can be traced historically from many standpoints. Most commentators favour a straight scientific appraisal, ignoring the esoteric adjuncts as an embarrassing and medieval excess. But by using this means, alchemy is robbed of its true meaning – the marriage of macrocosm with microcosm. Science must be seen in context as a holy art, rather than as an unholy interference with creation. Scientists and proto-scientists up until the dawn, or rather, twilight, of rational science, devoutly believed in the interelation of their studies with God; they harnessed their work with the yoke of prayer. This was especially important as the arts of metallurgy, herbal medicine, astronomy, astrology, and so on were considered to have been imparted by the Fallen Angels to humanity, according to Hermetic tradition. (197) This distrust of the scientist lives on today, based firmly upon the fear of knowing what should not be known, except by God.

Aristotle's theory of the four elements – which were seen to be in a state of flux, changing from one into the other – underlies the basic alchemical process. This theory can be demonstrated by fig. 20. A combination of air and fire results in heat, the combination of earth and water results in coldness. This schema gave rise also to the theory of the humours – the presiding elemental genius of the body by which individuals were judged to be phlegmatic, melancholic, sanguine or choleric, according to their makeup. All the elements were seen to derive from the *prima materia* – and indeed were subjected to the process by which they were returned to their prime condition. Yet the sum of the elements was the quintessentia or fifth element, a condition which was sought by alchemical means, by combining the elements in various processes. This can be seen in fig 21 which is a three-dimensional representation of the Great Work. When the elements are in balance, the quintessentia can result: the fifth element is itself a perfected mirror-image of the *prima materia* from which the other four derive. The numerous and lengthy processes to which the elements were subjected have been variously described both chemically and psychologically, as well as in mythological and symbolic terminology. However, since there is little space for a breakdown of the complex chemical processes here we must consider alchemy by means of the Emerald Tablet itself. The many emblem books of the seventeenth century – notably *The Rosarium Philosophorum* (290) and the Mylius Engravings (238) give a clear breakdown of the classical alchemical processes.

The following is a compressed meditation upon the Emerald Tablet.

The *prima materia* was understood to have been 'generated by fire, born of water, brought down from the sky by wind, and nourished by earth' (307) – the formation of matter, balanced by the elements, yet whose essential core – its DNA – remains a secret. All things created derive from its substance, yet its perfection is the achievement of the Great Work. The *prima materia* must be given over to the mother to be shaped or 'fixed'. When the 'child' is growing it must be purged of its separate elements in order that it grows strong: the soul and spirit of the *prima materia* are matured. Next, the correspondences between micro-and macrocosm must be comprehended: the 'youth' is sent to its father for instruction in matters sublime. When this is achieved the 'adult' returns to earth in order to practise this wisdom. The *prima materia* has been united with the quintessentia, which it mirrors, and discovers its adamantine purity and strength. This process is that by which everything is created and, if imitated with wisdom, can effect healing, long-life and illumination of the whole world. The guardian of this work is Hermes Trismegistos himself: the child of the philosophers and inheritor of their accumulated wisdom; the youthful initiate in the mysteries of both mother and father, God and Goddess; and the mature guardian of the mysteries, the Agathodaimon of all who seek to achieve the Great Work.

This meditation upon the text of the Emerald Tablet is offered as a working model for those who wish to go further in this Work. Alternatively, the reader may wish to work with the three unidentified concepts which are termed salt, sulphur and mercury. These are not to be taken only as physical or chemical substances, but apply respectively to the body, soul and spirit. Together with the glyph of fig 21 and the Emerald Tablet, the correspondences of these processes and their interrelation can be explored in meditation. Similarly, the classical terms for the main alchemical processes can be employed in a meditative manner, namely, the nigredo, albedo and rubedo which we shall be investigating later in this chapter.

Mercury, the metal of Hermes himself, is a bridge between the chemical substances employed in alchemy. Of all the metals, quicksilver (mercury) 'did not participate in the last stages of earth's densifying (but) remained a fluid.' (138) Just so, Hermes Trismegistos does not remain anchored in one mythos, but ranges throughout the systems and mythologies of many cultures, as messenger. The mercurial powers of Hermes are best assimilated under his symbolical representation as the Green Lion of the alchemical processes: his

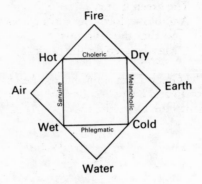

Figure 20: Aristotelian Table of the Elements

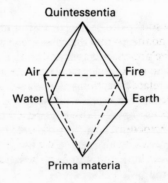

Figure 21: The Crystalline Structure of the Great Work

continual shape-shifting connects the many levels, systems and processes and produces a wealth of knowledge as set forth in the Emerald Tablet:

> The green lion is extremely agile
> And blows forth the sun's colours
> > So that the reflection
> > May be seen on the plain (6)

Hermes, as the Green Lion, explores the heights and depths: the heavens, the earth and the waters beneath the earth. His example is the pattern which the alchemist follows. (fig. 22)

Figure 22:   The Green Lion

Alchemy is the soul-price of the cosmos: it teaches us to relate the infinite to the mundane, to find the presence of the divine in the daily circle of being. The process is a spiritual code used – as is the Tree of Life – by those who seek the Stone, as a system of correspondences through which to relate everything micro- and macrocosmically. The search for the Stone consists in refining the soul, purging it of elemental influences, until all that remains is a single unit – a perfectly tuned microcosm, reflecting the macrocosm. All matter is a mystery: the processes of alchemy are a ladder wherewith to transcend time and space until one stands at the highest point of creation, which is God.

We have said that all matter is alive, in a mysterious manner. The 'deepening of the plane', whereby matter is despiritualized – a thing detestable to the Pythagoreans – seems an ominous possibility in our own time within the black alchemy of nuclear technology. The heavier radio-active elements, which have been derived from yet other elements, stand in danger of being totally cut off from the spiritual world. 'The descent of the spirit into matter has now reached a turning point in the earth and from now on it is man's task to recognise and release the spirit in matter. The descent of the spirit into matter reached a turning point at the element lead.' (209) The role of science in mitigating the sufferings of humanity has been vast, but when it loses the insight of its primal function within the cosmos, it loses faith with creation. Rudolph Steiner believed that science's role could be crucial:

> The initiate-ruler, the philosopher of personality, the priestly reconciler of knowledge and faith are equally unable to rescue modern humanity from the fruit of its own attainments. Only a man trained in the scientific thinking motivating the technological research and developments of modern civilisation can discover those *new* elements which must enter human consciousness if mankind is not to fall victim of its own achievements. (318)

Steiner obviously has little faith in the various modern fragmentations of the shaman – the esotericist, psychologist and priest – perhaps he looked to new alchemists who stood for planetary evolution, who combined spirit and matter, science and metascience.

This bringing together of all the disciplines of art, science and the spirit was the aim of the Rosicrucian manifestos. Francis Bacon's vision in the *New Atlantis* (1627) and his Great Instauration (1582 et seq.) propounded 'the universal and general reformation of the whole wide world through the renewal of all arts and sciences.' Subsequently the Royal Society was founded in 1660 but, short of it being the 'invisible college made manifest' after the Rosicrucian model, it soon became the cradle for rational science. Such 'externalisations of the hierarchy' rarely result in anything other than a talking-shop unless they are truly contacted. Yet these contacts have been not Inner spiritual beings, but creations of proto-scientists. From Rabbi Judah Leib's creation of the golem in sixteenth-century Prague (310) to Dr Frankenstein's monster is a long step: as far as Roger Bacon's Brazen Head is from the computer. The magician is credited with the creation of homuculi – a geni in a bottle, possibly a wild fundamentalization of the creation of the Child of the

Philosophers – yet what are we to make of conception *in vitro* and the other experimentations to which human flesh, with its divine spark, is subjected? Such creations are to be serviceable machines, obedient to their masters: but can such things ever be friends and counsellors after the fashion of the Inner guardians? Does the ghost in the machine answer back?

If spiritual symbols have been subverted to physical applications, as with the terminologies of God and Goddess, how terribly has the craft of alchemy been inverted that the habitations of the divine spark in matter should become scientific familiars? The ultimate materialism of the Great Work has hounded alchemy from the very beginning: not the inner gold of the spirit, but the outer currency of mundane commerce is demanded on request.

> All clamour aloud: 'We want to be rich!' Rich! Yes, you desire wealth and say with Epicurus: 'let us provide our bodies and leave our souls to take care of themselves. Even as Midas in the fable, we wish to turn all things to gold. 'So there are people who seek this gold in Antimony, but since they do not care for God, and have cast far away from them the love of their neighbour, they will look at the horse's teeth of Antimony forever without knowing a thing of its age and quality. Like the wedding guests at Cana, they may behold, but. . . know nothing.

So writes Basilius Valentinus in his *Triumphal Chariot of Antimony* (341)

Our search for the stone must continue: it promises healing, long life and illumination, not earthly gold. 'The Stone, the Light of the Earth, serves as a guide to all created things and makes hidden things manifest.' (197) Yet, what if it remains hidden itself? How are we to proceed? The only method is to take the path of the walkers-between-the-worlds, the way of the Master-Men who, by the uses of imagination, pass between the worlds in search of this precious thing, with wisdom as our guide.

THE WANDERING VIATICUM

Those who follow the alchemical path of the Western Way travel by signs and stories, as all good travellers from the Canterbury Pilgrims up to the benighted travellers in Italo Calvino's *Castle of Crossed Destinies* have done. (41) Those who want to make an alchemical excursion will perhaps first read accounts of such journeys for informative tips on how they are to proceed, only to find that they can make no sense of alchemical texts because they can only be read by means of symbolic keys. It take patience and determination to learn the symbolic language of the wise: the *disciplina arcani* of the mysteries kept no better guard from intrusion by the profane than this method of writing does. Yet, as Paracelsus says, 'resolute imagination can accomplish all things'. (134)

The problem arises: to whom should we go for guidance? Faced with the numerous commentaries on this and that text, the student of alchemy may well falter. While a more hardy traveller in these realms will assure the beginner that he or she knows as much about alchemy from individual resources and experience as the greatest commentator alive, this statement is hard to accept. Yet, we are all alchemists to some degree, transmuting our bodies and natures into something other by the ingestion of both food and ideas. Just as metabolism replaces all our cells so that we are physically reconstituted within seven years, so with our consciousness: our motivation shifts tack from necessity to necessity, all the time guided into new channels of experience as year succeeds year. Our progress in alchemical exploration depends very much upon input of ideas and experiences. Therefore it is doubly important that we study original texts, where possible, and carefully monitor what modern commentators tell us.

Where once we would have studied under physical guardians we must now learn to listen for the teachings of the inner guardians who ensure that the mysteries are transmitted. This may come about by virtue of our interest or study, but inner contacts or teachers have a way of arriving without announcement within our consciousness, as we have already seen in the previous chapter. Jung himself had many inner contacts, including one whom he called Philemon, of whom he wrote:

> Psychologically, Philemon represented superior insight. At times he seems to me quite real, as if he were a living personality. To me he was what the Indians call a guru. (He) and other figures of my fantasies brought home to me the crucial insight that there are things in the psyche which I do not produce, but which produce themselves and have their own life. Philemon represented a force which was not myself. (165)

Clearly, Jung has been pathwalking in a state of solitary discovery; he is unwilling to acknowledge rationally that his inner teacher could be real – he only 'seems' real. Nevertheless, this did not stop Jung from listening and recording, nor from writing up his own experiences for the benefit of other would-be travellers. It is a pity that later Jungians have rarely chosen to follow his example, got out of their armchairs and travelled thither themselves. The temptation to intellectualize about inner experience is great. Because Jung has opened up for the modern world the reality of archetypes, *as he experienced them*, many are now content to sit back and work from his findings rather than their own.

Jung wrote: 'only an unparalled impoverishment of symbolism could enable us to rediscover the gods as psychic factors, that is, as archetypes of the unconscious.' We have already spoken of how symbolism must be grounded in first-hand understanding: so it is with the archetypes of the inner worlds – we cannot presume to work with them at second-hand, nor relegate them to the unconscious. Such an understanding will help our reading of alchemical texts. The complex processes and strange symbolic beasts, kings and androgynes of alchemy are the signature of those inner energies we call the gods; they are not abstractions or productions of our psyches, working in some objective sense from a projected theatre of memory. Their effect is real, not illusory. Hidden under many guises these inner energies, called by psychology the archetypes, come through us – they do not originate within us, as Jung himself acknowledged. The poet W.B.Yeats corroborates this understanding:

> There are, indeed, personifying spirits that we had best call but Gates and Gatekeepers, because through their dramatic power they bring our souls to crisis, to Mask and Image. . . They have but one purpose, to bring their chosen man to the greatest obstacle he may confront without despair. (366)

Without such encounters, our alchemical quest cannot be maintained because, without these Gates and Gatekeepers, we cannot find our way onwards. The alchemical archetypes are, at base, our *neter* – the Egyptian term for archetype or salt – the *prima materia* of our search, the basis upon which the other elements work. We still say of certain characters about us whose daily intercourse leavens the lumpishness of life, that they are 'the salt of the earth:' so with our archetypes. Yet the *archai* – Greek for principles or beginnings – are 'something more universal than the elements.' (197) We need careful preparation in order to work with them in full co-operation. This is where the ground-work of correspondences comes in and where the reader can prepare the way for him or herself by the means we have suggested in chapter 4.

One means of preparation is the making of a talisman which must be seen, not as a good-luck charm method of fine-tuning. A talisman is 'a magical figure charged with the Force which it is intended to represent (286).' Israel Regardie's book *How to Make and Use Talismans* gives practical advice on their construction. However, whether they are made of paper, virgin parchment or precious metals, it is not the quality of the material which matters, but the quality of the meditation and concentration by which they are consecrated which counts. The Egyptian sculptor imbued each statue in a similarly talismanic way, by concentrating the divine energy of the god portrayed with its appropriate correspondences; the hieroglyph for sculptor was 'he-who-keeps-alive.' (55)

Another method of preparation is by means of music, whose subtle correspondences do indeed activate the *archai* in a universal manner, once the right harmonic permutations are discovered. Orpheus with his lyre was able to change the nature of beasts and men by the permutation of but seven strings. If you choose to work by means of music's alchemy, then he is the one to contact. The Head of Orpheus, like the Head of Bran the Blessed, is still singing for those who have ears to hear. In the book will be found a discography of suitable music, but at no time should recorded music, however beautiful, replace that which you make yourself:

> Remember that song is the most powerful imitator of all things. For it imitates the intentions and affections of the soul, and speech, and also reproduces bodily gestures, human movements, and moral characters, and imitates and acts everything so powerfully that it immediately provokes both the singer and hearer to imitate and perform the same things. (351)

Ficino sought to reproduce planetary correspondences by means of his Hermetic hymns. Fabio Paolini, a professor of Greek at Venice in 1589, wrote about the talismanic alchemy of music also, noting that although musicians in his own time were masterly skilful, 'none has produced effects superior to Orpheus.' (ibid).

For most people, the most immediate means of preparation will be the reading of the alchemical texts and the contemplation of alchemical emblems. These have a deep inner effect, as Jung himself recorded in his psychological study of alchemy (164). Just as the architectural language of medieval symbolism presented books in

stone in every cathedral, so the alchemical archetypes were portrayed as emblems, conveying initiatory clues. How shall we go
about working with these? Gerhard Dorn (floriat 1565–78), a
disciple of Paracelsus, advises on the means to approach the Great
Work thus:

> Through study one acquires knowledge; through knowledge,
> love, which creates devotion; devotion creates repetition and by
> fixing repetition one creates in oneself experience, virtue and
> power, through which the miraculous work is done and the
> work in nature is of this quality. (345)

Marie-Louise von Franz speculates that the 'study' spoken of above
means the actual reading of the alchemical texts – that exposure to
them can itself have an effect. Although the processes described,
verbally and pictorially, within the texts correspond to the chemical
admixture of various substances, they are also emblematic of the
inner human condition – which is what the psychological schools
have made their study.

Such intelligent reading and contemplation is the start of the
initiatory journey. In *The Chymical Wedding of Christian Rosenkreutz* (178) the hero, Rosenkreutz himself, describes his own initiation in such a way that only those who had themselves experienced it
could understand. Yet, if we meditate upon the hidden words and
images – 'fixing by repetition', as Dorn has it – we will find some of
the keys which we seek. In default of operational Mystery Schools
and mystery guardians, we are driven to seek for nourishment in the
mystery stories which remain to us. Did the world but know it, the
mysteries are scattered at our feet – whole initiatory systems which
wait for someone to exposit them after having travelled with the
archetypes which are their inner guardians. They are explored only
by meditating, by entering the story – just as the Classical Mystery
schools initiated their candidates, by making them live the mystery in
identification with the cult deity (cf. chapter 1).

The expositors, guardians and paradigms of the Great Work have
been the subject of these two volumes. Alchemy is the most total
expression of the Western Way, concerned as it is with the transmutation and perfection of consciousness. The Native Tradition's
guardians sought to effect the change from tribal to individual
consciousness, just as the Hermetic Tradition's guardians have
sought to transmute individual into cosmic consciousness. Both
shaman and magician have tried to interrelate the microcosm to the

macrocosm, in their different ways. Their roles have fragmented in diverse ways; their symbologies have varied with bewildering complexity, but we can trace the similarities and choose how we would wish to align our own inner journey towards the Great Work. The Foretime was motivated by a chthonic identification; its alchemy was effected by means of earth, wood and stone. Later ages looked to the celestial hierarchies for their integration in the Body of God, yet they still recognized the chthonic signatures of metals, the talismanic properties of all created things. The cauldron and alembic were both transformative vessels which met in the universal image of the Grail. Shaman and alchemist are connected by the same story involving the difficult inner-world journey of the initiate, his quest for otherworldly guides and for the drink which will bring healing, long-life and illumination to his tribe.

When esotericism is under attack, often the only survivor is the central story of the mystery which can masquerade merely as a folk-tale or be reinstated as an initiatory key, as necessary. In such a way is the esoteric wisdom of the Tarot said to have survived: what better place to hide the mystery than in a pack of cards, which can be found in the hands of any wandering rogue whose greasepaint hides the true nobility of a master? The marginal shamans of both Native and Hermetic traditions have survived as storytellers, troubadours and playwrights in order to transmit their inherited wisdom. So has the ancient role of the poet-shaman been instrumental in keeping alive the old traditions of transformation. And what matter if the mysteries become the stuff of a story by which to beguile the long winter nights, as long as they are still told and live in our hearts? It is to these faithful guardians – *the makars*, as the medieval Scottish poet, William Dunbar called his fellow-poets – that we must be grateful that we possess a traditional mystery system within the West, springing directly from our Native roots to flow into the Hermetic stream of alchemy.

Just as the Hermetic inner landscape harks back to the natural perfection of the Native Otherworld, so do the transformative images find their root in Paradise itself. The scenario in which the transformative symbol is sought, varies little from story to story. In the apocryphal text *The Apocalypse of Moses*, dated to about the early Christian era, we read how Seth, the inheritor of Adam's wisdom in Hermetic tradition, is sent by his father to obtain the oil of mercy from Eden. He is refused by the archangel Michael, but is promised that it shall be forthcoming 'to the holy people at the end of time.' (278) This oil of mercy is a healing oil which will restore Adam to his former wholeness but, although Seth does not obtain it for the healing of his father, he is promised that his line shall indeed produce a saviour who will administer healing to Seth's descendants. We have already seen how the Story of the Pearl is similarly associated with Seth's lineage (chapter 4): to possess the Pearl is to obtain paradise. These stories and the discovery of the Emerald Tablet (chapter 1), point to a quest to be undertaken, a challenge to be answered. They are the archetypal myths of the Hermetic quest for the divine spark's reunion with God in Paradise, whereby the world shall be healed and where there shall be no more death or ignorance.

From the Native Tradition sprang yet another such story – that of the Grail. There is no one source for this legend, although we can look to numerous references to the healing waters, springs or fountains of the Otherworld which brought wisdom and healing. We notice, too, the cauldron of transformation which variously pro- duced the food of one's desire, brought the dead to life and healed the sick. It is always in the possession of a Goddess of Sovereignty, maiden of the well or woman or otherworldly power. (219) Underlying the theme of the Waste Land – a paradigm of the earth's condition of disharmony in the cosmos – is that of the ravaged earth-mother who cannot give her bountiful gifts to the sovereign who is likewise a Wounded King. The Wounded King's champion is the untried hero who must somehow find the healing draught which will make his sovereign whole once more: he must seek to free the waters which are

Figure 23:   Alchemical King and Queen

chained by evil custom so that the Waste Land of the earth-mother may blossom once more. Then and only then can the Sovereign and his Sovereignty be united in alchemical union. (fig. 23)

Who can tell how many times this mystery has been expounded and in how many different ways? The healing draught which unites Sophia and Logos within Gnosis, Wounded Kings and Waste Land within the Grail corpus and Red King and White Queen within alchemy can only be caught in the vessel which the adept fashions for this purpose. It is krater, cup and stone. Those who achieve this height of the Great Work – the union of the Great Above and the Great Below – are granted to drink from the wandering viaticum by which the initiate is sustained upon the journey towards the apocatastasis when all things will have their healing. The draught that he or she drinks is for the healing of the world, not a magical potion which benefits only the seeker. This wandering viaticum – the way-bread and drink of the world – is like the alchemical Stone in that it is found in unlikely places, after great searching and cannot be retained for personal use. Like the kernel of the mystery-story which cannot be grasped by the ignorant, the Grail cannot be used for evil purposes – its healing cannot be mediated by the unworthy. Yet neither is it achieved by the pedant. Its healing comes only to the simple, to the holy-fool, the initiate who to gain eternal life, stands on the brink of the abyss and leaps lightly over with all the trust of his ancestor, the shaman.

The dimension of the inner quest for the transformative symbol is further deepened by the admixture of Native and Hermetic traditions at the nexus of Christianity when the Native stories of the poet-singer become fused with the Hermetic craft of the alchemist-magician. Makar and artificer, troubadour and guildsman, master-man and Qabalist, Grail-knight and Rosicrucian sage are caught up together in a marvellous exchange of material. The exponents of the Mystery Schools had been subsumed into Christianity, or else followed their own unorthodox ways of transmission and the Hermetic tide had not returned when the Grail legends were eventually written down. Celtic champion had become medieval knight in the quest for the transformative vessel. The Dux Bellorum, Artos, had become King Arthur, that most Christian king who'carried the image of the holy Mary, the ever-lasting Virgin, on his shoulder' at the Battle of Guinnion. (248) The Grail legends became the healing lance of spiritual chivalry. The Grail itself became identified with the cup of the Last Supper, or with the cruets in which Joseph of Arimathea caught the blood and water from the side of the Crucified Lord. Seth's mighty descendant had returned to redeem his people and give them, at long last, the oil of mercy. The people's native story entered the lists of the Christian story, cross-fertilizing with the hero-myths of all lands.

If the Grail legends are the epitome of Catholic Europe's inner-mysteries, then those of Christian Rosenkreutz are the underlying mysteries of Protestant Europe after the Reformation. They may seem to be a totally Hermetic invention, but their roots are deeper. In the tradition of the Master Men of Celtic tradition, Rosenkreutz enters the mountain of the goddess and lifts her veil – just as Thomas the Rhymer and Tannhauser do. (217) He has elements of Spenser's Red Cross Knight but, instead of vanquishing dragons and freeing maidens, he goes on a quest for inner wisdom and vouchsafes himself the champion of the ignorant, the sick and the tormented. In the *Chymical Wedding*, he both unites King and Queen, and is himself united with Lady Venus, who represents the inner wisdom. He can be identified with both Hermes, Christ and Perceval at the moment of accomplishment – whether of the Philosopher's Stone, the Redemption or the Grail, is for the reader to say.

Both sets of legends – those of the Grail and of Christian Rosenkreutz – show a remarkable similarity in dedication to the Great Work. The company of Arthur's Round Table and the Congregation of the Rosicrucians each meet once a year, respectively at Camelot during Pentecost, and in the House of the Holy Spirit at Christmas. Both swear to do good service to all who ask of it, freely and without favour. While Arthur's knights subdue dragons, quelling atavistic, evil customs in the land, Rosicrucians strive to heal the sick and counsel the ignorant. Evidently spiritual chivalry did not die at the Reformation and Renaissance. (6, 185)

The storytellers, the makars, who had once enjoyed an honourable place in society and lost it again, were able to return with the letters of learning after their names, having vindicated the mysteries and brought them to a new generation. It was time to return to the physical participation in the mysteries, within the boundaries of alchemy, magic and science. The fragmented shaman – smith, magician, astrologer, priest, poet, philosopher – was united in the person of the alchemist, once more under royal patronage to pursue the Great Work. It was a brief return of an ancient way of life which was to dissipate under the ignorance of the 'new learning', which despised the emblematic processes of the alchemical story and looked upon them as childish allegories which prefigured the glories of science. The transformative wisdom of the Grail was ignored in favour of a material end to all ills. The Stone of the Philosophers became so much rubbish again – unless, of course, it was capable of generating real gold or eternal life. The demise of alchemy's classical age was brought about by disbelief in its internalized mythological sequences. Neither Hermes, Christ nor Arthur were of interest, except as curious literary remains. The earth could return to Waste Land and the soul to perdition. Surely the makars were dead, and the wandering viaticum appeared not at all during this period – none were worthy to drink, because none were able to transform. Both Native and Hermetic traditions died back, to seed from the Inner in a later century, in our own time.

If the Foretime's wisdom is the natural resonance of the Native Tradition in our own time, so then is Alchemy the current resonance of the Hermetic Tradition for today. There is still much work of recovery to be done among those who are committed to the survival of the Western Way. Some of the fragments of tradition are so scattered as to be like the pieces of Osiris' corpse, to be gathered with much toil and sorrow. Yet, whatever has been lost in the physical world is still recoverable by means of meditation and analeptic memory. (cf. exercise 2, vol. I).

The Rosicrucian heritage connects the Grail and the Elixir of Life, spiritual chivalry and hermetic quest, physical and soul alchemy. The Rosicrucian and alchemical texts of the early seventeenth century unconsciously drew upon the Gnostic usages of early Christian Alexandria, via the medium of Islamically preserved alchemical wisdom. Thus, at a time when Christianity was further fragmented at the period of the Reformation into Catholic and Protestant, an old esoteric Christian impulse was able to permeate Europe. Up until the middle of the seventeenth century the patterns laid down at this period were virtually upheld throughout the Western world. Cut off from each other by cultural and religious boundaries, as though by the corridor of time, Catholic and Protestant Europe developed in totally different ways. The speculative Rosicrucianism of Northern Europe countered the much symbolically-curtailed Christianity which Protestantism presented: robbed of the sacramental liturgy, the esoterically unfulfilled turned to the transmutations of alchemy; deprived of the Virgin Mother, alchemists invoked Pan Sophia, the World Soul, the White Queen of the alchemical union. Meanwhile, in the Catholic South, where liturgical business went on as usual, philosophy and physics took on the pallor associated with Northern skies: the ascetic thinking of Descartes and Pascal countered the over-blown superstitions of a world-order with which science had no accord. Esoteric development seems to have progressed only in the north. The centre of esoteric attention moved from Italy to Germany where, from the time of Boehme and the Rosicrucians, until the time of Goethe and Steiner it continued unabated. The French estoeric revival only took place after the French Revolution. Greece never experienced a Renaissance due to its occupation by the Turks but, with pre-Revolutionary Russia, maintained the esoteric Christianity of the mystical Orthodox rite. Spain expelled its esoteric cabals in the fifteenth century. Britain, along with America, is currently undergoing a rediscovery of both Native and Hermetic traditions. Migrations of people and of ideas have shaped the esoteric development of the West: what one part of the world has rejected, another takes up as its saving idea and motivating force. In the cycles of recurrence and Inner resonance, the synthesis of one tradition with another brings us a closely-interlocking pattern in which to operate according to our ability and inclination.

We each have the potential to approach alchemy as our own study, according to our individual talents whether as poet, singer, magician, scientist or craftsman. Alchemy is crucially important to the future development of the West, which is still unable to adjust to either physical sexuality or inner polarity, let alone the interpenetration of microcosm and macrocosm. We have yet to plumb the deepest mysteries of reconciliation: it is a path walked in darkness, illumined only by the lantern of love.

THE CHYMICAL WEDDING

In an age which is concerned with revamping the old symbologies and archetypes, there is much dispute about the rightful position of divine masculine and feminine symbols, just as there has been a corresponding debate about the respective roles of men and women. In the esoteric world such disputes are rarer: the symbolisms of Lord and Lady, God and Goddess are the everyday currency of the Inner Planes. Let us proceed intuitively upon this ground and not attempt to use symbols as weapons. The Divine Masculine and Feminine are the two-sided door – Janus/Janua. In terms of developing consciousness, we come through the door which portrays the Goddess, for she is the primal image of our birth into the mysteries. If we refuse to pass through her mysteries we may not proceed upon our way: she stands at the entrance of the inward spiral of the Native Tradition. Our way out of the labyrinth is by means of her wisdom. On the reverse, inside the door is the God who stands at the end of the outward spiral of the Hermetic Tradition. We cannot emerge without the assistance of his knowledge. Just as these dual influences affect whole ages and cultures at different times, so too do we en-counter the God and Goddess at the appointed time in our own life-cycle. Our own parents tell us of Mother and Father, our own relationships, of wife and husband; our own children, of son and daughter. As we age physically, so our inner understanding appreci-ates the ever-youthening aspects of masculine and feminine, but this is merely one expression – the physical realization – of a complex set of polarities: the Inner world polarities are yet different again.

We spoke in volume one of the problems which can occur when the inner companion is projected upon a physical person. To avoid confusion, let us refer to figure 15 (p. 154) where the polarities and their levels are set our clearly. Each man stands under the macrocos-mic archetype of the Logos or God, and is capable of mediating that force; each woman stands under the macrocosmic archetype of the Goddess or Sophia, and is capable of mediating that force. As man is able to experience the love of a woman, the inspiration of his inner companion – the muse or sibyl – and behold the macrocosmic beauty of the Goddess, so, too, is woman able to experience the love of a man, the inspiration of her inner companion – the daimon or prophet – and behold the macrocosmic beauty of the God. Further, each polarity is able to mate on its own plane i.e. man with woman, prophet with sibyl, God with Goddess: each of these levels, which are mysteriously within us, are also capable of mating, but each partner must be aware of these levels in the first place, which is not the case in most modern relationships. The mating, in such cases, occurs only in the conjoining of flesh during sexual union – the other levels are not polarized and so cannot mate.

The alchemical understanding of the *coniunctio* is this very mating on every plane which produces the rebus or hermaphrodite of the Great Work – a reconciliation which prefigures the union of micro-cosm with macrocosm. This is at the heart of that lost tantra of the West, the secret of which is the highest working of alchemy.

To assume the roles of the White Queen and Red King is only

possible if both partners are initiates within the Great Work: this is the reason for the alchemist's working with his *soror mystica*, who was invariably his wife. Those who see the woman's role within the work merely as a conjuror's assistant – all tulle and tights – do not understand it at all. Yet neither is the *soror mystica* a passive agent in the operation. Indeed, if the operator is female, she will require the assistance of a *frater mysticus*.

But where does this leave the non-initiate who has married a partner who is not only ignorant of inner realities but positively refuses to believe in their existence? How does one come to a re-evaluation of one's relationship without tearing at the delicate webs of love which already bind one human being to another? The radical revisioning of male and female roles has had the same effect that science has had on a metaphysical perception of the world – it has sundered the work wrought on the looms of light, shattered the mirror of the mysteries, left us dissatisfied. Those who long to mate on higher levels with their partner and are unable, remain in a state of frustration which is not physical. They lack true sacramental union. 'Only those who are rightly married can go to the higher degrees,' writes Dion Fortune, in her study of laws of sexuality and polarity. (92) By 'right marriage', she does not mean legally-sanctioned but divinely-sanctioned partnership. This does not mean to say that partnerships should be abandoned when esoteric duty calls. The esoteric laws on this point are clear enough: whatever contracts are entered into must be abided by, especially when children are involved. The law regarding marriage is often mocked, but it reflects the understanding that marriage is a sacrament which one human being gives to another in the token of flesh. Who knows but if we go on quest for the Grail, which is the vessel of this polar-alchemy between the sexes, that it may be bestowed by the lover upon the beloved, that the wounds of Wounded Lord and Waste Land may be healed at last?

The royal way of alchemy is by no means easy to achieve. Opposites are difficult to reconcile. The Great Work is only achieved by intense effort and delicate preparation. No alchemist would casually throw his elements into the prepared bath with the abandon with which some people jump into bed with each other: the result of either operation would be negligible.

The seemingly irreconcilable division of opposites has been the subject of many myths and legends. The traditional story about the incestuous love of the sun for the moon, his sister, is one which finds its home within the alchemical and hermetic symbology. God sets sun and moon in the sky so that they follow each other around the heavens, never meeting, except at the moment of eclipse when they are seen to embrace. Yet the unsatisfied yearning of the sun and moon gives us light by day and night. 'Life is poured into all things through the moon and sun, and therefore they are called by Orpheus the vivifying eyes of Heaven.' (84) In an early Hermetic text, Hermes is addressed as one 'whose tireless eyes are sun and moon – that shine in the pupils of the eyes of men.' Hermes, the child of Sun and Moon, mediates the imagery of God and Goddess within the symbology of all myths, and so we perceive all things as partaking of these dual natures on many levels. Yet, in the *Revelations of St John* (chapter 22) we are told that there shall be no need for sun or moon in the Holy City, because the light of God will be shining in and through us: the need to steer by the celestial influences of either divine masculine or feminine will be over because we shall *be* the light itself.

We are yet earth-bound and not spiritual beings, however, and the neo-Pythagorean invocation to the Eternal Feminine is still appropriate to our needs:

> Honour be to woman on earth, as in Heaven, and may she be sanctified, and help us mount to the Great Soul of the world who gives birth, preserves, and renews – the Divine Goddess who bears along all souls in her mantle of light. (295)

Those who wish to work with these archetypes of reconciliation can employ many different scenarios drawn from whatever tradition they find appropriate. One such is the Gnostic *apocatastasis* when the Bride, Sophia, is raised up to her Bridegroom, the Logos. They form the gateway of the bridal chamber where they are to conjoin and, each holding out a curved hand, form an O through which the created hierarchies pass – mineral, vegetable, animal, human, angelic etc. When everything has passed within, their union takes place. Similarly, the reconciliation of the Shekinah with God can be visualized, after the Qabalistic Sabbath meditation of *yichudim*. The Assumption and Coronation of the Virgin is another image of this reconciliation: although her body and soul have been assumed to heaven, she is, with her Son, a bridge over which the whole creation may enter into the final unity of Paradise. (fig. 24)

Alchemy ultimately answers the challenge of dualism by not passing up the challenge of duality. The 'evil' nature of the flesh – a fear which lay at the very heart of many of the Classical mystery

Figure 24:   Alpha and Omega: Logos and Sophia – emblems of eternal hope

schools, was not resolved until alchemy became a working system. Here it was realized that the task of transmuting the fleshly envelope towards a higher spiritual plane of existence, could begin while one was yet still living, and that the effect of this transmutation could become a means of uniting the scattered Body of Light for the benefit of all creation. The unification of the alchemist and the *soror mystica* in the bridal-chamber and of the elements within the furnace were paradigms of this gathering-in.

The alchemical processes vary considerably from text to text: some relate the integration of two opposites – as in the *Rosary of the Philosophers* (290) – where Sun and Moon go through two sets of processes. Others represent the elements as being subjected to seven stages, corresponding to the seven-fold planetary system, rather as the Gnostic sects who were taught to traverse the seven spheres of the archons in order to arrive at the pleroma, purged of all the vices attributable to the guardians of each sphere. Some tell of the birth of the perfect Mercurius who emerges only at the end of this seven-fold cycle of transmutations through the nigredo, albedo and rubedo stages of the alchemical process – Hermes Trismegistos goes through the seven days of creation in reverse, to appear triumphant.

The black, the white and the red stages are the archetypal pattern, not only of alchemy, but also of the Native folk-story. Perfection is seen to reside in a combination of these three colours: the languishing prince or princess of the story can only marry one whose cheek is pale as the snow, whose lips are red as blood, whose hair as black as the raven's wing. This ancient motif is a feature of the Grail-knight's awakening from the unreal dream: he sees the blood in the snow as a black raven stoops upon its prey and remembers his quest. This symbolic key is far more complexly employed within alchemy where each stage has its own mythos. Some systems give further colours – the peacock's tail and the yellowing – but we shall only be considering these basic three.

In the *Nigredo*, the Wounded King encounters the Waste Land, Christ enters the tomb, Osiris is scattered by Set. The King of the alchemical process is sundered of his flesh and putrefaction sets in. In the *Albedo, a* sevenfold bath is prepared. The bones of the scattered one are restored by Isis, the White Mass of the Holy Mother is celebrated where the Virgin offers up her child, the Wounded King drinks of the Grail: the heavenly dew of the planets is bestowed. In the *Rubedo*, the glorified body is resurrected, Isis joins with Osiris to produce Horus, the Grail Knight succeeds his Wounded King and marries his master's daughter. The Stone of the Philosophers is achieved. (79)

Just as the alchemical elements were separated, purified, changed and reunited, so have the divine sparks of creation been separated from their source, changed by earthly experience; purified by the trials they encountered, they shall, likewise, return to the primal unity. The figures of Adam Kadmon in Qabala, of the Gnostic anthropos, and of elusive Mercurius in alchemy are paradigms of the same esoteric truth. Our touchstone is the symbol of the scattered Body of Light: be it Pearl, Grail, Philosopher's Stone.

Alchemy is the philosophy which enables us to transcend the limitations of mortality: our divine spark is transmuted into the elixir of life so that the physical vehicle becomes a temple in truth. To find and isolate the quintessentia – the undying part of ourselves – is the quest: like the oyster that forms a pearl, we must learn to live with irritation, toil and an inglorious life in order to achieve this quest. The transmutation of the earthly into the heavenly is, however, not only the concern of alchemy. In the daily transubstantiation of the mass, bread is offered at the altar and mysteriously becomes the Body of Christ. The moment of Redemption, whereby matter is given the potentiality of spiritual regeneration, is offered for all by one who is the high priest of these mysteries – a priest forever after the order of Melchizedek (Hebrews 5,6). Alchemy was able to claim 'the earthly philosopher's stone is the true image of the spiritual and heavenly stone, Jesus Christ.' (55) This was neither blasphemous nor alien to the Hermetic tradition; all who follow the way to cosmic consciousness and regeneration of matter use the bridges which tradition provides for us. Christ, partaking of both earthly and divine natures, was seen as such a bridge: his resurrection and the Assumption of his Mother figure frequently in alchemical emblems as symbolic of the achieved work. Significantly, the term *Corpus Christi* – the Body of Christ – has three meanings: the glorified body of Christ, the consecrated bread upon the altar, and the community of believers who form the macrocosmic body of Christ.

In the mythos of Christ is seen the meeting of two traditions. As Dionysius is torn to pieces by the Titans, or Orpheus by the Maenads, within the Native Tradition – itself a later paradigm of the ritual sacrifice in which the tribe partakes of the tortured body of John Barleycorn – so the ritual mythos of the Hermetic Tradition shows us the dissolving of the Red King in the alchemical bath of natron which turns to pure gold. There are many vegetation gods who bear names meaning verdancy: from the Mesopotamian Tammuz, to Osiris, who is the Green One, the drama unfolds. Gold-leaf hammered out thinly and held to the light will glow green and gold, like the green and gold lion, the Mercurius, in whom are hidden all the philosopher's secrets: the chlorophyll of the *prima materia*.

The foundation mysteries of the Native Tradition speak of the apportioning of the body of the Goddess to form the world: so the foundation mysteries of the Hermetic Tradition are those of the scattered God. Their reunion has been celebrated from Sumeria to Ireland: from ritual mating of the Goddess's representative with the King, the homage of the King to Sovereignty, to the Gnostic Bridal-Chamber. (217) Red King and White Queen are God and Nature, Christ and Sophia, Mercury and Venus – a chess encounter which is mate, death and remaking of creation in one.

> Syria has Adonis, Greece has Dionysius, Egypt has Osiris but these are merely the Sun of Wisdom. Isis is the sister, wife and mother of Osiris; Typhon cuts his limbs into pieces, but she binds them together. (307)

The stone which fell from heaven – the proto-Grail – is matter, personified by its guardian, the Anima Mundi or Sophia. Only when the quintessentia embraces the *prima materia* can the stone which is rejected become the keystone of creation. The Rosicrucian alchemists were correct in their appaisal of Christ as the philosopher's stone because he, of all created humanity, has achieved not only birth and death, but also resurrection in his created body.

The mysterious encounter of Christ in the depths of the Underworld which brought about the Resurrection can only be guessed at:

he brought his heavenly light, like that Star of Bethlehem at the place of his birth, into the darkness of the tomb. As one in human flesh, he embraced the human condition of death and dissolution, making it his sister and bride. Thus the laws of nature were altered in an inapprehensible way. The Shroud of Turin bears the imprint of this mysterious encounter – of which the initiate should be loath to speak to the unwise. Flesh was offered voluntarily for the redemption of all flesh: a sacrifice which could not be unacceptable. What Christ has done changes the laws of the created world for ever afterwards. (217) Word and Wisdom, Logos and Sophia have embraced – this side of the apocatastasis – but our Anima Mundi cannot rest from mantling 'the guilty globe' until the whole creation is returned to the primal unity: only then can she enter the eternal embrace of the Bridegroom.

The Golden Age Restored, an alchemical treatise, speaks of matter personified as the 'pure and chaste virgin of whom Adam was formed and created': the alchemist, like Christ, must choose her and say, 'her garments are old, defiled, and foul, but I will purge them, and love her with all my heart.' (307) The alchemical work is therefore one of planetary service for, only by dedication to the lot of the earth and those living on it, can the Great Work be achieved at last.

We have heard how the Emerald Tablet was found in the hands of Hermes Trismegistos, how the Oil of Mercy was eventually given to Adam's successors, how Adam passed to Seth the precious Pearl of gnosis: these are ultimately stories of the inheritance of an unworldly wisdom. Genetically we are part of the Body of Light: the two serpents upon Hermes' caduceus rule our every cell with their encoded spirals of DNA. The cup of gnosis waits to be held to our lips at the end of the quest. These are the esoteric paradigms of the hermeticist – the stories which our ancestral shamans once told and which have been reshaped by successive generations of travellers on the Western Way. This is the story which will be told until the sigh of the last blade of grass, when creation will run backwards as a succession of brilliant sparks in the darkness, into the abode of Light.

The sign of the Aeon is the Hermaphrodite – the rebus of alchemy. This being is the product of a union between Hermes and Aphrodite, the Sun and Moon, God and Goddess of Hermetic and Native Traditions. The totality of the two traditions is comprised of the Emerald Tablet of Hermes and the rose of Aphrodite. As the Native Tradition has come down to us via the shaman as poet/mystic/

quester, so has it been preserved within the wisdom of the Rosicrucian-alchemist, whose symbol is the rose of the Goddess upon the cross of the elements' regeneration. The Hermetic Tradition has been transmitted by the shaman as magician/philosopher, who follows the laws of the Emerald Tablet of the God, Hermes Trismegistos. The union of these disparate functions of the shaman is happening in our own time, where the two traditions meet in the New Aeon – the Aquarian Age.

There is much speculation about this phenomenon: will it be yet another projection of the Golden Age or merely the imagining of mystics at the fag-end of an esoteric era? The Aeon comes as a child: and, like the child Harpocrates, its finger is to its lip. It is a new creation, with the knowledge of both parents – Isis and Osiris – remembering both the nemetons of the Goddess and the temples of the God. It has been – and will be – many things. It is coming to birth while you read this page: the song is already woven between the chthonic sibyl and the celestial prophet.

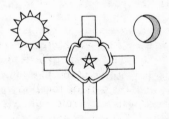

Figure 25:   Sun and Moon shine upon the Rose-Cross of the Great Work

EXERCISE 8 THE SHEPHERD OF STARS

'The ultimate ideal is for every human being to be psychically androgynous' (68) – *not*, we note, physically so. The meaning of this dictum can be realized within the following exercise. In exercise 6, you experienced the elements and learned to integrate them: in this exercise you learn to balance the male and female halves of your inner nature. Seated in meditation, visualize this scene before you.

You are standing, as it were, at the edge of the world. Before you are the two equilibrated pillars: to your left the white pillar – the merciful pillar of the Tree of Life, denoting the Divine Masculine energy which is positive and outer in its effect. To your right is the black pillar, the Pillar of Justice on the Tree of Life, denoting the power of the divine Feminine which is inner and negative in its effect. (Though not in any malign sense: *negative* here means restrictive – the polarized opposite of positive outflowing energy.) Behind the pillars is a vast night sky of deep indigo in which are the stars and planets; the heavenly bodies appear to have eternal stillness and yet to spin on their axes at the same time.

Begin by concentrating upon the individual force of the pillars: if it helps, rehearse the symbolism of a mythos you feel at home with and transfer its energy to the pillars, in order to focus on their effect. Do not hurry; allow the polarized forces to rise. Without touching either pillar, feel their interlocking energies as a magnetic field which is almost tangible. When the power is stabilized and firmly established, visualize the power of each pillar emanating as a ray, like the beam of a spotlight, into the heavens beyond you. At the point where the rays intersect a naked figure stands in an oval of polarized light. It is an adrogyne, formed of the dual energies – one half female, the other half male – either side of the body is composed of a completely perfect man and a completely perfect woman. The figure is beautiful with the power and purity of an angel, yet it is the sum of the pillar's energies in human form. A rainbow scarf swathes the body lightly.

It is sufficient to visualize the scene above, as you stand before the pillars, allowing any realizations to rise from within. But you may wish to go a stage further. The initiate of the mysteries has to 'pass between the pillars', or die to the world, in the mystical sense. The uninitiated can only read this mystery at its face value, perceiving the loss and sacrifice implied in this symbolic action. Yet the initiate gains more than is sacrificed at the dedicatory altar. The androgyne which stands behind the pillars is your potential self, perfected and balanced. When the time is ripe, and you feel prepared, step between the pillars, take the step forward into space, and stand in the twin rays. You are identifying with the potential and essential nature of the whole earth, representing its place in the cosmos as a balanced and thriving unit. As you stand in the starry vault, receiving the power of both pillars, before you appears the Shepherd of Stars, the guardian of flocks. He says, 'I am Alpha and Omega, the Guardian of the Gates, the Keeper of the Keys of Time.' Meditate upon his words: listen to any other words he may have to tell you. Beyond this point you may not go. Visualize yourself back before the pillars, feel the power return to the pillars and their force shutting down for this time. Seal off, in your usual way, making sure you are well earthed.

If you have a tarot pack of the more traditional kind you may find it helpful to contemplate trump twenty-one, the World, on which the androgyne appears, The Shepherd of Stars will appear in whatever shape is appropriate to your needs.

EXERCISE 9 REVITALIZING YOUR ROOTS

We are near the end of the book. If you have read both volumes and worked the exercises consistently you will have begun to walk the Western Way. Perhaps you will have set yourself a regular routine of meditation or practical work. You will then have discovered how much time and energy are diverted from other areas of your life. If this is the first time you have worked with or on the Inner planes you may be disturbed at the depletion of your energy: this is to be expected in the early stages, but everyone, from neophyte to adept experiences this depletion at some time or another, especially after prolonged periods of work. Your physical frame may be ill-suited to take the kind of battering that living on more than one level involves, and you may need to plan your work with care. Any period of prolonged exhaustion is dangerous and leaves the subject open to illness: if your energy is seriously depleted, a long holiday from Inner work is indicated. And that means a *complete* break.

This exercise is designed to help generate vitality and should be regarded as the psychic equivalent of glucose tablets — use it occasionally, but don't expect to survive for a long period on it. It is *not* to be regarded as a substitute for normal rest and refreshment.

Do you remember the great Tree of Tradition on which you found your clan totem? (ex.1, vol.I) This Tree is the axile tree of the Western Way, the central landmark which cross-intersects all levels of the tradition. It is an image which can be fruitfully meditated upon and worked with in many ways, but for this exercise we are going to draw on its vitality. There is no need to travel down the central bole of the trunk: if you have already worked the Clan Totem exercise, you should be able to visualize the Tree and be instantly there. Take your personal totem with you on this exercise, as your passport and strength.

Sit, relax and establish an easy rhythm of breathing. If you are tired and tense this is particularly important, so don't skim it. Five minutes of regular breathing will start to vitalize you in any case. Visualize the Tree before you. It is a beautiful day – just the kind of weather you like best. The earth is springy under your feet. Lay your hand on the trunk of the Tree and feel the green strength running beneath the warm bark. Acknowledge your belonging to the Tree of Tradition.

Turn and look about you. If you have travelled extensively in the Otherworld you may recognize certain features of the landscape. Beside the Tree, sitting on a low mound is the Guardian of Tradition. You may not have met him before: you will see him according to your ancestral alignment – there is no one way of seeing him. He is Guardian both of the Tree and of a natural spring which rises next to a slab of greenish stone. In his hands is a drinking horn.

Greet the Guardian and request to drink from the spring. He may challenge you and ask by what right you come to drink of the spring. In this case, show your totem of belonging. If it is acceptable – and he has the right to refuse you if he feels you are not true to the tradition – he will dip the horn into the spring and hand it to you. Drink and be deeply refreshed. The waters of the spring rise under the roots of the Tree itself, coming from the very depths of the Underworld realm of the ancestors. Return the horn with thanks and go back to the Tree itself. Sit with your back against its trunk, leaning back to share its pulsing vitality. Feel the strength seeping back into you. Enjoy this feeling of well-being and then return to your own time and place.

Certain kinds of devitalization occur because of the kind of inner tide which is running. The waning phases of the moon, the autumn and winter tides as well as personal bodily rhythms need to be taken into account – especially at the onset of menstruation or the menopause. Inner work, other than very general meditation work, should not be attempted if one is pregnant when all the physical and psychic energies should be engaged in nourishing the growing child. While male bodily rhythms are not so marked as female ones, men should likewise record and plot their own inner patterns of response.

Figure 26:   The Virgin Wisdom

AFTERWORD
Tomorrow's Tradition

Ultima Cumaei venit iam carminis aetas;
Magnus ab integro saeclorum pascitiur ordo.
Iam redit et virgo, redeunt Saturnia regna,
Iam nova progenies caelo demittitur alto.

Now comes the last age according to the oracle at Cumae:
the great series of lifetimes is renewed. Now comes the Virgin
goddess once again, the golden days of Saturn's
reign return and a new race descends from heaven.

Virgil: Eclogues

The sleeping place of the Age of Gold is in the depths of every
human heart.

J.C. Powys: Morwyn

We have come a long way, in space and time, since we set out on an
imaginary journey with a helpful guide at the beginning of volume
one. We have explored the inward spiral of the Native Tradition,
visited ancient places, either in person or in the imagination, performed meditations and visualizations, found an inner guide and
teacher, faced the guardians of the road and passed beyond them
through doors into inner worlds. There perhaps we have begun to
map out our own inner landscape, to seek the answers to questions
which have disturbed or fascinated us in our daily lives. Now, in
following the outward spiral of the Hermetic Tradition, we have
perhaps discovered, as was suggested in volume one, that the place
arrived at is no longer the same as that from which we began.

We stand on the verge of a new beginning which is neither a
millennial dream nor the desire for a lost Age of Gold, but rather a
nexus of traditions. The Native path has been walked almost to its
end: in places it is worn thin. The Hermetic way has been explored in
greater and greater depths. What, then, is the next likely step on this
road we have been following from Foretime to Futuretime?

There can, of course, be no single answer, nor any 'right' answer: each individual must decide for himself. Some suggestions have already been made within these pages. One which overrides all these is the step towards some new kind of magical discipline – one which is also, paradoxically, the oldest kind: a dimensionless, cosmic awareness which transcends all boundaries, all paths and all other disciplines. The mind has no limits: it can reach out beyond any boundaries of time and space we care to set. And it can communicate with others of the like disposition. Telepathy is no figment of the imagination, as many who read this will know already; a universal development of the power to communicate over vast distances may not be so far off. Above all we must recognise that there are no limits to what we can achieve other than those we set ourselves, no bolts and bars between the worlds except those we have personally hammered home. The soul is not a bird trapped in a cage: it can and does fly free – returning to its home after long voyaging. All the exercises and techniques in this book will be as nothing to this realization, nor will they work properly without its consent.

The ancients were right to attach so much importance to the idea of the vital spark that sought to rise above earthly confines, and as we have seen repeatedly it is a mistake to believe that this teaching meant that we should despise the body. Through its windows we can catch glimpses of the infinite, which to look upon otherwise would be like looking directly at the sun without protective glasses for our eyes. We see heaven through a darkened glass indeed, but as much for our own good as for any other reason.

This may come as a surprise to those who think that practitioners of esoteric disciplines seek only to transcend the physical. In truth if we are wise we will realize that our physical selves are of the utmost value. From their safe harbourage we depart on voyages of discovery and to them we return, as from any journey, to the welcome of home. Microcosmically, there is an echo here of the soul's longing for the place of its origin, wherever we may personally believe this to be. In our long search for the promised land, the paradisial home of our exiled states, we learn that there must always remain a point of contact with the roots of being. While we yet remain in incarnation the body is that point of contact for us.

So before flying forth towards whatever infinite realm you seek or are drawn, remember to be in tune with yourself as well as with the infinite. Make friends with your human chariot before you leave it behind; and be sure to return to its welcome embrace at your journey's end.

This two-volume book is by no means a complete course. If the Western Way is sufficiently appealing for you to work within its many traditions, then you will no doubt find that you have been walking it for some time already. You may wish to regularize your practice of its wisdom by joining a mystery school or magical group, or you may want to continue mapping your own way or participate in one of the living spiritual traditions. Whatever you decide, the most important thing is to *use* your acquired wisdom. All that we have tried to teach within the confines of these pages is worth nothing unless it is applied to your own lives on a daily basis. If the Western Way remains an abstract study in your hands, then it is likely to become an extinct tradition before long. Only when it is applied directly does it become real, multi-dimensional, a *path* rather than a concept. Our hope is that you will find useful ways of improving your perceptions and deepening your inner experience of the Western Way: indeed, we hope that you find better and more skilful ways of signposting it for others. It is said that the teacher and the taught comprise the teaching between them. The teaching is different for everyone: it is the individual reaction to it that reflects the ancient traditions from one generation to the next.

You should create your own programme of study, meditation and practice: these three disciplines form the basic components of an esoteric way of life. Study gives us the material to work with, meditation shows us new approaches to the work and helps fix our individual response in a symbolic way, practice grounds our inner experiences in outer reality. It is often the last of these which students of the Western mysteries find most difficult: to some extent ritual working fulfils a part of our practice, but the major part is inevitably going to fall within the bounds of our mundane life – the home, the office, in relationships. 'Solitary occult practice is fine – it's people who wreck everything' is a cry often heard on the lips of the beginner: try to prevent this by adopting a clear-headed approach to your fellows.

Everyday life is the best training ground of all. If you need to run to your inner teacher, tarot pack, or table of correspondences for a solution to every mundane problem, then you are not facing up to life's realities. To test this out, try to live one whole day in accordance with esoteric principles: eat and drink with total attention to the items being consumed, their taste, the goodness being derived from their digestion. See everyone you meet as possessed of the divine spark: each being is as much deserving as yourself. Even those who irritate you may possess qualities you never guessed at and which you might do well to imitate. Perform your daily tasks with total attention to the principle involved: cleaning the house is but an extension of self-clarification, and is itself a reflection of macrocosmic order. When faced with sudden decisions try to see the principles and choices before you as they a) affect you, b) affect others, c) affect the cosmos. Be as attentive to your moments of relaxation: rest hard as well as working hard: feel the cessation of work as the commencement of creative stillness which will in turn be the thrust-block of your work. At the end of one day so spent note down your responses: you may begin to understand just what is involved in the word *practice*.

Whatever material you choose to work with, let it be an expression of your own perception, not a revival which has to be learned like a part. If you have already started practical pathwalking, you will have discovered that the way feels right when you use your own compass and not some complicated device which has been patented by someone else. No one can make you an adept: that rank – which is really no more than a title given to one who has reached a stage of development within the scheme of creation – can only be awarded by you yourself, either in colloquy with an inner teacher or with the inner spark of divinity.

> God said to man: I have placed you in the world that you may more readily see what you are. I have made you neither earthly nor heavenly, neither a mortal nor a immortal being, in order that you, as your own sculptor, may carve features for yourself. You may degenerate into an animal, but by using your free will you may also be reborn as a god-like being. (67)

We have taken many things for granted in this book. The belief in other states of being and other worlds, other orders of creation above and beyond what we recognize in our normal functioning state. We have stated that mankind has a future; that it is not necessarily doomed to extinction – that it may in fact be on the verge of a wholly new development. That this is no mere speculation can be seen clearly enough if we look at the discoveries being made daily in quantum physics and other areas of scientific research which are the outer manifestation of Alchemy and are bringing creation in a full circle towards its beginnings.

But science is not enough: it fails to satisfy because it cannot answer the really important questions; its theories and laws, when added up, do not make up the sum total of creation – not even a tenth part of it. As esotericists we have ourselves to use as indexes of creation, alchemically perfecting the elements within us until they fit exactly into the puzzle of the cosmos.

It is not enough simply to be aware of these things, to enquire into them for the sake of curiosity alone. We have to be a living part of the process which transforms the scattered particles of the Body of Light into a wholly new and original being. Adam Kadmon must be built up, piece by piece; Osiris, Dionysius – all the wounded saviour gods – made whole; the Fisher King restored. But to do this, to help bring it about, we have to be functioning parts of the process. This underlines the importance of 'being in touch,' of being connected to the heart of the cosmos, knowing that there we will feel an answering touch, a note with which to resonate.

> None of the gods of heaven will ever quit heaven, and pass its boundary, and come down to earth; but man ascends even to heaven, and measures it; and what is more than all beside, he mounts to heaven without quitting the earth; so vast a distance can he put forth his power. We must not shrink then from saying that a man on earth is a mortal god, and that god in heaven is a mortal man. (302)

Towards this end we have given exercises and techniques aimed at connecting us to the infinite worlds around us, of bringing back the wisdom of the otherworld to our own dimension and making it a lasting part of our own eternal becoming. The techniques on their own mean nothing, without the commitment to the truths that stand behind them. To this end we have given much that is in the nature of an esoteric philosophy – a framework on which to hang the stuff of wonder. It is to these truths that we each dedicate ourselves as followers of the Western Way, whether in the end we call them gods or states of mind; and it is these fundamental axioms we have tried to bring before you through the intricate web of belief, practice and teaching which is the backbone of all traditions.

For choosing to believe in a universe with purpose we make no apology, assuming that those who read these pages share our belief. As the Zoroastrian magi believed, the universe is indeed a great chariot: it need not matter that we know little or nothing of the driver (who may well be ourselves collectively), only that it is proceeding towards a point of completion rather than destruction, and that we, as passengers, should be present when it arrives.

The image of the esotericist as black magician or harmless crank has been slow to fade. The shaman and shamanka, the magician and pathwalker – however we tend to see ourselves – are all subjected to this image. Friends, family, even your employer, may look severely on your efforts and brand you godless, cracked, perhaps even evil. Confronted with the esoteric many people react in an orthodox and fundamentally, exoteric way. You will have to weigh these disadvantages of following the Western Way; for even though a spirit of tolerance exists towards esotericism at present this does not mean that this will always be so. Fundamentalism is on the march again, witch-hunts and brainwashing have happened in this century: they are not just the record of an ancient past. Discretion and silence have kept the esoteric traditions from the uninitiated during such times of persecution; now that times are kind to us it is the responsibility of anyone walking the Western Way to ensure that the teaching is carefully practised and sensibly taught; that traditions are disseminated wisely and practically demonstrated to a world which may think them unnatural.

You may be doing nothing more than meditating in a small group or meeting at an ancient site for the festivals; or you may be teaching at open seminars or giving lectures and pathwalkings to beginners. Whatever you practise, *you* are the public image of the Western Way: people look to you to practise what you preach. You owe respect to the teachers – whether inner or outer – who have instructed you, and you certainly bear responsibility to those you seek to teach. We must all imitate the instructions contained in the Rosicrucian Manifesto: dress and behave in the manner of the country you live in, do not draw attention to yourselves, do not accept money for your services (which are of the Inner and not yours to sell), meet with your contemporary pathwalkers periodically, find one worthy person (at least) to whom you can transmit your tradition and what you have learned. Above all, always be true to your inner principles. The Tree of Tradition is rooted in the ancestral past; be true to that past and ensure that its branches grow strong in our own time and that fruit grows upon it for tomorrow's tradition.

This being said, what of that future? Where does esotericism go next? Can the Hermetic and Native traditions fuse to keep the former from hierarchical stasis and the latter from atavistic reversion to type? We believe that this fusion is now becoming manifest in many imperceptible ways; just as there will soon no longer be any clear boundary between East and West, so it will become harder and harder to see the join between Hermetic and Native traditions.

> Each race maintains its cultural traditions, and each cult survives until the faculties which it was designed to initiate have become the normal inheritance of the species. Then it ceases to be esoteric and becomes exoteric. . . As long as there are souls that require the discipline the cult lives on. (90)

This is exactly the case of the Native Tradition — elements of its wisdom may now be atavistic but until its lessons are assimilated it cannot be abandoned like a worked-out quarry. The Native Tradition's resonance is particularly strong at this time because much that has been esoteric is now becoming exoteric and thus available to all. The resonance of the Hermetic tradition is both for this time and for future ages: much remains which will be the work of competent pathwalkers to synthesize into forms more exoteric.

The barriers between East and West are melting also, though it will be generations before they are finally down. For those walking the Western Way initial contact with the roots of the western mysteries is recommended. A pull to the East may well be experienced: Eastern spiritual schools appear tempting and there may be incarnational links — but birth has placed us in the West. At a certain point the mysteries reach a plateau where all traditions are in accord. Already, with the fore-shortening of Eastern and Western margins, many new factors are coming into play. The seizure of Tibet by the Chinese in 1958 has had the unprecedented effect of sending forth a body of secret Tibetan teaching in the persons of fleeing lamas who are the living exponents of what will be a migrating native system into the West. The parallels between this exodus and that of the fabled Atlantean escape routes to the West are not inconsiderable. Then too a culture about to be overwhelmed sent forth emissaries into the world who may well have seeded the teachings of the Western mysteries. Such migrations have ever done their work of cross-fertilizing, and energizing dying traditions, providing a vast influx of new energy.

The fact that to gain esoteric training people have had to journey to the East, as in the story by Hermann Hesse with which we began has meant that Eastern teaching has not always been properly assimilated into Western life. The Tibetans who will now live their lives in the West bring their knowledge at first hand and are adapting it as usefully as they know, using their skilful means. (Anderson)

The ultimate solution of our world problem lies in ... a knowledge that is neither Eastern nor Western, but which is known to both. When we have joined hands with the Orient and when we have united the best thoughts of the East with those of the West, we shall have a synthetic and balanced teaching which will liberate the coming generations. (19)

Meanwhile our task as the guardians of the Western Way is to work towards a synthesis of Native and Hermetic traditions, taking the 'best thoughts' of each to form a new whole. Cosmic consciousness is the goal of tomorrow's tradition, built firmly upon the realizations of both Native and Hermetic ways: into cosmic consciousness, threading in and out of the maze to discover a new collective awareness.

The re-emergence of the Divine Feminine and the mingling of masculine and feminine energies, are elements which mark the birth of the Aquarian Age. At last the division of the paths is being ended; people are beginning to realize that there has only ever been one goal, even though there were many ways to reach it. The Western Way is not exclusive, it is just our most familiar path. Those who walk it must learn to think differently to the rest of warring humanity, must indeed relearn all we have forgotten since the Beginning, the Foretime, when living *was* life, was creation, was nature, was God. There is no great synthesis at this level, no simple answer. Finally, no philosopher's stone – unless it be ourselves. Only a new way of being, a possibility of realizing the truth of our place in the cosmos.

In looking to the future we have much to keep in mind, much to consider and meditate upon before we can be freed to explore the endless dimensions we have sought so long. As we look back along the winding maze of the Western Way we see many signposts. All are pointing the same way: *at us*. A long line of teachers stand behind us: another line stretches out into the future. We all stand as links in a chain of transmission which must not be allowed to fail. We ourselves are like solar systems, whole cosmologies, with fixed stars and wandering planets. There are no known limits to where we may go or how far we may travel. We stand with map and compasses in hand, ready to begin a new journey and we are, in some senses, our own guides, for that country is very familiar. All we have to do is step forth. That experience awaits you, in your own time and in your own way. May your journey be as happy and joyful as ours has been, and may you always return safely.

Hermes, offspring of Dionysos who revels
    in the dance
and of Aphrodite, the Paphian maiden of the
    fluttering eyelids,
you frequent the sacred house of Persephone
as guide through the earth of ill-fated souls
which you bring to their haven when their time
    has come,
charming them with your sacred wand and giving
    them sleep
from which you rose them again. To you indeed
Persephone gave the office, throughout wide
    Tartaros,
to lead the way for the eternal souls of men.
But, blessed one, grant a good end for the
    initiate's work. (13)

BIBLIOGRAPHY AND DISCOGRAPHY

Items are listed in numerical order and numbers will be found to correspond to those in the text. Those marked with letters after the publication details are to indicate the type of work. Thus: F = Fiction, G = General, J = Journal, P = Poetry, R = Recording, T = Text, M = Music, I = Instructional or Meditation tape.

(1) Abulafia, A., *The Path of the Names*, Berkley, Trigram, 1976 (T)

(2) Adams, H., *Mont St-Michel and Chartres*, London, Hamlyn, 1980 (G)

(3) Agrippa, C., *Occult Philosophy*, Wellingborough, Aquarian Press, 1975 (T)

(4) Ahern, G., *Sun at Midnight*, Wellingborough, Aquarian Press, 1984 (G)

(5) Albertus, Frater, *Alchemist's Handbook*, Routledge & Kegan Paul, 1976 (G)

(6) Allen, P.M., ed., *A Christian Rosenkreutz Anthology*, New York, Rudolf Steiner Publication, 1968 (G)

(7) Allen, R.H., *Star Names: their lore and meaning*, New York, Dover Books, 1963 (G)

(8) Anderson, W., *Open Secrets, a Western Guide to Tibetan Buddhism*, Harmondsworth, Penguin, 1980 (G)

(9) *Apocalyptic Spirituality*, ed. and trans., B. McGuinn, London, SPCK, 1979 (T)

(10) *Apocryphal New Testament*, ed. and trans., M.R. James, London, Oxford University Press, 1924 (T)

(11) Apuleius, *The Golden Ass*, trans., Robert Graves, Harmondsworth, Penguin Books, 1950 (T)

(12) Ashcroft-Nowicki, D., *The Shining Paths*, Wellingborough, Aquarian Press, 1983 (G)

(13) Athanassakis, A.N., trans., *The Orphic Hymns*, Missoula, Mont., Scholars Press, 1977 (T)

(14) St Augustine, *The City of God*, Harmondsworth, Penguin Books, 1972 (T)

(15) *Aurora Consurgens*, ed., M.-L. von Franz, New York, Pantheon Books, 1966 (T)

(16) Bacon, F., *Advancement of Learning and New Atlantis*, London, Oxford University Press, 1906 (T)

(17) *The Bahir*, trans. A. Kaplan, New York, Weiser, 1979 (T)

(18) Baigent, M., Lincoln, H., and Leigh, R., *Holy Blood, Holy Grail*, London, Cape, 1982 (G)

(19) Bailey, A.A., *The Externalization of the Hierarchy*, London, Lucis Press, 1957. (G)

(20) Bailey, A.A., *The Rays and the Initiations*, Lucis Press, 1960. (G)

(21) Bailey, A.A., *A Treatise on White Magic*, London, Lucis Press, 1934 (G)

(22) Bamford, C., 'Natureword, the Hermetic Tradition and Today' in *Natureworld* by R.A. Schwaller de Lubicz, Mass., Lindisfarne Press, 1982 (G)

(23) Banks, N.N., *The Golden Thread*, London, Lucis Press, 1963 (G)

(24) Barbault, A., *Gold of a Thousand Mornings*, London, Neville Spearman, 1975 (G)

(25) Bausch, W.J., *Storytelling: imagination and faith*, Twenty-Third Publishers, Mystic, Conn., 1984 (G)

(26) *The Holy Bible*, (R.S.V.), London, Nelson, 1966 (T)

(27) Blake, W., *Poetry and Prose*, ed. G. Keynes, London, Nonsuch Library, 1975 (P)

(28) Blakeley, J.D., *Mystical Tower of the Tarot*, London, Watkins, 1974 (G)

(29) Blavatsky, H.P., *The Secret Doctrine*, London, Theosophical Publishing House, 1970 (G)

(30) Bolton, J.D.P., *Aristaeus of Proconnesus*, London, Oxford University Press, 1962 (G)

(31) *Book of Enoch*, trans. R.H. Charles, London, SPCK, 1982 (T)

(32) Bronstein, H., *A Passover Haggadah*, Harmondsworth, Penguin, 1974 (G)

(33) Bruno, G., *The Expulsion of the Triumphant Beast*, trans. A.D. Imerti, New Brunswick, Rutgers University Press, 1964 (T)

(34) Budge, E.A.W., *Osiris: The Egyptian Religion of Resurrection*, New York, University Books, 1961 (G)

(35) Burckhardt, T., *Alchemy: Science of the Comos, Science of the Soul*, trans. W. Stoddart, London, Stuart & Watkins, 1967 (G)

(36) Burton, U. and Dolley, J., *Christian Evolution: Moving Towards a Global Spirituality*. Wellingborough, Turnstone, 1984 (G)

(37) Butler, E.M., *The Myth of the Magus*, Cambridge, Cambridge University Press, 1979 (G)

(38) Butler, E.M., *Ritual Magic*, Cambridge, Cambridge University Press, 1979 (G)

(39) Butler, W.E., *Apprenticed to Magic*, Wellingborough, Aquarian, 1962 (G)

(40) Caldecott, S., *The Treasures of Tradition*: in *Resurgence* no. 102, January-February 1984 (J)

(41) Calvino, I., *The Castle of Crossed Destinies*, London, Secker, 1977 (F)

(42) *Cambridge History of Judaism volume I: The Persian Period*, ed. W.D. Davies and L. Finkelstein, Cambridge, Cambridge University Press, 1984 (G)

(43) Casaubon, M., *A True and Faithful Relation Of What Passed For Many Years Between Dr. John Dee and Some Spirits*. Glasgow and Portmeirion, Antonine Publishing Company Ltd. with Golden Dragon Press, 1974 (T)

(44) St Catherine of Siena, *The Dialogues*, London, SPCK, 1980 (T)

(45) Chapman, V., *Bladdud the Birdman*, London, Rex Collings, 1978 (F)

(46) Chevalier, G., *The Sacred Magician – a Ceremonial Diary*, Frogmore, Paladin, 1976 (G)

(47) Chretien de Troyes, *Conte du Graal*, trans. R.W. Linker, Chapel Hill, University of North Carolina, 1952 (T)

(48) Christian, P., *The History and Practice of Magic*, London, Forge Press, 1952 (G)

(49) Christie-Murray, D., *A History of Heresy*, London, New English Library, 1976 (G)

(50) *Cloud of Unknowing*, ed. E. Underhill, London, Stuart and Watkins, 1970 (T)

(51) Colquhoun, I., *The Sword of Wisdom – MacGregor Mathers and the Golden Dawn*, London, Neville Spearman, 1975 (G)

(52) Coomaraswamy, R.P., *The Destruction of the Christian Tradition*, London, Perennial Books, 1981 (G)

(53) Cooper, J.C. *The Illustrated Encyclopedia of Traditional Symbols*, London, Thames & Hudson, 1978 (G)

(54) Corbin, H., *The Man of Light in Iranian Sufism*, Shambhala, Boulder, Colarado and London, 1978 (G)

(55) Coudert, A., *Alchemy: The Philosophers' Stone*, London, Wildwood, 1980 (G)

(56) Court, S., *The Meditators' Manual*, Wellingborough, Aquarian, 1984 (G)

(57) Critchlow, K. *Temenos and Temple*, in *Temenos*, I, 1981 (J)

(58) Crowley, A. 777, privately printed by Ordo Templi Orientis, n.d. (T)

(59) Cumont, F., *The Mysteries of Mithras*, New York, Dover Publications 1956 (G)

(60) Danielou, A., *Shiva and Dionysius*, New York, Inner Traditions Int., 1984 (G)

(61) Dante, *The Divine Comedy*, trans. L. Binyon, London, Agenda, 1979 (T)

(62) Dart, J., *The Laughing Saviour*, New York, Harper & Row, 1976 (G)

(63) Davidson, G., *A Dictionary of Angels*, New York, Free Press with Collier-Macmillan, 1967 (G)

(64) De Borron. R., *Joseph d'Arimathie*, ed. W.A. Nitze, in Roman de L'estoire dou Graal, Paris, Classiques Français du Moyen Age, 1927 (T)

(65) Dee, J., *The Hieroglyphic Monarch*, New York, Samuel Weiser Inc., 1975 (T)

(66) De Jong. H.M.E., *Michael Maier's Atalanta Fugiens: Sources of an Alchemical Book of Emblems*, Leiden, E.J.Brill, 1969 (G)

(67) Della Mirandola, P., *On the Dignity of Man, On Being and the One, Heptaplus*, Indianapolis, Bobbs-Merrill, 1965 (T)

(68) Denning, M. and Phillips. O., *The Magical Philosophy* (5 Volumes) St Paul. Llewellyn Pubs, 1974–1981 (G)

(69) Dionysius the Areopagite, *The Divine Names and the Mystical Theology*, trans C.E. Rolt, London, SPCK, 1940 (T)

(70) Dionysius the Areopagite, *The Mystical Theology and the Celestial Hierarchies*, trans. and ed. The Shrine of Wisdom, Fintry, Shrine of Wisdom, 1949 (T)

(71) *Dream of Scipio*, trans. R. Bullock. Wellingborough, Aquarian, 1983 (T)

(72) Drower, E.S., *The Secret Adam: A Study of Nasoraean Gnosis*. Oxford, Oxford University Press, 1960 (G)

(73) Eliade, M., *History of Religious Ideas vol. I: From the Stone Age to the Eleusian Mysteries*, London, Collins, 1979 (T)

(74) Eliade, M., *History of Religious Ideas vol II: From Gautama Buddha to the Triumph of Christianity*, Chicago, University of Chicago Press, 1982 (T)

(75) Ellwood, R.S., *Religious and Spiritual Groups in Modern America*. New Jersey, Prentice Hall Inc., 1975 (G)

(76) Ellwood Post, W., *Saints, Signs and Symbols*, London, SPCK 1962 (G)

(77) Epstein, P., *Kabbalah: the way of the Jewish Mystic*, New York, Weiser, 1978 (G)

(78) Every, G., *Christian Mythology*, London, Hamlyn, 1970 (G)

(79) Fabricius, J., *Alchemy*, Copenhagen, Rosenkilde and Bagger, 1976 (G)

(80) Ferguson, J. *Illustrated Encyclopedia of Mysticism and the Mystery Religions*, London, Thames & Hudson, 1976 (G)

(81) Ferguson, J. *Jesus in the Tide of Time*, London, Routledge & Kegan Paul, 1980 (G)

(82) Ferguson, M., *The Aquarian Conspiracy*, London, Routledge & Kegan Paul, 1981 (G)

(83) Ficino, M., *The Letters of Marsilio Ficino vols I – 3*, London, Shepheard Walwyn, 1975–1981 (T)

(84) Figulus, B., *A Golden and Blessed Casket of Nature's Marvels*, London, Vincent Stuart Ltd., 1963 (T)

(85) Fleming, D.L., *Contemporary Reading of the Spiritual Exercises*, St Louis, Institute of Jesuit Sources, 1980 (G)

(86) Fludd, R., *The Origin and Structure of the Cosmos*. Edinburgh, Hermetic Source Works, 1982 (T)

(87) Fontenrose, J., *Python*, Berkeley, University of California Press, 1959 (G)

(88) *Forms of Prayer for Jewish Worship*, ed. Assembly of Rabbis of the Reform Synagogues of Great Britain, 1977 (T)

(89) Fortune, D., *Applied Magic*, Wellingborough, Aquarian, 1962 (G)

(90) Fortune, D., *The Cosmic Doctrine*, Wellingborough, Aquarian, 1976, (G)

(91) Fortune, D, *Esoteric Orders and their Work*, St Paul, Llewellyn Press, 1978 (G)

(92) Fortune, D., *Esoteric Philosophy of Love and Marriage*, Wellingborough, Aquarian Press, 1970 (G)

(93) Fortune, D., *Moon Magic*, Wellingborough, Aquarian, 1956 (F)

(94) Fortune, D., *The Sea Priestess*, Wellingborough, Aquarian, 1957 (F)

(95) Fortune, D., *The Secrets of Dr. Taverner*, St Paul, Llewellyn Press, 1979 (F)

(96) Fortune, D., *The Training and Work of an Initiate*, Wellingborough, Aquarian 1930 (G)

(97) Fouquet, J., *The Hours of Etienne Chevalier*, London, Thames & Hudson, 1972 (T)

(98) French, R.M., *The Way of the Pilgrim*. London, SPCK 1930 (G)

(99) Gadal, A. *Sur Le Chemin du Saint-Graal*, Haarlem, Rozekruis Pers, 1960 (G)

(100) Garrison, J., *The Darkness of God: Theology after Hiroshima*, London, SCM Press, 1982 (G)

(101)   Giraldus Cambrensis, *The Journey through Wales*, trans. L. Thorpe, Harmondsworth, Penguin, 1978 (T)

(102)   Godwin, J., *Athanasius Kircher*, London, Thames & Hudson, 1979 (G)

(103)   Godwin, J., *The Golden Chain of Orpheus*, in *Temenos* 4 and 5, 1984 (J)

(104)   Godwin, J., *Mystery Religions and the Ancient World*, London, Thames & Hudson, 1981 (G)

(105)   Godwin, J., *Robert Fludd*, London, Thames & Hudson, 1979 (G)

(106)   *Golden Verses of the Pythagoreans*, trans. Editors of the Shrine of Wisdom, Fintry, Shrine of Wisdom, n.d. (T)

(107)   Gorman, P., *Pythagoras*, London, Routledge & Kegan Paul, 1979 (G)

(108)   Gorres, I.F., *Broken Lights*, London, Burns & Oates, 1964 (G)

(109)   Grant, F.C., *Hellenistic Religions – The Age of Syncretism*, New York, Bobbs-Merrill, 1953 (G)

(110)   Graves, R., *Adam's Rib*, London, Trianon Press, 1955 (G)

(111)   Graves, R., *Greek Myths*, London, Cassell, 1958 (G)

(112)   Graves, R. and Patai, R., *Hebrew Myths*, London, Cassell, 1963 (G)

(113)   Graves, R., *Seven Days in New Crete*, London, Cassell, 1949 (F)

(114)   Gray, W.G., *Inner Traditions of Magic*, London, Aquarian, 1970 (G)

(115)   Gray. W.G., *Magical Ritual Methods*, Toddington, Helios, 1971 (G)

(116)   Gray, W.G., *Western Inner Workings*, New York, Weiser, 1983 (G)

(117)   Green, M., *Experiments in Aquarian Magic*, Wellingborough, Aquarian, 1985, (G)

(118)   Green, M., *Magic in the Aquarian Age*, Wellingborough, Aquarian, 1983 (G)

(119)   Greene, B and Gollancz, V., *God of a Hundred Names*, London, Gollancz, 1962 (G)

(120)   Greer, M.K., *Tarot For Your Self: a Workbook for Personal Transformation*, North Hollywood, Newcastle Publications Company Inc., 1984 (G)

(121)   Grossinger, R., *The Alchemical Tradition*, Berkeley, North Atlantic Books, 1983 (G)

(122)   Grossinger, R., *The Night Sky*, San Francisco, Sierra Club Books, 1981 (G)

(123)   Guénon, R., *Crisis of the Modern World*, London, Luzac, 1975 (G)

(124)   Guénon, R., *Symboles Fondamentaux de la Science Sacrée*, Paris, Gallimard, 1962 (G)

(125)   Guirdham, A., *The Great Heresy*, Jersey, Neville Spearman, 1977 (G)

(126) Guthrie, W.K.C., *Orpheus and Greek Religion*, New York, W.W. Norton, 1966 (G)

(127) Halevi, Z., *Adam and the Kabbalistic Tree*, London, Rider, 1974 (G)

(128) Halevi, Z., *Kabbalah: Tradition of Hidden Knowledge*, London, Thames & Hudson, 1979 (G)

(129) Halevi, Z., *A Kabbalistic Universe*, London, Rider, 1977 (G)

(130) Halevi, Z., *The Work of the Kabbalist*, London, Gateway Books, 1985 (G)

(131) Hall, M.P., *The Adepts in the Western Esoteric Tradition*, Los Angeles, Philosophical Research Society, 1949 (G)

(132) Hall, M.P., *Magic*, Los Angeles, Philosophical Research Society, 1978 (G)

(133) Hall, M.P., *The Secret Teachings of All Ages*, Los Angeles, Philosophical Research Society, 1975 (G)

(134) Hargrave, J., *The Life and Soul of Paracelsus*, London, Gollancz, 1951 (G)

(135) Harner, M., *The Way of the Shaman*, New York, Harper & Row, 1980 (G)

(136) Haughton, R., *The Catholic Thing*, Dublin, Villa Books, 1979 (G)

(137) Haughton, R., *Tales from Eternity: The World of Faeries and the Spiritual Search*, London, Allen & Unwin, 1973 (G)

(138) Hauschka, R., *The Nature of substance*, London, Rudolph Steiner Press, 1983 (G)

(139) Hawkridge, R., *The Wisdom Tree*. New York, Houghton Mifflin Co., 1945 (G)

(140) Heller, A., *Renaissance Man*, London, Routledge & Kegan Paul, 1978 (G)

(141) *Hermetic Journal* ed. A. McLean. issn. 0141 6391, Edinburgh, 1978 (J)

(142) Hesse, H. *The Glass Bead Game*, London, Cape, 1970 (F)

(143) Hildegard of Bingen, *Meditations*, trans, G., Uhlein, Santa Fe, Bear & Co 1983 (T)

(144) Hoeller, S.A., *The Gnostic Jung and the Seven Sermons to the Dead*, Wheaton, Theosophical Publishing House, 1982 (G)

(145) Hoffman, E., *The Way of Splendour: Jewish Mysticism and Modern Psychology*, Boulder, Shambhala, 1981 (G)

(146) *Homage to Pythagoras*, Lindisfarne Newsletter 1981, West Stockbridge (J)

(147) Hope, M., *Practical Egyptian Magic*, Wellingborough, Aquarian, 1984 (G)

(148) Hope, M., *Practical Techniques of Psychic Self-Defence*, Wellingborough, Aquarian, 1983 (G)

(149) Houselander, C., *Letters*, London, Sheed & Ward, 1965 (G)

(150) Huizinga, J., *The Waning of the Middle Ages*, Harmondsworth, Penguin, 1955 (G)

(151) Huxley, A., *The Perennial Philosophy*, London, Chatto & Windus, 1946 (G)

(152) Iamblicus., *On the Mysteries*, trans. T. Taylor, San Diego, Wizard's Bookshelf, 1984 (T)

(153) Jackson-Knight, W.F., *Vergil: Epic and Anthropology*. London, Allen & Unwin, 1967, (G)

(154) Jacobs, L., *Jewish Mystical Testimonies*, New York, Schoken Books, 1976 (T)

(155) St John of the Cross, *Four Poems*, trans, Y. Orta, Oxford, Carmelite Priory, Boar's Hill, 1984 (T)

(156) Johnston, W., *Christian Mysticism Today*, London, Collins, 1984 (G)

(157) Jonas, H., *The Gnostic Religion: The Message of the Alien God and the Beginnings of Christianity*, Boston, Beacon Press, 1963 (G)

(158) Jones, D., *Epoch and Artist*, London, Faber, 1959 (G)

(159) Jones, P., *Physics as Metaphor*, London, Wildwood, 1983 (G)

(160) Julian of Norwich, *Revelations of Divine Love*, Wheathampstead, Anthony Clarke, 1973 (T)

(161) Jung, C.G., *Answer to Job*, London, Routledge & Kegan Paul, 1954 (G)

(162) Jung, C.G., *Archetypes and the Collective Unconscious*, London, Routledge & Kegan Paul, 1968 (G)

(163) Jung, C.G., *Memories, Dreams and Reflections*, London, Collins and Routledge & Kegan Paul, 1963 (G)

(164) Jung, C.G., *Psychology and Alchemy*, London, Routledge & Kegan Paul, 1968 (G)

(165) Jung, C.G., *Word and Image*, ed. A. Jaffe, New Jersey, Princeton University Press, 1979 (G)

(166) Jung, E. and Von Franz, M., *The Grail Legends*, London, Hodder, 1956 (G)

(167) Kaplan, A., *Meditation and the Bible*, Maine, Weiser, 1978 (G)

(168) Kaplan, A., *Meditation and Kabbalah*, York Beach, Weiser, 1982 (G)

(169) Keen, M., *Chivalry*, New Harlem, Yale University Press, 1984 (G)

(170) Kempis, T., *The Imitation of Christ*, trans. R., Dudley, Wheathampstead, Anthony Clarke, 1980 (T)

(171) Kerenyi, K., *Apollo*, Dallas, Spring Publications, 1983 (G)

(172) Kerenyi, K., *Asklepios*, New York, Pantheon Books, 1959 (G)

(173) Kerenyi, K., *Gods of the Greeks*, London, Thames & Hudson, 1951, (G)

(174) Kerenyi, K., *Hermes, Guide of Souls*, Zurich, Spring Books, 1976, (G)

(175) Kerenyi, K., *The Heroes of the Greeks*, London, Thames & Hudson, 1959 (G)

(176) Kierkegaard, S., *For Self-Examination and Judge for Yourselves*, trans. W. Lowrie, Oxford, Oxford University Press, 1941, (G)

(177) Klibansky, R., *Continuity of the Platonic Tradition*, London, Warburg Institute, 1939, (G)

(178) Knight, G. and McLean, A., *Commentary on the Chymical Wedding of Christian Rosenkreutz*, Edinburgh, Magnum Opus Hermetic Sourceworks, 1984 (T)

(179) Knight, G., *Experience of Inner Worlds*, Toddington, Helios, 1975 (G)

(180) Knight, G., *A History of White Magic*, London, Mowbrays, 1978 (G)

(181) Knight, G., *Occult Exercises and Practices*, Wellingborough, Aquarian, 1982 (G)

(182) Knight, G., *The Practice of Ritual Magic*, Wellingborough, Aquarian, 1979 (G)

(183) Knight, G., *A Practical guide to Qabalistic Symbolism*, Toddington, Helios, 1965 (G)

(184) Knight, G., *The Rose-Cross and the Goddess*, Wellingborough, Aquarian, 1985 (G)

(185) Knight, G., *The Secret Tradition in Arthurian Legend*, Wellingborough, Aquarian, 1984 (G)

(186) *Kore Kosmou*, trans. A. Kingsford and E. Maitland, Minneapolis, Wizard's Bookshelf, 1977 (T)

(187) Lacarriere, J., *The Gnostics*, London, Peter Owen, 1977 (G)

(188) Lambert, M.D., *Medieval Heresy*, London, Edward Arnold, 1977 (G)

(189) Lang-Sims, L., *The Christian Mystery*, London, Allen & Unwin, 1980 (G)

(190) Le Roy Ladurie, E., *Montaillou*, London, Scolar Press, 1978 (G)

(191) *Lenten Triodion*, trans. Mother Mary and Archimandrite K. Ware, London, Faber, 1977 (T)

(192) Lewis, C.S., *The Business of Heaven*, London, Fount, 1984 (G)

(193) Lewis, C.S., *The Discarded Image*, Cambridge University Press, 1964 (G)

(194) Lewis, C.S., *Til we Have Faces*, London, Fount, 1978 (F)

(195) Lievegoed, B.C.J., *Mystery Streams in Europe and the New Mysteries*, New York, Anthroposophic Press, 1982 (G)

(196) Lindisfarne Letter no 9. *Poetry and Prophecy*, West Stockbridge, 1979 (J)

(197) Lindsay, J., *The Origins of Alchemy in Graeco-Roman Egypt*, London, Frederick Muller, 1970 (G)

(198) Lindsay, J., *The Troubadours*, London, Frederick Muller, 1976 (G)

(199) Lionel, F., *The Seduction of the Occult Path*, Wellingborough, Turnstone, 1983 (G)

(200) Lossky, V., *The Mystical Theology of the Eastern Church*, Cambridge, James Clarke & Co. Ltd., 1957 (G)

(201) Love, J., *The Quantum Gods*, Compton Russell Element, Tisbury, Wilts., 1976 (G)

(202) Lucian, *The Syrian Goddess*, Constable, 1913, (T)

(203) Lurker, M., *Gods and Symbols of Ancient Egypt*, Thames & Hudson, 1974 (G)

(204) *Mabinogion*, ed. and trans. Lady Charlotte Guest, John Jones, Cardiff, 1977 (T)

(205) McClain, E.G., *The Pythagorean Plato*, Nicholas Hays, 1978 (G)

(206) McGregor-Mathers, S.L., *The Book of the Sacred Magic of Abra-Melin the Mage*, Wellingborough, Thorsons, 1976 (G)

(207) McIntosh, C., *Rosy Cross Unveiled*, Wellingborough, Aquarian Press, 1980 (G)

(208) McLean, A., *A Compendium on the Rosicrucian Vault*, Hermetic Research Series, 12 Antigua Street, Edinburgh, 1985 (G)

(209) McLean, A., 'A Hermetic Origin of the Tarot Cards?' in *Hermetic Journal*, vol. 21, Autumn 1983 (G)

(210) McLean, A., *Journal of Rosicrucian Studies I*, Autumn 1983, 12 Antigua Street, Edinburgh (G)

(211) McLean, A., 'Robert Flood's Great Treatise of Rosicrucian Science' in *Hermetic Journal* No. 17, Autumn 1982 (G)

(212) McLean, A., 'A Rosicrucian Alchemical Mystery Centre in Scotland' in *Hermetic Journal* No.4, Summer 1979 (G)

(213) McLean, A., *The Western Mandala*, Hermetic Research Series, 12 Antigua Street, Edinburgh, 1983 (G)

(214) McWaters, B., *Conscious Evolution*, Wellingborough, Turnstone Press, 1983 (G)

(215) Macrobius, *Commentary on the Dream of Scipio*, Columbia University Press, New York and London, 1952 (T)

(216) Malory, Sir Thomas, *Le Mort d'Arthur*, Harmondsworth, Penguin Books, 1969 (T)

(217) Matthews, C., 'The Rosicrucian Vault as Sepulchre and Wedding Chamber' in Stewart, B. *The Initiation of the Underworld*. Wellingborough, Aquarian Press, 1985 (G)

(218) Matthews, C., *The Search for Rhiannon*, Frome, Brans Head, 1981 (P)

(219) Matthews, C., 'Sophia as Companion on the Quest' in *At the Table of the Grail*, ed. J. Matthews, Routledge & Kegan Paul, 1983 (G)

(220) Matthews, J., *At The Table of the Grail*, Routledge & Kegan Paul, 1983 (G)

(221) Matthews, J., *The Grail, Quest for the Eternal*, Thames & Hudson, 1981 (G)

(222) Matthews, J. and Green, M., *The Grail Seekers Handbook*, Wellingborough, Aquarian Press, 1986 (G)

(223) Mead, G.R.S., *Apollonius of Tyana*, University Books, New York, 1966 (G)

(224) Mead, G.R.S., *Fragments of a Faith Forgotten*, New York, University Books, 1960 (T)

(225) Mead, G.R.S., *Mysteries of Mithras*, Theosophical Publishing Society, 1907 (G)

(226) Mead, G.R.S., *Orpheus*, J.M. Watkins, 1965 (G)

(227) Mead, G.R.S., *Thrice Greatest Hermes*, J.M.Watkins, 1964 (G)

(228) Mead, G.R.S., *Vision of Aridaeus*, Theosophical Publishing Society, 1907 (G)

(229) Meltzer, D., *Six*, Santa Barbara, Black Sparrow Press, 1976 (P)

(230) Menahem Nahum of Chernobyl, *Upright Practices*, New York, Paulist Press, 1982 (T)

(231) Merry, E., *I Am: the Ascent of Mankind*, Rider, 1944 (G)

(232) Merton, T., *Asian Journals*, Sheldon Press, 1944 (G)

(233) Merton, T., *Seven Story Mountain*, Sheldon Press, 1975 (G)

(234) Miller, R., *Continents in Collision*, Amsterdam, Time-Life, 1983. (G)

(235) Milton, J., *Complete Poetry*, New York, Anchor Books, 1971 (P)

(236) Moore, V., *The Unicorn: William Butler Yeats' Search for Reality*, New York, Macmillan, 1954 (G)

(237) *Munificentissimus Deus (Pope Pius XII)*, Daughters of St Paul, Derby, New York, 1950 (T)

(238) Mylius, J.D., trans. P. Tahta, *Alchemical Engravings*, Magnum Opus Hermetic Sourcebooks, Edinburgh, 1984 (T)

(239) *Nag Hammadi Library*, trans. J.M.Robinson, Leiden, Brill, 1977 (T)

(240) Nahman of Bratislav, *The Tales*, Paulist Press, New York, 1978 (T)

(241) Needleman, J., *Lost Christianity*, New York, Doubleday, 1980 (G)

(242) Needleman, J. ed., *Sword of Gnosis*, Baltimore, Penguin Books, 1974 (G)

(243) Nennius, *British History and the Welsh Annals*, London and Chichester, Phillimore, 1980 (T)

(244) Newman, J.H., *The Arians of the 4th Century*, E.Lumley, 1871 (G)

(245) Nicholas of Cusa, *The Vision of God*, New York, 1960 (T)

(246) Origen, trans. Gasser, M., *An Exhortation to Martyrdom and Other Writings*, London, SPCK 1979 (T)

(247) *Orphic Hymns*, Text, trans., and Notes by A.M. Athanassakis, Missoula, Montana, Scholars Press, 1977 (T)

(248) Otto, W.F., *Dionysius, Myth and Cult*, Bloomington, Indiana University Press, 1965 (G)

(249) Ovid, *Metamorphoses*, trans. M.M.Innes, Harmondsworth, Penguin Books, 1955 (T)

(250) *Oxford Classical Dictionary*, ed. N.G.K. Hammond, and H.H. Scullard, London, Oxford University Press, 1970 (G)

(251) *Oxford Dictionary of the Christian Church* ed. F.L. Cross and E.A. Livingston, London, Oxford University Press, 1957 (G)

(252) *Oxford Dictionary of Nursery Rhymes*, ed. I. and P. Opie, London, Oxford University Press, 1951 (G)

(253) Paracelsus, *The Archidoxes of Magic*, Askin Publishers, 1975 (T)

(254) Paracelsus, *Selected Writings*, ed, J. Jacobi, New Jersey, Princeton University Press, 1951 (T)

(255) Patai, R., *The Hebrew Goddess*, New York, Avon Books, 1978 (G)

(256) Pausanius, *Guide to Greece*, trans. P. Levi., Harmondsworth, Penguin Books, 1971 (T)

(257) Pelikan, J., *Vindication of Tradition*, New Haven and London, Yale University Press, 1984 (G)

(258) *Perlesvaus: The High History of the Holy Grail*, trans. S. Evans, J.M.Dent, 1911 (T

(259) Perry, M., *Psychic Studies*, Wellingborough, Aquarian Press, 1984 (G)

(260) Perry, W.N., *A Treasury of Traditional Wisdom*, Allen & Unwin, 1971 (G)

(261) Philo of Alexandria, *The Contemplative Life*, Paulist Press, 1981 (T)

(262) Pindar, *The Odes*, C.M. Bowra, Harmondsworth, Penguin Books, 1969 (T)

(263) Piske, L., *The Actor and His Body*, Harrap, 1975 (G)

(264) *Pistis Sophia*, ed. G.R.S. Mead, New Jersey, University Books, 1974 (T)

(265) Plato, *The Collected Dialogues* ed., E. Hamilton, New Jersey, Princeton University Press, 1973 (T)

(266) Plato, *The Republic*, trans. D. Lee, Harmondsworth, Penguin Books, 1955 (T)

(267) Plato, *Timaeus and Critias*, trans. D. Lee, Harmondsworth, Penguin Books, 1965 (T)

(268) Plotinus, *The Enneads*, trans. S. Mackenna, Faber, 1956 (T)

(269) Plotinus, *Enneads*, trans. Stanbrook Abbey, Callow End, Worcester, n.d. (T)

(270) Plutarch, *Moralia V*, 'Isis and Osiris' trans. F.C. Babbitt, London, Heinemann, Cambridge, Mass., Harvard University Press, 1957 (T)

(271) Plutarch, *Moralia VI* 'On the Sign of Plato' trans. P.H. De Lacy and B. Einarson, London, Heinemann, Cambridge Mass., Harvard University Press., 1968 (T)

(272) Ponce, C., *The Game of Wizards*, New York, Penguin Books, 1975 (G)

(273) Ponce, C., *Papers Towards a Radical Metaphysics – Alchemy*, Berkeley, California, North Atlantic Books, 1983 (G)

(274) Potok, C., *The Book of Lights*, Heinemann, 1982 (F)

(275) Potok, C., *The Chosen*, Harmondsworth, Penguin Books, 1970 (F)

(276) Powys, J.C. *Morwyn or the Vengeance of God*, Village Press, 1974 (F)

(277) *Quest of the Holy Grail*, trans. P. Metarasso, Harmondsworth, Penguin Books, 1969 (T)

(278) Quinn, E.C., *The Quest of Seth*, University of Chicago, 1962 (G)

(279) Quispel, G., *Secret Book of Revelation*, Collins, 1979 (G)

(280) Raine, K., *Defending Ancient Springs*, Oxford University Press, 1967 (G)

(281) Rakoczi, B.I., *Fortune Telling*, MacDonald, 1970 (G)

(282) Reeves, M., *Joachim of Fiore and the Prophetic Future*, SPCK, 1976, (G)

(283) Regardie, I., *The Complete Golden Dawn System of Magic*, Phoenix, Falcon Press, 1984 (G)

(284) Regardie, I., *Foundation and Practice of Magic*, Wellingborough, Aquarian Press, 1979 (G)

(285) Regardie, I., *The Golden Dawn*, Saint Paul, Llewellyn Publishers, 1971 (G)

(286) Regardie, I., *How to make and use Talismans*. Wellingborough, Aquarian Press, 1981 (G)

(287) *Rider Book of Mystical Verse*, ed. J.M. Cohen, Rider Books, 1983 (G)

(288)   Roberts, R., *Tarot Revelation*, Privately Printed, L.C. 80–50329. n.d. (G)

(289)   Robertson, S.M., *Rosegarden and Labyrinth*, London, Routledge & Kegan Paul, 1963 (G)

(290)   *The Rosary of the Philosophers*, ed. Adam McLean, Edinburgh, Hermetic Sourceworks, 1980 (T)

(291)   Rudolph, K., *Gnosis*, Edinburgh, T. and T. Clark Ltd., 1983 (G)

(292)   Schaya, L., *Universal Meaning of the Kabbalah*, London, Allen & Unwin, 1971 (G)

(293)   Scholem, G.G., *Major Trends in Jewish Mysticism*, New York, Schoken Books, 1961 (G)

(294)   Schuon, F., *Esotericism as Principle and as Way*, Bedford, Perennial Books, 1981 (G)

(295)   Schure, E., *The Great Initiates*, New York, Mackay, 1913 (G)

(296)   Schwaller de Lubicz, R.A.S., *Nature Word*, West Stockbridge, Lindisfarne Press, 1982 (G)

(297)   Schwaller de Lubicz, R.A.S., *The Opening of the Way*, New York, Inner Traditions Int., 1981 (G)

(298)   Schwaller de Lubicz, R.A.S., *Sacred Science*, New York, Inner Traditions Int., 1982 (G)

(299)   Schwaller de Lubicz, R.A.S., *Symbol and the Symbolic*, New York, Inner Traditions Int., 1978 (G)

(300)   Schwartz-Bart, A., *The Last of the Just*, Harmondsworth, Penguin, 1984 (N)

(301)   Schweighardt, T., *The Mirror of Wisdom*, trans. D. McLean in *Hermetic Journal* no. 25 (T)

(302)   Scott, W., *Hermetica* vol. I. Boulder, Hermes House, 1982 (T)

(303)   Scruton, R., *From Descartes to Wittgenstein*. London, Routledge & Kegan Paul, 1981 (G)

(304)   Serrano, M., *El/Ella: Book of Magical Love*, London, Routledge& Kegan Paul, 1973 (G)

(305)   Serrano, M., *Nos: Book of the Resurrection*, London, Routledge & Kegan Paul, 1984 (G)

(306)   Serrano, M., *The visits of the Queen of Sheba*, London, Routledge & Kegan Paul, 1960 (G)

(307)   Shumaker, W., *The Occult Sciences in the Renaissance*, Berkeley, University of California Press, 1972 (G)

(308)   Silverberg, R., *The Realm of Prester John*, New York, Doubleday & Co., 1972 (G)

(309)   Sinclair, J.R. *The Alice Bailey Inheritance*, Wellingborough, Turnstone Press, 1984 (G)

(310) Singer, I.P., *The Golem*, London, Deutsch, 1983 (N)

(311) Slade, H., *Contemplative Meditation*, London, Darton Longman & Todd, 1977 (G)

(312) Smith, M., *Jesus the Magician*, London, Gollancz, 1978 (G)

(313) Solomon, J., *The Structure of Matter*, Newton Abbot, David & Charles, 1973 (G)

(314) Sorabji, R., *Time, Creation and the Continuum*, London, Duckworth, 1983 (G)

(315) Southwell, R., *Poetical Works*, London, John Russell Smith, 1856 (P)

(316) Spence, L., *Occult Sciences in Atlantis*, London, Aquarian Press, 1970 (G)

(317) Steiner, R., *Atlantis and Lemuria*, New York, Anthroposophical Publications Co., 1923 (G)

(318) Steiner, R., *The Course of My Life*, New York, Steiner Books, 1977 (G)

(319) Steiner, R., *Evolution and Consciousness*, London, Rudolph Steiner Press, 1979 (G)

(320) Steiner, R., *Occult Science, an Outline*, London, Rudolph Steiner Press, 1979 (G)

(321) Steiner, R., *The Occult Significance of Blood*, London, Rudolph Steiner Press, 1967 (G)

(322) Stewart, R.J., *The Underworld Initiation*, Wellingborough, Aquarian Press, 1985 (G)

(323) Stewart, R.J., *The Waters of the Gap*, Bath, Bath City Council, 1981 (G)

(324) Szekeley, E.B., *The Gospel of the Essenes*, London, C.W. Daniel, 1976 (G)

(325) Taylor, T., *Selected Writings*, ed. K. Raine, Princeton, Princeton University Press, 1969 (T)

(326) Teilhard de Chardin, *Hymn of the Universe*, London, Collins, 1965 (G)

(327) Teilhard de Chardin, *Towards the Future*, London, Collins, 1975 (G)

(328) *Temenos*, ed. K. Raine, 47 Paultons Square, London SW3 5DT. issn 0262 4524, 1981 et seq. (J)

(329) Temple, R., *Conversations With Eternity*, London, Rider, 1984 (G)

(330) Tillyard, E.M.W., *The Elizabethan World Picture*, London, Chatto & Windus, 1943 (G)

(331) Tolstoy, N., *The Quest for Merlin*, London, Hamish Hamilton, 1985 (G)

(332) Trinick, J., *The Fire-Tried Stone*, London, Stuart & Watkins, 1967
       G)

(333) Underhill, E., *Mysticism*, New York, Dutton and Colne, 1961 (G)

(334) Underkircher, F., *Le Livre du Cueur d'Amours Espris*, London,
       Thames & Hudson, 1975 (T)

(335) Unterman, A. *The Jews: Their Religious Beliefs and Practices*,
       London, Routledge & Kegan Paul, 1981 (G)

(336) Urmson, J.O., *Concise Encyclopedia of Western Philosophy and
       Philosophers*, London, Hutchinson, 1960 (G)

(337) Vaughan, H., *The Complete Poems*, ed. Alan Rudrum. Harmonds-
       worth, Penguin, 1976 (P)

(338) Vaughan, T., *The Works of Thomas Vaughan*, New York, Univer-
       sity Books, 1968 (T)

(339) Vermaseren, M.J., *Cybele and Attis*, London, Thames & Hudson,
       1977 (G)

(340) Vermaseren, M.J., *Mithras, the Secret God*, London, Chatto &
       Windus, 1963 (G)

(341) Versluis, A., *The Philosophy of Magic*, London, Routledge & Kegan
       Paul, n.d. (G)

(342) Vidal, G., *Julian*, London, Heinemann 1964, (N)

(343) Virgil, *The Eclogues*, Harmondsworth, Penguin, 1980 (P)

(344) Von Eschenbach, W., *Parzival*, trans. A.T. Hatto, Harmondsworth,
       Penguin, 1980 (T)

(345) Von Franz, M.L., *Alchemical Active Imagination*, Irving, Spring
       Books, 1979 (G)

(346) Von Franz, M.L., *Alchemy*, Toronto, Inner City Books, 1980 (G)

(347) Waddell, H., *Songs of the Wandering Scholars*, London, Folio
       Society, 1982 (P)

(348) Waite, A.E., *The Brotherhood of the Rosy Cross*, New York,
       University Books, 1961 (G)

(349) Waite, A.E., *The New Encyclopedia of Freemasonry*, New York,
       Weathervane Books, 1970 (G)

(350) Walker, B. *Gnosticism*, Wellingborough, Aquarian Press, 1983 (G)

(351) Walker, D.P., *Spiritual and Demonic Magic*, London, University of
       Notre Dame, 1969 (G)

(352) Wang, R., *The Qabalistic Tarot*, Maine, Weiser, 1983 (G)

(353) Warden, J., *Orpheus: the Metamorphosis of a Myth*, Toronto,
       University of Toronto Press, 1982 (G)

(354) Ware, T., *The Orthodox Church*, Harmondsworth, Penguin, 1963
       (G)

(355) Ware, K., *The Orthodox Way*, London and Oxford, Mowbrays,
       1979 (G)

(356) Wasson, R.G., *The Road to Eleusis*, New York, Harcourt Brace Jovanovitch Inc., 1978 (G)

(357) West, M.L., *The Orphic Poems*, Oxford, The Clarendon Press, 1984 (G)

(358) Whone, H., *Church, Monastery, Cathedral*, Tisbury, Compton Russell Element, 1977 (G)

(359) Wilby, B., *New Dimensions Red Book*, Toddington, Helios Books, 1968 (G)

(360) Wilson, P.L., *Angels*, London, Thames & Hudson, 1980 (G)

(361) Watt, R.E., *Isis in the Graeco-Roman World*, London, Thames & Hudson, 1971 (G)

(362) Yates, F., *The Art of Memory*, London, Routledge & Kegan Paul, 1966 (G)

(363) Yates, F., *Giordano Bruno and the Hermetic Tradition*, London, Routledge & Kegan Paul, 1971 (G)

(364) Yates, F., *Occult Philosophy in the Elizabethan Age*, London, Routledge & Kegan Paul, 1979 (G)

(365) Yates, F., *The Rosicrucian Enlightenment*, London, Routledge & Kegan Paul, 1972 (G)

(366) Yeats, W.B., *Autobiography*, New York, Collier-Macmillan, 1974 (G)

(367) Zoroaster, *The Chaldean Oracles*, Wellingborough, Aquarian, 1983 (T)

DISCOGRAPHY

(368) Abelard, P., *Planctus Jephtha*, Studio der Fruhen Musick, Reflexe 1C 063–30–123 (M)

(369) *L'Agonie du Languedoc*, Studio der Fruhen Musick with Claude Marti, Reflexe 1c 063–30–132 (M)

(370) *The Art of the Psaltery*, Les Musiciens de Provence with Maurice Guis, Arion ARN 36613 (M)

(371) Ashcroft-Nowicki, D., *The Halls of Osiris*, Sulis Music, BCM 3721, London WC1N 3XX (I)

(372) Ashcroft-Nowicki, D., *The Journey of the Fool*, Sulis Music, BCM 3721, London WC1N 3XX (I)

(373) Bearns, R and Dexter, R., *The Golden Voyages tapes 1—4*, Awakening Productions Inc.

(374) Chants d'Exil, Boston Camerata, Erato Stu 71429 (M)

(375) Dowland, J., *Songs, Books III*, Consort of Musicke, Oiseau-Lyre I DSLO 508–9, 528–1 & 531–2 (M)

(376) Dunstable, J., *Motets*, Hilliard Ensemble, HMV ASD 1467 031 (M)

(377) Gesualdo, *First Book of Madrigals*, Consort of Musicke, Oiseau-Lyre HO 128–1 (M)

(378) Hildegard of Bingen, Abbess, *A Feather on the Breath of God*, Gothic Voices, Hyperion A66039 (M)

(379) Hovhaness, I., *Fra Angelico* op.220, Unicorn Records UNS 243 (M)

(380) Hovhaness, I., *St Varten Symphony* op.80, Unicorn RHS 317 (M)

(381) Kindler, S and Warner, P.L., *Lemurian Sunrise*, Waterfall Music 105 (M)

(382) Knight, G., *The Calling of King Arthur*, 8 Acorn Avenue, Braintree, Essex (I)

(383) Knight, G., *Contacting the Western Masters*, 8 Acorn Avenue, Braintree, Essex (I)

(384) Knight, G., *Dion Fortune's Magical Battle of Britain*, 8 Acorn Avenue, Braintree, Essex (I)

(385) Knight, G., *Dion Fortune's War Letters*, (2 tapes), 8 Acorn Avenue, Braintree, Essex (I)

(386) Knight, G., *The Phaidon Scripts*, (2 tapes), 8 Acorn Avenue, Braintree, Essex (I)

(387) Knight, G., *Visions of Lost Atlantis*, 8 Acorn Avenue, Braintree, Essex (I)

(388) Lassus, O., *Lagrimi di San Pietro*, Consort of Musicke, Oiseau-Lyre DSDL 706 (M)

(389) Lawes, W., *Dialogues, Psalms and Elegies*, Consort of Musicke, Oiseau-Lyre DSLO 574 (M)

(390) Matthews, C. and J., *Walking the Western Way*, Sulis Music, BCM 3721, London WCIN 3XX (I)

(391) Mozart, W.A., *The Magic Flute*. (Zauberflöete) Berlin Philharmonic (Boehme) DG 138 981–3

(392) *Music from the Time of the Popes at Avignon*, Jean-Claude Malgoire and the Florigeum Musicium de Paris, CBS 76534 (M)

(393) *Music in Christian and Jewish Spain*, Hesperion XX, Reflexe lC 163–30–125/26 (M)

(394) *Music of Ancient Greece*, Atrium Musical de Madrid HM 1015 (M)

(395) Orff, G., *Trionfi*, BASF 59–21346–3 (M)

(396) Pinter, J., *Secrets from the Stone*, Sona Gaia Productions C123 (M)

(397) Scriabin, A., *Symphonies 1–3*, Melodiya 80030 XHK (M)

(398) Upper Astral, *Crystal Cave: Back to Atlantis*, New World Cassettes AM109 (M)

(399) Vaughan-Williams, R., *Job: a Masque for Dancing*, HMV 2673 (M)
(400) Vaughan-Williams, R., *The Sons of Light*, Lyrita SRCS 125 (M)

Contact Addresses

GROUPS AND ORGANIZATIONS

The following groups give training or instruction, Membership is often by examination only, although some of these organizations also provide seminars or tapes for those who have no wish to be affiliated to a formal society.

SHAMANIC/NATIVE TRADITION

The Centre for Shamanic Studies: Box 673, Belden Station, Norwalk, Connecticut, 06852, USA.
The Australian Shamanic Centre, PO Box 193, Lidcombe, New South Wales, Australia 2141.
The Green Circle, BCM–SCL Quest, London WC1N 3XX

GNOSTIC

Lectorium Rosicrucianum, Bakenessergracht, 11–15, Haarlem, Holland.
The Gnostic Society, PO Box 3993, Los Angeles, California 90028, USA.

WESTERN MYSTERIES/QABALA

Servants of the Light Association, PO Box 215, St Helier, Jersey, Channel Island.
Builders of the Adytum, 5105 Figueroa Street, Los Angeles, California 90042, USA.
Society of the Inner Light, 38 Steele's Road, London NW3 4RG.

A tape containing further exercises and practical material entitled
WALKING THE WESTERN WAY is available from Sulis Music
and Tapes BCM 3721, London, WC1N 3XX.

Index